Ann Vanderhoof is a writer and magazine editor whose work has appeared in publications in the United States and Canada. She was the founding editor of the award-winning Canadian magazine *Cottage Life* and is also the senior editor of Ports Cruising Guides, a series of guidebooks for boaters. She lives with her husband, Steve Manley, in Toronto.

An Embarrassment of Mangoes

A Caribbean Interlude

Ann Vanderhoof

BANTAM BOOKS

LONDON • TORONTO • SYDNEY • AUCKLAND • JOHANNESBURG

AN EMBARRASSMENT OF MANGOES
A BANTAM BOOK: 0 553 81555 5

First publication in Great Britain
Published by arrangement with Broadway Books, a division of the
Doubleday Broadway Publishing Group, a division of Random House, Inc.

PRINTING HISTORY
Bantam edition published 2005

1 3 5 7 9 10 8 6 4 2

Copyright © Ann Vanderhoof 2003
Map © David Cain

The right of Ann Vanderhoof to be identified as the author of this
work has been asserted in accordance with sections 77 and 78
of the Copyright Designs and Patents Act 1988.

Every effort has been made to obtain the necessary permissions
with reference to copyright material, both illustrative and quoted:
should there be any omissions in this respect we apologize and shall
be pleased to make the appropriate acknowledgements in any future edition.

Set in 11/14pt Garamond by
Falcon Oast Graphic Art Ltd.

Bantam Books are published by Transworld Publishers,
61–63 Uxbridge Road, London W5 5SA,
a division of The Random House Group Ltd,
in Australia by Random House Australia (Pty) Ltd,
20 Alfred Street, Milsons Point, Sydney, NSW 2061, Australia,
in New Zealand by Random House New Zealand Ltd,
18 Poland Road, Glenfield, Auckland 10, New Zealand
and in South Africa by Random House (Pty) Ltd,
Endulini, 5a Jubilee Road, Parktown 2193, South Africa.

Printed and bound in Great Britain by
Cox & Wyman Ltd, Reading, Berkshire.

Papers used by Transworld Publishers are natural, recyclable
products made from wood grown in sustainable forests. The
manufacturing processes conform to the environmental
regulations of the country of origin.

FOR STEVE

Contents

Part Three

As I write this, back in the real world, back in an office, back home, back up against a deadline, I glance down at the mousepad to my right, and I am filled once again with powerful longing. The pad is printed with a picture of a laughing woman stripping off a wetsuit on a golden beach. Her hair is streaked blond, her shoulders broad on an otherwise slender frame, muscular shoulders that look like they know how to work. She is completely relaxed, and radiates happiness. The slice of beach in the photo is deserted—pristine, private, no one and nothing on it, except for a pile of snorkeling gear in the sand at the woman's feet. Behind her, the sea is turquoise glass, on which sits a lone boat with a white hull and a tall mast that has impaled the sky's single puffy white cloud like cotton candy on a stick.

The woman does not appear to be looking at anyone, to even realize that her photo is being taken. She is just plain damn happy.

That woman is me.

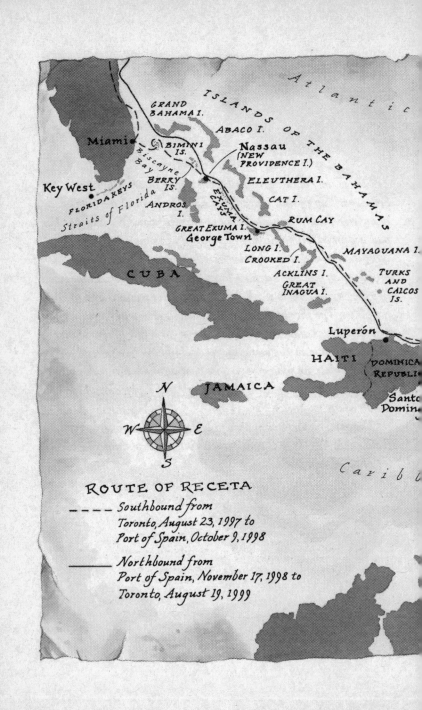

Atlantic

GRAND
BAHAMA I.

ISLANDS OF

ABACO I.

Miami

BIMINI
IS.

Biscayne
Bay

Nassau
(NEW
PROVIDENCE I.)

THE BAHAMAS

BERRY
IS.

Key West

FLORIDA KEYS

ELEUTHERA I.

EXUMA CAYS

Straits of Florida

ANDROS
I.

CAT I.

RUM CAY

GREAT EXUMA I.
George Town

LONG I.
CROOKED I.

MAYAGUANA I.

CUBA

ACKLINS I.

TURKS
AND
CAICOS
IS.

GREAT
INAGUA I.

Luperón

HAITI

DOMINICA
REPUBLI

JAMAICA

Santo
Domin

N

W   E

S

Carib

ROUTE OF RECETA

- - - - Southbound from
Toronto, August 23, 1997 to
Port of Spain, October 9, 1998

———— Northbound from
Port of Spain, November 17, 1998 to
Toronto, August 19, 1999

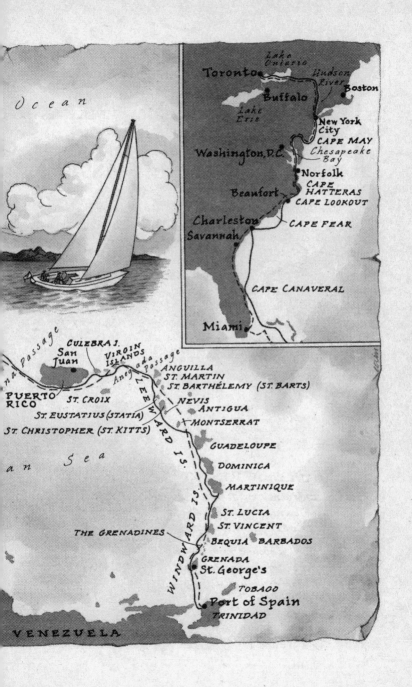

Ocean

Lake Ontario
Toronto
Hudson River
Boston
Buffalo
Lake Erie
New York City
CAPE MAY
Chesapeake Bay
Washington, D.C.
Norfolk
CAPE HATTERAS
Beaufort
CAPE LOOKOUT
Charleston
CAPE FEAR
Savannah

CAPE CANAVERAL

Miami

na Passage
CULEBRA I.
San Juan
VIRGIN ISLANDS
ANGUILLA
ST. MARTIN
ST. BARTHÉLEMY (ST. BARTS)
Anegada Passage
PUERTO RICO
ST. CROIX
NEVIS
ANTIGUA
ST. EUSTATIUS (STATIA)
MONTSERRAT
ST. CHRISTOPHER (ST. KITTS)
GUADELOUPE
an Sea
DOMINICA
MARTINIQUE
ST. LUCIA
ST. VINCENT
THE GRENADINES
BEQUIA BARBADOS
GRENADA
St. George's
TOBAGO
Port of Spain
TRINIDAD
LEEWARD IS.
WINDWARD IS.

VENEZUELA

Conversion Charts

LIQUID MEASURES

US MEASURES	FLUID OUNCES	IMPERIAL MEASURES	MILLILITRES
1 teaspooon	⅙	1 teaspoon	5
2 teaspoons	¼	1 dessertspoon	10
1 tablespoon	½	1 tablespoon	15
2 tablespoons	1	2 tablespoons	30
¼ cup	2	4 tablespoons	56
⅓ cup	2⅔		80
½ cup	4		110
⅔ cup	5	¼ pint/1 gill	140
¾ cup	6		170
1 cup/½ pint	8		225
1¼ cups	10	1/2 pint	280
1½ cups	12		420
2 cups/1 pint	16	generous ¾ pint	450
2½ cups	20	1 pint	560
3 cups/1½ pints	24		675
3½ cups	27		750
3¾ cups	30	1½ pints	840
4 cups/2 pints	32		900
4½ cups	36		1000/1 litre
5 cups	40	2 pints/1 quart	1120
6 cups/3 pints	48	scant 2½ pints	1350
7 cups	56	2¾ pints	1600
8 cups	64	3¼ pints	1800
9 cups	72	3½ pints	2000/2 litres
10 cups/5 pints	80	4 pints	2250

SOLID MEASURES

US AND IMPERIAL	METRIC EQUIVALENT
1 oz	25 grams
1½ oz	40
2 oz	50
3 oz	60
3½ oz	100
4 oz/¼lb	110
5 oz	150
6 oz	175
7 oz	200
8 oz/½lb	225
9 oz	250
10 oz	275
12 oz/¾lb	350
16 oz/1lb	450
1¼lb	575
1½lb	675
1¾lb	800
2 lb	900
2¼lb	1000/1 kilo
3lb	1kg 350g
4lb	1kg 800g
4½lb	2 kilos
5lb	2kg 250g
6lb	2kg 750g

OVEN TEMPERATURE EQUIVALENTS

FAHRENHEIT	CELSIUS	GAS MARK	HEAT OF OVEN
225°	110°	¼	Very cool
250°	120°	½	Very cool
275°	140°	1	Cool
300°	150°	2	Cool
325°	160°	3	Moderate
350°	180°	4	Moderate
375°	190°	5	Moderately hot
400°	200°	6	Moderately hot
425°	220°	7	Hot
450°	230°	8	Hot
475°	240°	9	Very Hot

An Embarrassment

of Mangoes

Island Time

The market ladies sell spice necklaces—garlands of cloves, cinnamon bark, bay leaves, cocoa beans, mace, and nutmeg—that are irresistible. I now have them hanging all around the boat, making it smell spicy and delicious. Mangoes are in season, and literally falling off the trees—an embarrassment of mangoes, to someone from the north. We feel duty bound to try as many varieties as we can.

—Journal Entry, July 1998

*I*N THE DISTANCE, THE HILLS on Hog Island are soft black silhouettes against a paler starlit sky the color of shark's skin. Fish skip across the ocean surface in front of our small inflatable dinghy, each one a quick metallic sparkle in the beam of my flashlight. The air is heavy, warm, scented—partly a salty sea smell, from the shiny-wet rock wall close to us on one side, which has just been uncovered by the falling tide; but partly, too, the smell of lush land floating out from the dark hillsides, the fragrance of white frangipani and blooming spice trees.

Steve points our dinghy at the taller of the island's rounded hills, and from my perch in the bow, I begin a slow, measured count, just loud enough for him to hear over the burble of the outboard: "Onnnnne Mississippi . . . twooooo Mississippi . . . threeeee Mississippi . . ." When I reach "tennnnnnn Mississippi," Steve pulls the tiller to turn us toward the second, smaller hill, farther to the north. Within seconds now, if I've counted at the correct speed, my flashlight should pick up a pair of cantaloupe-sized white floats bobbing on the ocean ahead of us. About 20 feet apart, they mark a deep-water route that threads between patches of coral reef lying just below the surface. We had timed the turn during daylight, when the sea was serene and the sun high overhead, when we could clearly see the sapphire ribbon of safe water between the dappled yellow-green reefs.

"Slow it down, *slow it down*, I don't see the floats yet," I call back to Steve, panning my light nervously in wide arcs. We *have* to spot the floats before proceeding. If we don't follow a line straight between them, we will almost certainly grind to a halt on the reef, damaging both it and our prop, and impaling the dinghy on the coral spikes—a far-from-appealing idea in a small rubber boat, in the darkness, on the ocean. He cuts the throttle.

We are heading home from dinner out with friends on the night of my forty-sixth birthday, and this thread-the-needle-in-the-dark dinghy trip is what heading home now involves. Because home these days is a 42-foot sailboat named *Receta*, which currently floats off the southeastern coast of Grenada, in a protected bay behind these shallow reefs. She has carried us to the Caribbean from Toronto, where we lived and worked until a year ago, and where we'll return a year from now—2,100 miles south as the crow flies, but much, *much* farther as the sailboat travels.

"There. Got 'em." The white balls gleam as I flick my light from one to the other so Steve can see the gap. We're right on course. The anchorage opens up ahead, between a short finger of "mainland" Grenada on one side and a barely disconnected thumb of land, Hog Island, on the other. The masts of maybe twenty boats inscribe gentle arcs in the night sky, but I can pick *Receta* out from her neighbors by the *T* that glints near the top of her mast when I shine my light on it. I had placed that *T* there myself seven months earlier in Key Biscayne, Florida. Steve had winched me up the mast, and with both arms and both legs wrapped around it so tightly that the muscles ached for days afterward, I had peeled the backing off pieces of reflective tape and slapped them hurriedly on the metal, desperate to be lowered back down to sea level as quickly as possible. At the time, the reflective *T* was just an excuse to make the trip 50 feet above the water's surface; the *real* reason was to prove to myself I could do it if I had to. At the time, it was still hard to imagine we would actually ever use the *T* to help us find our way home at night.

As the dinghy putts closer, Steve kills the engine so we glide the last few feet to *Receta*. The *slip-slap-slip-slap* of our wake on the hull dies away, and quiet seems to resettle on the darkness. In fact, the night is incredibly noisy—but the piping of thousands of tree frogs is by now an accustomed background sound, as ordinary and unremarkable a part of the summer night as the hum of an air conditioner once was. I grab the boat's swim ladder, tie the dinghy to a cleat, and climb into the cockpit. We're home.

A bus comes hurtling around the curve past Nimrod's rum shop every ten minutes or so, and while you wait you can watch Hugh Nimrod lettering a sign under the spreading ginnip tree next to the shop, his hands steady but his eyes a gentle haze of rum. If Hugh is inside serving a customer, there are always the goats to watch, the spindly young ones suckling on their mamas, who continue to graze intently up and down the roadside, pointedly ignoring the kids they drag along.

The morning is cool and green, the sun not yet risen high enough behind the mountains to feel its heat. It's market day for us, and we have zipped across the turquoise bay in the opposite direction from last night and tied our dinghy to the long skinny dock at Lower Woburn—a village of a hundred or so people, a handful of tiny stores, a few chickens and goats, and a riotous profusion of banana, mango, coconut, breadfruit, and papaya trees. The local fishermen and lobster divers don't bother with the dock;

they just pull their heavy wooden boats up on the sliver of beach and run a line to a palm tree, leaving the dock free for kids to cannonball off the end or fish with their handlines, and for people like us to tether our dinghies when we come ashore.

A couple of minutes' walk up the road from the dock brings us to Nimrod's, where the bus stops—but, then again, the bus will stop almost anywhere along the winding road if you wave, or point, or scratch your nose, or slow your pace even a fraction, suggesting you just *might* be tempted into a ride. "Bus stop" is a flexible concept in Grenada, sensibly dictated by the driver's bottom line, since public transit is privately, individually owned. You can get off most anywhere too, of course; just rap your knuckles on the metal frame of the bus when you're ready.

The first bus to slide to a halt outside Nimrod's this morning is named *All Eyes on We*—perfectly acceptable grammar on this island, where objective pronouns are scarce as snow. Like all its public-transit counterparts, *All Eyes on We* is a minivan, and the driver's assistant—the conductor kid, we call him—throws open the side door for us to climb onboard. "Good morning," Steve says immediately to the bus at large, loud enough to be heard over the high-volume soca tunes issuing from the van's speakers. "Okaaayyyy," "Good morning," "Okay, okaaayyyyy," the other passengers reply. People here are expected to say good morning and good afternoon to others on public transportation. To *strangers*. It's simply good manners.

During the school year, the morning buses are jammed with kids in their neat uniforms. But today, in the row in front of me, one very little girl sits by herself, no older sibling sandwiched in next to her. Four years old at most, she sits quietly, looking straight ahead, very neatly turned out in a little red jumper and sporting a wonderful assortment of baubles in her elaborately braided hair: plastic cars, trains, planes, pumpkins, hearts, and balls, along with a rainbow of ribbons tied in careful bows.

Without anyone signaling a stop, the bus pulls over about a mile down the road from Nimrod's, in front of a church preschool. The teenage conductor kid—old enough to be packing an attitude—gently lifts the little girl down, helps her put on her tiny backpack, and then takes her by the hand and slowly walks her around the van to the path at the front of the church. From there, she skips off toward the building, a blur of red jumper and flying braids. The rest of the passengers wait patiently as this sweet, slow scene unfolds—no restlessness, no checking of watches, no mutterings about being late for morning appointments. On island time, it doesn't matter. Most days, I don't even bother to wear a watch.

Besides walking little girls to preschool, the conductor kid collects fares when passengers disembark and hands down their bags and packages. He also orchestrates the seating as the bus begins to get more crowded. Once every inch of the bench seats is occupied, he pulls down little tip-up seats that fill the aisle. The van is absolutely, completely full now, and I'm sure it won't stop for anyone else. But no—someone gestures from the roadside, and now the conductor kid is a magician, whipping a cushion out of thin air and placing it over the gap between a tip-up seat and a bench seat to create a place for the new arrival to settle her ample self. Steve's regular game on bus trips to town is to keep a running body count; the prize so far goes to the kid who managed to cram twenty-two bodies into a twelve-person van.

It's perhaps only 5 straight-line miles from Nimrod's to the center of St. George's, Grenada's capital, where the market is. But describing it as 5 straight-line miles doesn't capture the essence of the half-hour trip: the ricocheting of the van through the curves, the driver beeping a firm "keep clear" to anyone who might be approaching from the other direction, since none of Grenada's roads appears to be wider than one-and-three-quarters lanes. A wall of tropical vegetation rises up before us as we enter each hairpin turn, so thick I can feel its damp coolness on my face.

Splashes of color jump out of the green—clusters of thimble-sized orange flowers on the flamboyant trees, and brilliant magenta bougainvillea. As we whip around the bends, I lurch into the unlucky women on either side of me, leaving a sticky sheen of perspiration on their cool, well-powdered skin.

Driving is a bit cavalier here. One Friday afternoon, our driver pulled to the side of the road across from a rickety one-room frame building that, like most every business along this road, is "licensed to sell spiritous liquors." Without a word, the conductor kid trotted across the road, returning a minute later with a bottle of Royal Stout. The driver took a couple of grateful gulps and drove on. Nobody blinked.

The other evening, we heard on the news that anyone in Grenada who has more than thirty driving tickets is going to have his (or her, although we rarely see a woman behind the wheel) license suspended. That would be 3,000 Grenadians, the announcer said, set to lose their licenses. This, mind you, in a country where the number of driver's licenses issued totals only about 18,500.

Finally, St. George's opens up before us—gleaming white buildings with orange and red tile roofs arranged around a curve in the Caribbean Sea, the quintessential Caribbean capital. St. George's is built into the island's substantial hills, with the sea on one side of town and the protected harbor on the other. No one calls it the harbor, though. "Dey on deh Carenage," you'll be told if you ask directions to, say, police headquarters. "Deh Carenage" is where the big sailing ships were careened in centuries past—turned on their sides at low tide so their bottoms could be cleaned of barnacles, caulked, and repaired before they headed out to sea again, having exchanged the ballast of tiles they arrived with for cargoes of spices, coffee, fruit, and rum. Our bus teeters at the top of an impossibly steep street, until a white-gloved policeman gives the signal for the driver to descend toward the water.

"Mangoes. Look at my lovely mangoes." "Christophene. Don't you need christophene?" "Good morning, darlin'. Stop, take a look." "My avocados deh best. Take a taste." The bus disgorges us into a confusion of musical voices at the end of the route: the public market at the foot of Market Hill. Huge brightly colored umbrellas at rakish angles create pockets of shade amidst the hot white light. The tables underneath hold carefully arranged pyramids of tomatoes and limes, bundles of elephant ear–like callaloo leaves, brilliant orange wedges sliced from monstrous green-skinned pumpkins. On the ground are stalks of bananas and plantains in every stage of ripeness—fluorescent green to creamy yellow to almost solid black—and piles of mysterious, hairy, arthritic-looking roots.

The smell of spices is so strong I can taste them. Heaps of gnarled ginger overflow their trays and vie for table space with finger-long pieces of cinnamon and mauby bark tied in neat bundles, pungent allspice berries, sharp little cloves, glossy mahogany nutmegs, and broom-sized bunches of gray-green thyme. And everywhere, *everywhere*, the sweet perfume of mangoes hangs in the air. It's mid-August, the last glorious gasp of mango season, and every market table groans with them. We've been devouring them greedily, a couple of times a day. Sometimes we do as we see the locals doing along the roadside, when they take a break from their work: cut slabs off the sides with a pocketknife, then pull the flesh from the skin with their teeth. But I also slice them and squirt them with lime for breakfast, turn them into salsas and salads, bake them into sweet crisps. With every mango I use, I stand over the sink and suck the last bits of sweetness off the flat seed, leaving fragrant, sticky trails of juice dripping off my chin. I have become a mango glutton, and I start to worry if my supply drops below half a dozen.

Today, I beetle toward one of my favorite market ladies, who does business from beneath an enormous lemon-yellow umbrella that came her way courtesy of Benson & Hedges. She's resplendent in her stop-sign-red T-shirt and pants covered by a leopard-print apron, with a ball cap in the colors of the Grenadian flag—red, yellow, green—on her head. "Four for $4 EC, darlin'," she says, pointing to the plump yellowy-orange mangoes stacked on her table. "What are they called?" I ask, because here, a mango is not simply a mango; at least half-a-dozen varieties are available in the market on any one day, and I'm trying to learn the differences. "Sealawn," she says, drawing out the second syllable like a musical refrain, and the name seems fitting, since we're surrounded by the sea and lush greenness. I know there's a place called Seamoon toward the north end of the island; I envision the bountiful Sealawn right next to it, covered with heavily laden mango trees. "Sealawn," I repeat as I load four into my backpack. She laughs her approval.

I also buy a fragrant bunch of what I've learned to call "shadow benny," a lovely nickname from the French patois that colors the language on this English-speaking island. Coupled with the lilting accent, the dropped letters, the missing pronouns, the islocentric vocabulary, and the high-speed delivery, it makes conversation a challenge. *Chadon bene*—shadow benny—means "good tea," she tells me, since a tea made from its slender, sawtoothed leaves cures flu, pneumonia, constipation, and other ailments. My shadow benny, though, is destined for a mango salsa: In taste and smell, it's a dead ringer for cilantro, or coriander, a close relative.

Our next stop is the fish market, a modestly sized building on the waterfront. There's no sign to identify it—it's next door to the abattoir, which *is* helpfully signed to alert the unwary—but is hard to miss since the vendors spill out onto the sidewalk, their scarred wooden tables lined with bloody hunks of kingfish, whole red snappers neatly side by side, and buckets of slender, silvery ballyhoo.

On our way, we run into a couple of other sailors we know, a pair from Texas. "You just missed the excitement," he says. "One guy just chopped off another guy's hand with a machete. Over a woman."

Back home, business would have stopped cold for hours while the area was marked off with yellow crime-scene tape, reports taken, a cleanup crew mopping and sanitizing while people gossiped and gaped. Here, the hand was simply put on a bed of ice—the same ice that had been holding raw fish minutes before—and sent with its owner to hospital. The market was back to normal within minutes, the flies resettled on the snappers, the vendors resettled in their seats. But the Texas couple is empty-handed: "Somehow we just didn't feel like buying any fish," he says.

We are not deterred. There are no stray appendages in sight when we step into the market's cool, dim interior, and we immediately stop to admire a gorgeous whole yellowfin tuna. The vendor leaps to his feet, and as soon as Steve indicates the thickness we want, slices thick red steaks off the fifty-pound fish with quick swipes of his cutlass, as the long, curving machete is called here. I have just a moment's hesitation, wondering where that cutlass had been a few minutes earlier, but Steve is exuberantly unconcerned. With the tuna the equivalent of $1.80 a pound, it's all I can do to stop him from buying the whole damn fish. Dinner tonight has clearly been decided.

On the way back toward our homeward bus, we poke into one more shop. Unlike the market, here the prices are posted, and I see the sign above one of the bins. "Ceylon Mangoes," it says. Or Sealawn, in the lilting voice of an islander. I laugh as broadly as my favorite market lady.

When Steve raps on the roof, *My Heart Desire* lurches to a stop in front of Nimrod's, and the conductor kid hands down our backpacks and my canvas cooler bag. A little time perched on one of Nimrod's three stools, schmoozing with Hugh and gulping a cold drink, is required before returning to the dinghy dock. Nimrod's is the closest thing to a convenience store in Lower Woburn, and customers wander in and out to buy one thing or another, or have a glass of rum. An old-fashioned wooden case on the counter holds baked goods while the shelves behind are dotted with just a few essentials: cooking oil, rum, fruit juice, rum, evaporated milk, rum, insecticide, rum. Whenever he gets a chance, Hugh puts aside his paintbrush and the sign he's working on to join his customers in a glass, while his slender, sad-faced wife, Bernadette, stoically keeps the place running. Besides getting customers their groceries, she takes in laundry, sends faxes, and prepares vats of chicken curry, which she scoops into large, thin pancake-like roti breads, wraps into neat packages, and sells at lunchtime. We occasionally see her heading off to church in the afternoon in a flowered dress, Bible in hand, while Hugh waits for her to disappear around a curve in the road so he can return to his schmoozing and his rum.

On our first visit, Hugh unearths from the back room a set of fat, dusty oversized ledgers with cracked covers. "Dey been signed by those who cross deh bridge," he says in his soft voice, and he insists we turn their pages to get a sense of the tradition—whatever it is. We haven't seen a bridge anywhere in Lower Woburn. The ledgers, which date back more than a decade, don't shed much light, even though verses, drawings, and oblique references to the difficulty of "crossing deh bridge" are sprinkled among the signatures of other cruisers.

Eventually, Hugh swears us to secrecy—and brings out a wooden model of a suspension bridge that he sets on the counter. There are spots for rum cups on each side. "Ready to cross?" He fills the cups to the brim with rum from Clarke's Court distillery, just down the road, while Bernadette puts glasses of water alongside. Hugh makes a sweet toast of welcome and friendship to those who come to this little village on the coast. He then indicates we have to down the rum in one go—demonstrating with his own cup, of course. Bernadette just looks on. I pick up my cup and gulp. Jesus. This is why rum was once called "kill devil." This is the local overproof stuff, fresh out of the still, no aging in barrels to temper the raw fire. I cough and sputter and grope for the water that Bernadette has prudently provided. She gives a little knowing smile: I wouldn't be able to spit out the word right now to ask for it myself. While Steve, his eyes watering only slightly, joins Hugh in a second, I sneak a peek at the bottle: 138 proof, 69 percent alcohol.

We have crossed the bridge. We have arrived.

Back on board, the shopping put away, I slide off *Receta*'s stern ladder into the water to swim just before sunset, as I do every afternoon, so I can watch, up close, the sea change color—the blue surface becoming streaked with rose and mauve as the sun sinks. Here, not quite 12 degrees north of the equator, sunset comes early, even in August. The sun is here one minute, below the horizon the next, and I am left to do my last lap around the boat in a pool of deepening gray, clutching an old toothbrush. I haven't entirely given up the obsessive multitasking of my old life: As I swim, I scrub off the tiny barnacles determined to get a foothold along the waterline of our hull. I then shower in the cockpit, using fresh water that was heated by the sun while we were at the market.

Steve claims tonight's dinner is the best I've ever cooked—on land or water—though in truth I do almost nothing: mince a little market ginger and garlic, add a couple of splashes of soy and olive oil, and let that thick yellowfin tuna sit in the mixture for just a few minutes; steam some rice, and turn one of the "Sealawn" mangoes into a salsa the color of the sunset. Meanwhile, on the small gas barbecue mounted on *Receta*'s stern rail, Steve quickly grills the fish, and it is dazzling: Seared on the outside and barely cooked inside, it has a sensuous, almost silken texture, the sweet salsa a perfect counterpoint to its fresh sea taste. Seven months later, another tuna, this one a blackfin we catch ourselves eleven islands farther into our journey, finally supplants tonight's as the best thing Steve has ever tasted from my kitchen. But until then— even after lobster season opens a few weeks from now—the yellowfin will remain first in his affection.

After we do the dishes—by hand, in one small pan of water, since every drop of fresh water we use now has to be caught when it rains or ferried aboard in jerry cans—I go up on deck to look at the sky and cool off in the breeze: doing nothing, doing everything. I've even taken to sleeping in the cockpit on still nights, when no wind disturbs the sultry air, the heat lies like a heavy blanket, and Steve gives off a million BTUs in our berth below. Not a building is visible on either mainland or island shore—no houses, stores, hotels, or restaurants—so there are no lights to dim the stars embroidered on the dark velvet overhead. The breeze is gentle and, as always, the piping frogs sing.

This is what I traded my Day-Timer and business clothes for a year ago. This is what my daily life has become. Ann of a Thousand Deadlines has slowly, surely, been left behind.

Part One

The Five-Year Plan

Your courage is like a kite. Big wind raises it higher.

> Fortune Cookie, Toronto, Canada;
> November 1996

Relinquishing fears now allows you to succeed.

> Fortune Cookie, Port of Spain, Trinidad;
> November 1998

PERHAPS THE HARDEST THING, we realized in hindsight, was making the decision to go.

It had started as idle, dreamy chat in the bleak days of January and February, the time of year I detest in Toronto, when all the color is sucked out of the city, and even the snow looks gray and tired. As I do.

I left for work in the dark and returned home in the dark. On the rare days the sun bothered to show itself, it was a pale lemon pretender, offering little warmth and barely brightening the gunmetal surface of Lake Ontario. When I cooked dinner in the evening, Steve would catch me warming my hands over the stove, and, later, huddling over the heating vent in our bedroom while I read. It's a very sad sight, he would say. I looked like the little match girl rather than a successful magazine editor. I didn't care. I longed to be too hot.

Steve—three years younger than me, all hard angles and sharp edges on the outside, a romantic softie within—was my partner in work as well as life. A small-town Ontario boy, he'd relocated to the city to go to art college in the seventies and never left. For the past few years, we'd been working for the same magazine, and it was hard to tell most days where business ended and private life began. We operated in separate spaces: he, the freelance art director, from a crammed studio tucked into the back of the second floor of our house; me, the editor, at the magazine's main office, a fifteen-minute drive away. But we speed-dialed each other incessantly and flung e-mails and electronic story layouts back and forth all day long. When people asked how our relationship could survive our working together, I'd exclaim about the virtues. "How many people have a chance to see firsthand how really good their spouses are at what they do?" That was on the good days.

The rest of the time, I drove home in the cold at night, freezing and fuming, replaying the day, and arrived ready to rant: about the sloppy writers, the uninspired stories, the cheapskate publisher, the blown deadlines and, especially, the talented but unreasonable art director. "Turn it off, the office is closed," Steve would say. And I would—for at least a full minute. Our work and our personal lives were inseparable.

And there never seemed to be enough hours for both. Every day required a battle plan. Besides the magazine, we squeezed in other publishing projects that we worked on together—including a small ongoing series of guidebooks for boaters on the Great Lakes that Steve published himself. They took a backseat to the other stuff and were, like their publisher, often late. Meanwhile, I was ruled day and night by my watch and the to-do lists in my Day-Timer. "I can barely brush my teeth without a deadline," I joked to friends. But increasingly I didn't find it funny.

On the surface, Steve remained calm and unruffled, letting the pressure swirl around him, seemingly as casual about business deadlines as he was about his standard business attire (T-shirt and jeans no matter what, unless the weather permitted shorts or required a sweatshirt). "It will all get done," he'd tell me, "whether you stew about it or not." Yet I knew he was growing more and more resentful of the constant demands on his time and his perpetual state of overcommitment. Not to mention what he swore was "ten months of winter a year."

His solution was thrown out casually—just another sensible suggestion, like telling me I should crank up the thermostat when I complained about the cold. "So let's take a break and sail south to the Caribbean for a couple of years," he said.

Right. Escaping work and winter for a couple of years sounded wonderful—but escaping on a *sailboat*? Was he *nuts*? Sure, I needed a break—we both did—but did he think I had somehow been miraculously grafted onto someone else's sea legs?

I had never set foot on a sailboat until one of my first dates with him, and it was hardly an auspicious beginning to a relationship, let alone a sailing career. Having taught himself to sail and fallen in love with sailing a few years earlier, Steve had planned a romantic afternoon for two on his boat on the lake. In fact, we didn't even get away from the dock, after he backed over one of his mooring lines leaving the slip and wrapped it on the propeller. ("I was too busy trying to impress you," he told me later.) Our second sailing date wasn't much better: It was aborted at the marina's fuel dock, when he discovered one of the boat's hoses had become detached, filling the bilge with gasoline. I, meanwhile, had identified sailing as an activity where things frequently go wrong.

When he did eventually get me out on the lake, I loved the feeling of being propelled by the wind, the total quiet except for the water gurgling past, the sense of freedom that came with leaving land (and land-based concerns) behind. But I only loved it on days when the lake was flat and the breeze gentle. My nervousness increased in direct proportion to wind strength, and so did my tendency to seasickness. I was most definitely not a natural sailor.

I didn't react instinctively to the wind—or to the movement of the boat. "You can't teach an old dog new tricks," I'd mutter, lurching into the companionway and simultaneously barking a shin and a shoulder.

One August, several years after we had bought a house and moved in together, I had a routine checkup with my doctor. As she was examining me, she suddenly asked in all seriousness, "Is your husband beating you?" She was staring at my assortment of multicolored sailing bruises, which I'd become accustomed to having all summer long. I still had not developed anything that could remotely be called sea legs.

By the time Steve popped his "let's sail south" suggestion about five years later, I had fewer bruises and a few more basic skills, but not much else had changed in my relationship with sailing. Steve, meanwhile, had become an even more competent and confident sailor. He now raced the boat every Wednesday night in Toronto's harbor, and also entered longer weekend races on Lake Ontario when he could get crew. He knew better than to look to me to fill that role.

However, not wanting to focus on my personal shortcomings, I cleverly decided to point out a few other niggling drawbacks to his "let's sail south" idea instead. Like money. We were both self-employed; there was no company or educational institution offering sabbaticals, no family trust fund, no cash reserves or investments to help pay for a midlife break from the working world. So how were we going to finance this little adventure?

And that's how the Five-Year Plan was born: "Let's think about sailing south five years from now," Steve said, "and in the meantime we'll see if we can put together enough money." Mostly the Plan would involve paying down the mortgage on our house, which would involve the ever-popular concepts of fiscal restraint and concerted savings.

"Sure," I said to Steve. *Stay calm*, I said to myself. *Five years is a long way off. This doesn't mean you're agreeing to sail into the sunset. We can always use the money to do something else.* And I had to admit, in the short term, having the Plan would allow us to fantasize on the cold, tough days about making the great escape.

When we arrive at Smith Island on the Eastern Shore of Chesapeake Bay, it is just before dusk. Rakish clouds with underskirts of gray scuttle across the sky. The public dock at the island's main town of Ewell, where we tie *Receta*, is a mere six inches above water level, and it's still not high tide; the main street is already awash ankle-deep. Neat white clapboard houses with red or green shutters are scattered along both sides, but there's not a soul in sight—and no other boats at the dock—just a family of ducks paddling up the flooded roadway.

By far the most off-the-beaten-path spot we've stopped at since leaving Toronto two months ago, Smith Island, Maryland, is one of only two inhabited offshore islands in Chesapeake Bay. The other is Tangier Island, a little farther to the south and just across the Virginia state line. Isolated from the mainland 11 miles away, Smith's 400 or so residents make their living by crabbing and, in winter, oystering, as they always have. In fact, the current residents are direct descendants of the island's original settlers who came here in 1657. Almost half the population of Ewell has the same last name, Evans. "Visitors are well advised not to make jokes or ask too many questions about this," says William Warner, writing about Tangier and Smith in *Beautiful Swimmers*, his Pulitzer Prize–winning elegy to the watermen and crabs of Chesapeake Bay. I've been reading it at night, and annoyingly recounting snatches to Steve (since he's already read it himself) as we sail down the bay. I suspect Smith Island would be unusual at any time, but it is *particularly* unusual on this chill, blustery October weekday when we are the only visitors and an abnormally high tide laps across the carefully tended lawns.

We pull on our deck boots and wade up the deserted main street, eventually coming upon a lone crabber who, with the help of a young woman, is unloading the day's catch into the back of a pickup. Blue crabs have been constantly on our minds lately because the most common method of catching them commercially is the crab trap, and crab traps and boats don't mix. The traps lie on the bottom of the bay, the location of each one marked on the surface by a small round buoy about the size of an overgrown grapefruit, which is attached to the trap below by a rope. During the summer and early fall, Chesapeake Bay is positively *littered* with them. "Watermen who normally set out 200 crab pots in the 1970s now work with 500 to 1,000 to get approximately the same catch," Warner tells us. The last thing we want to do is run into one of those ropes and catch it on our prop, for an unpleasant reprise of our Toronto harbor date.

So one of us spots and one of us steers as we slalom from anchorage to anchorage down the bay. We're particularly fond of the crabbers with the blue buoys—almost impossible to see in the waves until we're right on top of them, at which point we have to zigzag quickly away, the sails flapping inelegantly from the unplanned change in direction. Steve figures the only way to get even for the stress of constant crab-trap watch is to devour as many crabs as possible. There's no way we're going to walk by a truck full of them on Smith Island and not buy some to cook ourselves.

"How much are they?" I ask the young woman hefting traps. She relays the question to the man in oilskins in the bed of the pickup, who shouts back an incomprehensible answer. The island's isolation has allowed a distinctive dialect to survive, with outmoded words and grammatical constructions from seventeenth-century England. To our ears, it sounds like the crabber is gargling marbles with a Shakespearean southern drawl. "Thirty-five dollars for number one jimmies," the woman translates. Number one jimmies are the big fat prime male crabs, the ones served steamed in restaurants; but even given that, the price seems high for buying direct from the supplier—higher, in fact, than we've sometimes paid when eating out. "Wannem?" The man in the pickup pushes a basket scrabbling with live crabs toward the pickup's rear gate.

It's only then that I realize the price isn't for a dozen—our usual consumption—but for *an entire bushel basket*. I'd be up all night steaming and picking the meat out of seventy or eighty crabs. And even Steve, whose lean build belies his near-legendary appetite, can't see devouring *that* many. "Can we buy just a dozen?" Nope, it's all or none. We politely decline and wade on.

Maybe it's a good thing. Friends had recounted the difficulty of steaming crabs in the small galley of a cruising boat; one of theirs had escaped on its way to the pot and disappeared behind the stove. "When we finally rooted him out, he had a death grip on our propane line," Wayne had told us.

A woman stands on her front porch, hands on hips, watching the egret that has abandoned the marshes to fish the main street. "Excuse me, is there a restaurant in town?"

She points down the street. "Ruke's Store, 'cept it's closed. He went home to have dinner."

That doesn't sound promising. "It's the only place; he'll be back 'fore long to open up."

We splash around the village some more, until we spot a wind-hardened man unlocking the store, then wander in behind him. As we slide into one of the old-fashioned booths that fill a corner of the general store, he tells us we still can't get dinner: The cook is trapped at home by the exceptionally high water.

"Happens three times a year or so now," he explains. "You have to wait 'til a nor'wester blows through and ends it." Some people blame global warming—as the sea warms, it is rising and nibbling away at the land—others say the island is sinking. Whichever,

37

Smith is now just a foot above sea level, and the island's graveyard has been so badly flooded at times that coffins have been sent floating down the main street.

"There is little doubt that Smith Island is the champion of the Chesapeake in soft crab production," *Beautiful Swimmers* had informed us. To be here and not try one would be for Steve like being in Burgundy and not trying the local wine.

The joy of a softshell is eating the entire fried-crisp thing. But there's only about a one-day window between when a crab discards its old shell and when the new shell has hardened too much to eat, so the harvest has necessarily evolved into a precise science. With practiced eyes, the watermen cull the "busters," which have begun to shed, and the "peelers," which are just about to. And then they wait. The moment the crabs molt, they are put on ice and rushed to market.

The ones that arrive in front of Steve, once the tide turns and the cook arrives, are so perfect he has no intention of sharing more than one measly bite with me: dredged in flour and panfried gloriously crisp on the outside, yet soft and melting inside, with no trace of hardness from the start of a new shell. We end up ordering a platter of three additional softshells, and demolish every last buttery-sweet bite. Meanwhile, I have first inhaled my own crabcake dinner, giving up only the one requisite taste to Steve that fair trade requires. The cake is almost pure crab inside its golden exterior, held together by a bit of mayo, a wisp of seafood seasoning, and not much else. I'm determined to buy some crabmeat—already steamed and out of the shell—before *Receta* leaves the Chesapeake and replicate them onboard myself.

The ducks are gone when we walk back to the boat, and the wind is up. The nor'wester is on its way.

In one corner: The security of a job, a steady income, a home, a daily routine—comfortable, safe, predictable.

In the other corner: Escape from work, winter, and daily routine; the excitement and risk of the unknown—tempting, and more than a little scary.

The five years of the Five-Year Plan were ticking down. The mortgage was smaller, the work rut deeper. The stream of boating catalogs and books coming into the house had grown to a torrent. (Steve's economizing for the Five-Year Plan did not extend to cutbacks on "educational materials.") He was soaking up information like a bilge pad under a leaky diesel: on oceangoing sailboats, sailing gear, maintenance and repairs, passage-making strategies. By now he had also put numbers on how much sailing to and through the Caribbean would cost: $1,000 to $1,500 per month. "That's only $18,000 a year, max," he said jubilantly. "Staying here would cost us way more."

Yeah, and he'd better build in a big cushion for when we came back and didn't have any work. Did we—particularly I—really have the nerve to put our careers on hold? If we dropped out now, in our forties, how would we get back in the market and earn a living when we returned?

And there were other concerns. We don't have any children, but we do have aging parents—mine were approaching their eighties; Steve's their seventies. How could we think about placing ourselves out of easy reach?

Even as I raised objections, I knew I was moving closer to needing a change. I had been editing the same magazine for seven years, and it had become all-consuming. My whole identity was defined by what I did to make a living, and I didn't like that. Steve was focused on the fact that we were growing older; he watched friends put things off until "later" when, they said, they'd have more money and fewer responsibilities; by the time "later" came, they were no longer in good health and and no longer able. "I never want to find ourselves in that position," Steve said. "I never want to say, 'If only . . .'"

Four years into the Five-Year Plan, we decide to start shopping for a larger boat. *This still doesn't mean you've agreed to sail off into the sunset*, I tell myself. *It's not like you've set a date to quit your job and leave town.*

We find her in Maine, an aging 42-foot sailboat with classic lines and a fine pedigree. She appears out of the gloom of a boatyard shed, her varnish gleaming despite a patina of dust, her graceful hull proclaiming speed and elegance and calling our names. She is the first boat we look at, and the one that six months and many boatyards later becomes ours.

Not even sure exactly what to inspect when shopping for a boat, I lie down on one of the dust-covered, teak-slatted seats in the cockpit and stretch out to my full length (admittedly, only five feet, two inches). I know little about evaluating sail plans and hull condition, but I do know the importance of being comfy for a nap. Steve, meanwhile, examines *under* the other seat, checking storage capacity; he lounges on the coaming beside the wheel, to judge the comfort factor while steering; he inspects the stainless-steel fittings and—on his hands and knees—the condition of the nonskid surface on the deck. People fall in love in different ways.

Inside, we go through her with flashlights. The oiled teak that lines her cabins gives her a richness and warmth. So what if the upholstery is a nubby weave in early-eighties-rec-room turquoise-and-orange stripes? Cushions can be replaced. Traditional glass prisms are set into her deck to refract sunlight into the cabins, a bit of boat-building finesse missing on newer sailboats. So what if her electronics are out of date? A bonus, says Steve: He can buy the new ones he wants, without guilt. Her sleekness—and Steve's notebooks full of research—suggest she will sail extremely well. She is a sloop, with the bonus of a removable inner forestay, Steve explains, so she can fly three sails—a mainsail, a jib or headsail, and a staysail—giving us several options, an advantage in heavier winds. She will be fast, as befits a design based on an old racing hull, but also comfortable. So what if she doesn't have the space of a more modern cruising boat? We can create more storage by taking out the second toilet (two toilets on a *boat*, when we don't even have two toilets at home?) and an extra berth. *Surely* we will never need to sleep seven.

The list of changes grows long enough to make our wallets quiver, but we both feel a powerful affinity for this boat. For Steve, the graphic designer, to be happy, the form of something must be as pleasing, as perfect, as the way it functions. "Just look at those lines," he says longingly, returning for one last lingering glance as we get ready to leave the shed. I can picture myself cooking in her snug little galley; entertaining at her varnished table, which can easily seat eight (I've already counted); and curling up with Steve in the berth in her aft cabin. The usual practice of referring to boats in the feminine has always grated on me, and I've always made a point of saying "it." But this lovely boat demands to be personified. She is sleek and elegant, but also strong and heavy, built for the ocean. She inexplicably gives me confidence—a word previously nonexistent in any sentence that also contained the words "Ann" and "sailboat."

I am still nervous in any wind much stronger than a zephyr, have never handled any boat larger than a dinghy by myself, have never spent more than two consecutive weeks living on a sailboat—and have never *ever* sailed at night. All of which makes me an extremely unlikely candidate for a two-person, two-year sailing trip. But here we are in Maine, soon to make an offer on a sailboat to do exactly that.

The Tartan Marine Company produced thirty-four 42-foot sailboats between 1980 and 1984; the one in Maine is hull number 14, and the name emblazoned on her narrow transom is *Diara J*. Sailing lore is unequivocal in the matter of boat names: It's bad luck to change them. But we have no connection with *Diara J*—a conflation of the names of the first owner's children, the boat broker told us. The J is an ugly visual afterthought—a child who must have arrived after the boat—and particularly offensive to Steve. Perhaps we would have stuck with the name anyway, though, had we not heard the guys around the boatyard talking. "That pretty boat," they'd say as they climbed the ladder before the sale to add yet another coat of varnish to the gleaming wood-work, "that pretty boat with a name that looks like 'diarrhea.'"

Receta—pronounced with two short e's—means recipe in Spanish. "Because she has all the right ingredients," I tell everyone who asks. But there's more to it than that: I love to cook. Even after—or especially after—my most grueling days at work, I make dinner from scratch, to relax. I'm always playing in the kitchen, trying new recipes, experimenting, and Steve is a willing subject. We both *love* to eat.

When *Receta* arrives in Toronto on a truck from Maine, we add two more years to the Five-Year Plan. After all, we need time to get to know each other. And make (and pay for) all those easy changes.

The first 844 miles of our trip to the Caribbean—from Toronto to the southern end of Chesapeake Bay—are a relentless barrage of new places, new people, and new problems. Every day, in fact, brings a new situation to be tackled, something that didn't previously exist in my limited repertoire of boating skills. "How about a day that qualifies as quiet and uneventful?" I complain to my journal. We seem to have merely replaced our work pressures with a new set of stresses. Still, something is changing: My daily coffee intake has plummeted to one small cup before we get underway each morning instead of the maybe eight hefty mugs I used to consume each day. The stimulation of the new is replac-ing caffeine.

We're not only expending huge amounts of mental energy, but also doing *much* more physical, burn-the-calories type work. Two weeks after we started out, I had stepped on the scales at a yacht club where we stopped and discovered that without even trying I weighed less—by a good five pounds—than I had at any time in my adult life. Skinny-to-start-with Steve has had to punch another hole in his belt to hold his slumping jeans around his narrowing waist.

Maneuvering the boat through the twenty-nine locks of the New York State Canal System and the one federal lock connecting Lake Ontario to the Hudson River was the first new-to-both-of-us challenge, complicated by a 65-foot-long battering ram overhanging *Receta* by 10 feet at the bow and stern: Since sailboats can't go through the canal with their masts up, we are carrying it on deck. The trick is to avoid shish-kebabing other boats while keeping clear of the rough lock walls. "I guess you want me to do the driving," Steve says, knowing full well what my response will be. I've yet to maneuver *Receta* in close quarters, and I figure a crowded, concrete chamber coated in black-green slime is no place to start. We pick up only one small scratch before being spit out into the Hudson six days after we pulled into the first lock. Next up is what has historically been one of the world's busiest harbors, and with the mast in its proper place once again, we sail under the George Washington Bridge and into New York City, tacking back and forth across the river until the Statue of Liberty, her torch thrust into the air, comes into view ahead, welcoming two more new arrivals.

For me, it's a thrilling homecoming. I was born and raised in New Jersey; my family still lives here. Docked on the Jersey side of the river overlooking the Manhattan skyline, we uncork champagne to celebrate with Mom and Dad and family friends. "You'll see and hear from us as frequently as ever," I had promised when Mom and Dad had worried about our heading off, imagining us far away and out of reach. I hope that by delivering on that promise so quickly, by having made it, seemingly effortlessly, all the way to their home turf by boat, they will be more relaxed about our trip.

I'm careful, though, to hide my nervousness about the next phase: my first passages on the Atlantic Ocean, necessary to get us down the New Jersey coast. "I'm getting tired of the word 'exhilarating,'" I tell Steve after we complete an intense little stretch of ocean around the very bottom of the state. The recommended route here, through a maze of shallow, shifting sandbars, takes us nerve-wrackingly close to the rocky coast at Cape May—so close that from *Receta's* cockpit we can smell the bacon and eggs cooking in the resort town's kitchens.

"Your parents think this is all my idea," Steve said after we broke the news to the family. "They think I'm trying to kill you." I'm not sure what horrified them most: my taking up a lifestyle that seemed fraught with danger, my no longer being at the other end of a phone any minute of the day, or my giving up a good job. Steve's parents are more sanguine: They ask if they can come visit.

Staying had begun to seem as terrifying as leaving. Better to take the risk and go, we decided, than forever regret not going. There would never be a time that would be absolutely right, and if we waited for it, we would wait forever. Now, when we—and our parents—were healthy was as good a time as any.

Despite my fears, I had slowly come around to the idea that a boat, which combines the means of getting to a destination with the place to stay when you arrive, would make it possible to travel for an extended stretch. And one aspect of traveling this way was particularly appealing: It would mean having a kitchen with us wherever we went. We'd no longer have to limit our food purchases in exotic destinations to what we could chill in a hotel ice bucket, prepare with a Swiss Army knife, and consume with our fingers.

The Five-Year—now Seven-Year—Plan had worked. We had no debts. The mortgage was paid off, so we could rent our house for a source of income. We were completing new editions of two of Steve's guidebooks, which would be on the market while we were gone, for another source of income. We'd even built up a small cash cushion. But we'd also increased our guesstimate of what the trip would cost: $1,500 to $2,000 a month—not including the equipment we still needed to buy for *Receta* along the way. On top of that, I'd padded on a lavish security blanket to allow for lots of phone calls home and occasional flights to visit parents.

The word drifted out to colleagues, and the endless stream of questions began. How could we give up two highly coveted jobs and just sail over the horizon? How would we survive when we returned, jobless and out of the loop? *What would we do?* It was both unnerving and enlightening that so many concerns revolved around our *work*. I heard whiffs of words like "reckless." I caught wind of a betting pool on how long it would be—how soon, actually—before we turned back.

I hedged when people asked how long we'd be gone. "One year, maybe two," I said. I didn't want anyone to think I'd failed if I chickened out and we returned after one year.

Item in Day-Timer: Reduce contents of house owned by two packrats to a pile of useful possessions that will fit into a 42-foot sailboat that is only 12 feet, 3 inches across at her widest point. Most of *Receta*, in fact, beyond her bulging midsection, is *much* narrower.

"How many T-shirts do you think I'll need?"

I was ready to throttle him. "How the hell would I know? Have I ever done this?" If I was stressed out before, now I was strung so tightly you could pluck chords in my neck. The last guidebook still wasn't finished (Steve and his deadlines), and the property manager we'd hired had already rented our house. The first couple who walked through the door snapped it up, so there was no leeway in our timetable: We had to be completely moved onto *Receta* in three weeks.

While Steve wrestled with paring down his T-shirt collection on breaks from his computer, I packed up the rest of the house. Which cookbooks should I take? Could I live with just one frying pan? Would my wineglasses survive onboard? Each item required a decision before it went into a box: Was it destined for the storage locker we'd rented, the yard sale planned at Steve's parents' house, the recycling depot, the garbage, or *Receta*?

The smallest pile was the one for *Receta*.

As I gamely tried to consolidate a whole pantry's worth of condiments and spices into a row that would fit on one tiny shelf, it suddenly hit me: For the next two years, I would be cooking three meals a day in a space barely four feet square. No dishwasher, no food processor, no microwave, no electric coffeemaker; just a three-burner propane stove with a Lilliputian oven and a top-opening fridge and freezer with one-fifth the capacity of the one at home.

While Steve continued to mouse around at his Mac, I gradually moved our downsized possessions aboard. I had everything tidily stowed by the time he finally started packing and moving his own stuff. "That locker was for my tools," he said, swinging open a cupboard door in *Receta*'s aft cabin. It was neatly piled with wine bottles, each one carefully swathed in bubble wrap and labeled. He tried another, less-accessible spot. More wine. "I was gonna put my engine spares there," he said with dismay. He lifted the cushions on the forward berth to get at the locker there. It was filled with nonperishable food, and more wine. *Surely* he didn't expect me to leave good food and our (admittedly mediocre) wine cellar behind? The snarling that ensued did not bode well for the two years to come.

As our August departure approached, the daily to-do lists in my Day-Timer became more intimidating than any I ever had at the office: Get physicals, eye exams, dental checkups. Arrange out-of-country medical insurance. Work with family doctor on contents of onboard medical kit. Reassure parents that we really do know what we're doing while doubting that we really do. Assemble navigational charts and cruising guidebooks. Buy new laptop and equip with software that will allow us—we hope—to stay in touch via e-mail with friends (including the two who are handling the guidebook distribution business while we're gone). Reassure parents, who are not yet on e-mail, that there are indeed telephones throughout the Caribbean. Enroll in first-aid and CPR course. Reassure parents again. Sign powers of attorney to allow our accountant to handle our finances while we're away. See lawyer and prepare living wills, just in case. Reassure parents (and self) again. Find a buyer for my car and convince Steve's parents to store his. See every last friend we've got in the city, to say good-bye. Try not to think about all the things I'll soon be required to do that I've never done before. Like sail at night.

We cut things so close to the deadline that we're on the deck locking the back door of our empty house as our new tenants are on the porch unlocking the front. I've lost ten pounds from stress, and my excruciatingly well-organized self is trailing loose ends in all directions. When Carol, the property manager we hired, tracks me down two days after we move out, she inquires sweetly, "Did you realize you rented the house with a load of your clothes still in the dryer?"

Chesapeake Bay Crabcakes
(IN THE STYLE OF RUKE'S STORE)

What makes these cakes so delicious—besides the freshest possible crabmeat—is their meaty texture: They are almost entirely crab inside, with just enough bread crumbs to hold them together. The cakes are rolled in crumbs before frying, which gives them a crispy golden exterior. Serve with lemon quarters and tartar sauce, if you like.

SERVES 2–3

1 pound fresh lump crabmeat, drained
1 teaspoon Dijon mustard
6 tablespoons mayonnaise
1 large egg, beaten
¼ cup finely minced onion
2 tablespoons finely chopped flat-leaf parsley
1 teaspoon Worcestershire sauce
¼ teaspoon hot sauce (or to taste)
2 teaspoons fresh lemon juice
1 teaspoon Old Bay Seasoning
Freshly ground black pepper
1 cup fine bread crumbs or matzoh meal (approx.)
Butter and/or oil for shallow frying

1. Mix together all ingredients except the bread crumbs and the butter or oil. Add just enough crumbs—about 4 tablespoons—so the crab mixture holds together. Taste and season with additional lemon juice, hot sauce, and pepper as required.
2. Form into 6 cakes. Roll cakes in remaining crumbs. Place on a baking sheet lined with waxed paper and refrigerate for about an hour.
3. Heat a small amount of butter or oil (I like to use a

combination) in a large skillet. Fry until golden brown on both sides, about 5 minutes per side. Drain on paper towels.

Tips:
- The cakes can be deep-fried if desired.
- Make bite-size cakes to serve as hors d'oeuvres. They can be fried early in the day and refrigerated, then reheated briefly on a baking tray in a 350°F oven. Makes 25–30 hors d'oeuvres.

In the Marshes

Of course, just hearing the names of some of the places on the
Intracoastal Waterway will never ease anyone's mind about the trip:
Dismal Swamp, Alligator River, Lockwoods Folly, Cape Fear River,
Mosquito Lagoon, Haulover Canal, several Hell Gates . . .

> Jan and Bill Moeller, The Intracoastal Waterway:
> A Cockpit Cruising Handbook, 1997

TURN LEFT AT THE BOTTOM OF Chesapeake Bay and
you're in the Atlantic, turn right and you enter the
Intracoastal Waterway. *Receta* turns right.

The Intracoastal Waterway—the ICW—is the highway from
the Chesapeake to Miami, the watery equivalent of I-95. Also
called "the Ditch," it was created to provide a protected inside
route for those—like us—who don't want to go out on the open
ocean when they don't have to. Officially, the ICW starts in
Massachusetts, goes all the way down the East Coast (though the
stretch through New Jersey isn't maintained at depths suitable for
cruising boats), and then across the Gulf Coast to Texas. But the
heart of the waterway is from Mile 0, at Norfolk, Virginia, at
the bottom of Chesapeake Bay, to Mile 1,095 at Miami: a winding ribbon of rivers, creeks, and man-made canals just inland of
the ocean. This narrow ribbon, protected by barrier islands and
low coastal mainland, ties together pieces of American history—
Revolutionary War battlegrounds, the haunts of pirates and

smugglers, plantations once worked by slaves, Civil War forts—as it passes storied cities such as Charleston, Beaufort, Savannah, and St. Augustine.

Occasionally, the route crosses gloriously open water—Albermarle Sound, Pamlico Sound—but mostly the ICW is too narrow for us to sail. The channel between the red and green markers has space for two boats to pass but often not much more, with shoals or deadheads or both off to the sides. The channel markers wear crowns of thorns, jumbles of sticks that mark the home of osprey and their offspring. October is too late for young to be in the nests, but sometimes an adult glares down its curved beak at us as we motor by, or one soars overhead, a fish clutched in its talons.

And all along the waterway, herons stand stick-still in the shadows at the shoreline, flapping off with an annoyed *skronk* once they realize they've been spotted. Mistletoe decorates the treetops in the Alligator River in North Carolina, a novelty for northerners like us who only see it hanging in doorways at Christmas. We smooch in the cockpit every time we spot it. (Now I know how boating accidents happen in the South.) When Steve yells "dolphin" on the Pamlico River, I snap to attention but don't see anything, and I'm sure it's just a trick: He realized I had my eyes closed behind my sunglasses and was trying to put an end to my mid-morning nap. But, no, a slick gray back curves above the surface ahead of us, and soon three bottlenose dolphins are whistling by alongside, alternately diving and arcing, crisscrossing our bow wave with syncopated grace.

The water is a just-polished mirror as we motor down Russell Creek toward Beaufort, North Carolina. Suddenly it's broken by twenty or thirty fins: dolphins all around us this time, curving into the air in a slow-motion ballet that continues for half a mile. We are passing through a dolphin nursery area.

This is what I had hoped for back in Toronto when I finally

convinced myself to leave. Even though most stretches of the waterway only require one person on deck to steer, neither of us wants to go below even for a couple of hours to tackle some chore. "Forget it," I tell Steve. "I might miss something." Besides, we have a deal—the first one to spot an alligator gets to decide what we eat for dinner for a whole week—and I don't trust him.

One night, at anchor in the Neuse River off Oriental, North Carolina, small crackling noises resonate steadily through *Receta's* hull. It's a frightening sound, as if her fiberglass is slowly crumbling apart beneath us and the tea-colored river will soon begin pouring through the cabin floor. We search nervously for the problem, lifting up the access panels in the floor so we can inspect the bilges for cracks, and running our hands along the hull at the backs of lockers, checking for dampness. Nothing. The noise continues but we don't appear to be sinking, so we eventually try to ignore it, have dinner, and start studying the section of the guidebook about the next day's stretch of waterway. And there it is: Don't be alarmed, the guide warns, by the "disturbingly loud" noise that "often goes on all night long." It's only krill—small, shrimplike creatures—munching the algae off *Receta's* bottom. "Eat, eat," says Steve, encouraging them mightily. The more they eat, the less we'll have to scrub.

Most nights we anchor in swift-running tidal creeks off the main channel. From our anchorage in Taylor Creek, at Beaufort, I can walk across the barrier island at low tide to the broad beach that faces the Atlantic. Chestnut-colored wild horses with shaggy manes roam the tidal flats, as they've done since the forties, when they were put here by a local doctor and left to fend for themselves after he died. Hundreds of shorebirds—sandpipers, sanderlings, ruddy turnstones—scurry past like fast-moving windup toys, as if they know they've got limited time to make their rounds before the flats are again covered by the sea. On the beach, I hunt for shells—and find a necklace of fragile white coins, the egg case of a whelk

—until I begin to worry that the tide will start rising and strand me.

Granted, settling into this new way of life is requiring more adjustment than just getting used to not having a two-storey house to rumble around in, with a dishwasher, telephone, TV, VCR, and unlimited supplies of hot water and electricity. I'm a morning person, Steve's not, and his body clock has been winning. *Receta* is usually the last boat out of an anchorage in the morning. And as I begin to hear the *clank, clank, clank* of other anchor chains being raised, my stomach starts to churn. *Those boats* know *how long it takes to get to the next good stopping place. They're going to get there* first *and there won't be* any *space left when we arrive. We need to get underway* now. Steve, meanwhile, is just getting his second eye open and thinking about rolling out of bed and enjoying a coffee.

In Worton Creek a few weeks ago, I was *determined* to get underway with "the übercruisers," as Steve has dismissively dubbed the early-risers. So I shook him awake at 6:30, listened to the grumbling, pried him out of the berth, and considered it a major accomplishment when we were actually ready to hoist anchor at eight. *Receta* seemed sluggish as I motored forward so he could pull in the anchor chain. "Goose it," he called back to me from the bow, and I revved up the engine. But it was as if we were moving through thick, gooey chocolate syrup.

And then the syrup congealed. We were stuck fast in Worton Creek mud.

Lake Ontario doesn't have tides, so I wasn't used to thinking about them. In my eagerness for an early start, I had overlooked one very important point: We had come into Worton Creek at high tide. At 8 a.m. the next morning, the tide was falling, and the corner of the creek we were sitting in no longer had the five feet of water *Receta* requires.

It wasn't until early afternoon that the tide had risen enough to allow us to pop free and push very slowly through the muck.

During the intervening six hours, I got to practice cultivating patience—never one of my defining characteristics—and stew about losing whatever leverage I had with Steve on matters relating to early awakenings and early starts. He, meanwhile, yawned extravagantly and grinned like the Cheshire cat.

Clearly, I'm going to need more patience if I'm to be happy in this new lifestyle. Just the daily act of anchoring is exhausting my limited supply. Figuring tide, current, and *Receta*'s 23,000 pounds into the anchoring equation is new to Steve. He likes to think it through. Carefully. Slowly. This is an admirable characteristic, but at the time he's exercising it, I'm bristling with impatience to get the hook down, since after that I can relax. I realize that the better the spot we choose to anchor, the more likely we are to have a relaxing evening without having to worry about the anchor dragging or *Receta* swinging too close to another boat when the tide reverses. But as we circle the anchorage a second time, and I watch someone else take the spot I had suggested on the first pass, I'm about ready to explode.

By the time we reach the Waccamaw River across the South Carolina line, Spanish moss drips from the trees like fringe on a pale-green shawl draped around an elegant southern lady.

There's no question we're in the South now, with grits on every menu and accents like warm honey. "We don't care how you do it in the North" is emblazoned on bumper stickers in Beaufort, South Carolina (pronounced *Bew-fort*, and not to be confused with *Boh-fort*, North Carolina), and cocktail napkins in Savannah, Georgia (just off the waterway, nine miles up the Savannah River). And far too many Confederate flags hang stubbornly, aggressively from the rural homes we pass on the banks of the canals and rivers.

We've been seeing the flat-bottomed skiffs for a couple of days now, sitting low in the water off the channel, with one or two men onboard tossing nets over the side. From a distance, the nets look like ballet dancers' sequin-studded skirts—billowing, swirling, sparkling as the sun catches the droplets that spin from them into the air. In fact, Steve has taken to spying on the men in the skiffs through binoculars as we motor past, studying how they throw, getting the nets to hang for a few seconds in midair, opened in a perfect circle, before they settle gracefully into the water.

This isn't idle admiration. The men in the boats are shrimping, and buried in the locker under the foot of our berth is a brand-new, still-in-the-package cast net, presented to Steve what seems a lifetime ago in Toronto, as a going-away gift from friends. He's been dying to try it.

Unfortunately, he's not exactly sure *how*. The printed directions that come packaged with it are bewilderingly complex, and the helpful hints are not at all helpful when you're living on a boat. ("An excellent way to practice, without getting wet, is to throw the net in your backyard . . . You can practice from ground level or you can use a pickup tailgate . . . An old tire makes an excellent target for improving your aim. Remember, practice makes perfect.") One can only pick up so much by snooping through binoculars.

Our planned stopping point today is Five Fathom Creek, near McClellanville, South Carolina, which turns out to have a lot less water than its name implies. As we inch in on a rising tide—*note to self: Check tide tables before setting departure time*—a commercial shrimping boat is coming out the creek, its nets dangling from outriggers like huge bat wings. Looking east, shoulder-high marsh grass extends to the horizon, unbroken by even a single tree; from water level, the creeks that cut through it are invisible. When another big shrimper glides by in the distance, it looks like a combine adrift on a sea of wheat. If I didn't know better, I'd swear we were anchoring in the middle of the prairie.

But Steve's not interested in anchorage aesthetics. He's spotted one of those flat-bottomed skiffs just ahead. Faster than you can say jambalaya, he's got *Receta*'s hook down and has dug out his net to see if he can get a lesson. "Fishermen don't always like it when you horn in on their territory," I warn when he climbs into *Snack*, as we'd named our 9½-foot inflatable dinghy.

But Orland T. Cooper was a high school teacher, and he's delighted to take a student under his very southern wing. His two Coke coolers are almost full of shrimp, and he was about to call it a day anyway. "When the tide's up," he explains, "the shrimp retreat into the marshes where their food is. You don't get many then."

Orland has anchored his boat—an aging cabin cruiser—and rigged his well-worn skiff so it can be pulled back and forth by a rope strung between the poles he's staked on the edge of the marsh. Late sixtyish, wiry, with the sun-baked look of someone who's spent a lifetime outdoors, Orland tells Steve the stakes mark where he's put hockey pucks of fish-meal bait. "You need a license to bait," he says. "I got mine after I stopped teaching, when the integration came along." Steve never does find out what, exactly, Orland taught, but almost certainly it wasn't multiculturalism or race relations. Steve's net was made in China, and Orland inspects it approvingly. "Nobody can outfish a Chinaman," he says.

A good net thrown well settles into the water wide open, Orland explains, thus enveloping as many shrimp as possible. When you tug the net closed, the inch-long lead weights that line the circumference are drawn together and keep the shrimp from escaping. What Steve couldn't see through the binocs is that shrimpers use more than their hands to throw the net: They also use their teeth. ("This product contains lead, a chemical known to cause cancer," the instructions with Steve's net warn. "Do not place the product in your mouth.")

"Put the loop of the line over your left wrist"—so you don't lose the net when you throw it—"and then drape the net over your left hand." Orland demonstrates. "Then reach down and grab part of the bottom edge—not a lead weight—in your teeth, and grasp farther along the bottom with your right hand." The actual toss is kind of a cross between a frisbee throw and a tennis backhand. Orland's ruddy face cracks into a grin. "Now don't forget to open your mouth."

During the lesson, he insists Steve take a couple of breaks in his cabin cruiser—one for some jug wine and one for tea and cookies—and stuffs him with stories of life in the Carolina marshes. "This one's a favorite around here," he says, launching into a tale about two "British lads."

"They were cruising at the low end of the scale, in an old World War I lifeboat, and got caught in a wicked storm off the coast. They holed up belowdecks to ride it out. Meanwhile, the wind pushed them right through the inlet here and into one of these creeks that weave through the marshes. When one of the boys finally came topside for a look, he told the other they'd washed up in Kansas."

I can believe it.

It's almost dusk when Steve roars back to *Receta*, his jeans and sweatshirt plastered with bits of marsh—strands of weed, splotches of creek mud, and hairlike pink shrimp feelers—to exchange a plastic bag bulging with shrimp for a couple of bottles of our wine. "For my pal Orland," he says, as he grabs the wine and hands over the sack. I'm duly impressed—even when he confesses Orland had to supplement his student's catch with his own shrimp so we'd have enough for dinner.

What to make is easy: shrimp and grits. I've been keen to cook hominy grits since buying a box at the Piggly Wiggly grocery store (motto: "Big on the Pig") in Georgetown, South Carolina, a couple of days earlier. The only problem is that unlike store-bought shrimp, Steve's haven't come sorted by size. Some are truly jumbos . . . and some are barely salad shrimp. Which makes the shelling, deveining, and, particularly, timing the cooking a little tricky. I complain to the supplier, who's by now pinching off the last of the shrimp heads in the cockpit. Given that he's just delivered the freshest shrimp I'm ever going to eat, he's not the least bit sympathetic.

Eating shrimp just an hour out of the water is a revelation. The first thing we notice is their texture. They're meaty and firm, with none of the mushiness that affects their brethren that have spent a lot more time on ice. When I bite into my first one, it almost pops. And then there's the smell: clean, fresh, the essence of shrimp without any undertones of fishiness. They are set up perfectly by the mound of soft grits underneath, ribboned with melted cheddar.

As we wind the rest of the way through the marshes of South Carolina and Georgia, Steve no longer needs encouragement to get underway early. He wants time at the end of the day to cast before dark. Rock Creek brings stir-fried shrimp with garlic and ginger; Herb Creek, red-curry shrimp with coconut milk; New Teakettle Creek, shrimp in garlic butter; Shellbine Creek . . . cheese omelets. Damn: The wind's too strong for shrimping.

Steve's making it look easy now, but he's taking far too much credit for being the great provider. One evening I decide to go along in the dinghy and try casting myself. I thoroughly soak us both with marsh water before I manage to throw the net so it lands wide open. I can't wait to haul it in to see what I've got. "Let it settle for a few seconds," says the expert. "Okay, now, tug it closed and bring it in." Four measly shrimp. I try another equally unproductive cast, and since I have my heart set on pad Thai for dinner, I turn the net back over to Steve. By the time it's dark, he's brought in enough that we can even give a bag to another couple, who have dinghied up the creek from their own boat to join us on *Receta* for drinks.

The marshes give us solitude, though, as well as dinner. There are so many bends and twists that even if another sailboat anchors nearby it is usually out of sight, only the tip of its mast visible across the marsh grass. One evening, *Receta* sits alone under a vast sky that has been brushed top to bottom across the horizon with fat strokes of reds and pinks. Another night, we are the only witnesses when a half-dozen hungry dolphins work the shallow edges of the creek, hoovering up their shrimp dinner as Steve scoops up ours.

We're moving south, but we're not outrunning winter.

I look like the Michelin Man and I can barely clamber up and down the companionway. I'm swaddled in a full set of thermal underwear, jeans topped with rain pants, a fleece pullover topped with a down ski jacket topped with a foul-weather jacket, two pairs of socks, gloves, and a wool toque.

Under the toque, my hair is greasy and desperately in need of washing. Although it's possible to take a hot shower on *Receta*, it's not easy. Water is heated onboard by the engine via a heat exchanger, and it's a fair distance from the hot-water tank, which is aft, under the cockpit, to the head, far forward, where the shower is. By the time the water coming out of the showerhead is even tepid, I'm shivering; by the time it's approaching hot, I've already wasted so much water, I can't enjoy it. Plus, there's the cleanup. One drawback of *Receta*'s lovely traditional oiled teak interior is the head. Modern cruising boats of similar size have a separate molded-plastic shower; *Receta*'s shower is part of the head itself—which means the toilet, teak-trimmed counter, teak-trimmed walls, and floor (with teak grate) get soaked when you use it, despite the valiant efforts of a shower curtain—which means you need to wipe the entire head dry when you're finished, or mildew will sprout everywhere. In warm weather, in isolated anchorages, we showered in the cockpit, using a solar shower (essentially a heavy-duty plastic bag with a nozzle; fill it with water and leave it out to heat in the sun all day). Larger towns like Annapolis and Beaufort (*Boh-fort*) have shoreside showers for cruisers, but we haven't anchored off a lot of "larger towns" lately. A daily shower these days simply isn't worth the trouble.

One more night of record-cold November temperatures, the radio tells us. One more night of disgusting dirty hair. For the first time since we left Toronto, I wish I were curled up in our warm bed at home.

We droned along, 50 or so miles a day, 5½ miles an hour, the engine doing the work, often with one sail up to give us whatever assist from the wind we can get. The only variation in the deep thrum of the diesel comes when we need to slow down to wait for a bridge to open or goose it up to reach a bridge before it closes. Opening bridges are the bugbear of the ICW, eighty-five of them between the Chesapeake and Miami, as many as twelve in one day's travel. Some open only on the hour, some on the half hour, some every twenty minutes, some not at all during morning and afternoon rush hours, and some on a mysterious schedule apparently known only to the bridgemaster and completely unrelated to what's printed in our guidebook. Missing a bridge means endless circling until the next opening. More than mere annoyance, it can be downright tricky when the channel is narrow and the tidal current is sweeping in or out. Steve is always at the helm when we approach a closed bridge.

"*Receta*. Be careful." The cockpit speaker of the VHF radio had squawked to life as we circled in front of the highway bridge at Wrightsville Beach, North Carolina. "This is *Kairos*, the boat ahead of you. Don't follow me. We just touched bottom."

Thump. "*Kairos*, this is *Receta*. Too late. We're aground." Right in the channel, I might have added.

Piss. I hadn't even been anxiety-ridden about this stretch of the waterway. It was tomorrow's—the shallow, tricky Cape Fear River

with its multiple inlets, strong currents, and confusing buoyage—
that I was dreading.

This was the last bridge we'd planned to go through today; I
had been so looking forward to being at anchor on the other side.
But now our keel is firmly stuck in a ridge of sand that the current
had deposited along the channel's inside edge.

We don't know *Kairos*, don't think we've even seen the boat
before this afternoon. But, like us, they have been waiting for the
Wrightsville Beach bridge to open. It's the second in a particularly
odious one-two combo of bridges. The first opens on the half-
hour; this one opens only on the hour; and with 4.8 nautical miles
between them, it's impossible for a sailboat to catch consecutive
openings. We got to Wrightsville Beach with twenty minutes to
wait before the next opening—twenty minutes for Steve to circle
in a narrow channel with a lively breeze and an even livelier
current pushing us around—and now, hard aground.

"I don't think I can tow you off." *Kairos* on the radio again, a
male voice, with a bit of a twang, apologetic, as if it's his fault for
leading us astray. "If I get close to you, I'm afraid I'll go aground
too."

"Tell him no problem," Steve says to me. "And tell him to *get
going* or he'll miss the bridge and have to wait another hour, too."

Steve has raised the mainsail and unfurled the jib, sheeting
them both in tightly to heel *Receta* over to one side and lessen our
draft. One side of the deck is now almost touching the water. But
his tactics aren't working: The current is too strong, pushing us
farther into the sand. Unlike on Worton Creek, we can't just wait
for the tide to rise: It will be well after dark by then, and it would
be decidedly unwise to spend the night parked in a channel.

"TowBOAT U.S., TowBOAT U.S., this is *Receta*." It's time for
professional help.

Five minutes later, the nice men from TowBOAT U.S. have
pulled up alongside—seems this is a popular spot for them to wait

for business—and it takes them a scant twenty minutes more to "prop-wash" the sand out from under *Receta* and tow us free, giving us plenty of time to circle some more before the next bridge opening. When the driver hands me their bill for $432, I hand it back with a demure smile—and our no-limit towing insurance card. "*Everybody* goes aground at some point on the ICW," experienced cruisers had told us way back in New York. "If we see you later and you tell us you didn't go aground, we'll know you're liars. Buy towing insurance." The official TowBOAT U.S. card had caught up with us via a mail drop from home just days before.

We're still rehashing our no-harm-done-to-wallet-or-boat adventure—"only to my ego," mutters Steve—as we get settled in the anchorage on the other side of the bridge. "Hey, *Receta*, catch. You need these." Two cans of Coors fly from a dinghy into our cockpit. Which is how we make face-to-face acquaintance with Todd and Belinda on *Kairos*.

First-time cruisers just a few years younger than we are, they too had decided to take a time-out from careers that were growing increasingly stressful. He is gregarious, upbeat, quick to laugh, a practical, hands-on, do-it-yourself guy—and a gentle romantic. He had proposed to Belinda on the bow of their boat as they were sailing along the western shore of Chesapeake Bay, their home waters—on a day he just happened to have a minister friend in the cockpit who could perform the ceremony when she said yes. Belinda, meanwhile, is his perfect foil: She seems quiet at first, almost subdued, and then slowly reveals a steel-trap mind, and a sly and wicked wit. We like them immediately.

Their break is open-ended. "We'll see how we feel, how we like cruising, how the money holds out," Todd says. For Belinda, heading off on a sailboat was as much a leap of faith as it had been for me. She seems to have no more confidence in her sailing abilities than I have, and just as many anxieties. Their short-term plan is much the same as ours too: Florida by Christmas, the

Bahamas in the New Year, and then, as hurricane season approaches, decide where to go next.

We don't see them again until we've crossed into Florida in early December, but we frequently meet up in anchorages after that as we hopscotch our way down the state. Over potluck dinners, we share experiences, the friendship grows, and a loose plan develops: Let's cross together to the Bahamas—our first big ocean passage.

Low-Country Shrimp and Grits

Grits (a.k.a. hominy grits) are ground, skinned white corn kernels. They're a staple of Carolina cooking, found at both high-end restaurants (wild mushroom grits with oyster stew are a first course at Charleston's renowned Peninsula Grill) and in local luncheonettes (where a standard breakfast includes eggs, sausage patties, biscuits, and grits). We love them plain—with just a lump of butter and perhaps some freshly grated Parmesan—as a comforting, warming, stick-to-your-ribs alternative to potatoes or rice. But we never pass up an opportunity to have them with fresh shrimp piled on top.

SERVES 4

For the shrimp
  2 tablespoons butter or oil
  1 small onion, thinly sliced
  1 clove garlic, minced
  ½ red bell pepper, thinly sliced
  ¼ pound mushrooms, sliced
  1–1½ pounds shrimp, shelled and deveined
  1 tablespoon freshly squeezed lemon juice
  2 tablespoons chopped flat-leaf parsley
  Salt and freshly ground black pepper
  Hot sauce

For the grits
   1 cup milk
   2 cups water
   ¾ cup quick-cooking grits
   ¼ teaspoon salt
   ½–¾ cup grated cheddar cheese

1. To make the shrimp, heat butter or oil in a large frying pan. Sauté onion and garlic until soft. Add mushrooms and red pepper and sauté until mushrooms give up their liquid.
2. Add shrimp and stir fry until just done, about 2–5 minutes, depending on size. (The shrimp should be just opaque inside.) Sprinkle with lemon juice and parsley, and season to taste with salt, pepper, and hot sauce.
3. In the meantime, cook the grits: Bring milk and water to a boil in a large, heavy saucepan. Slowly add grits and salt, whisking constantly. Reduce heat to low, cover, and cook until grits are thickened, about 6 minutes, stirring occasionally. Remove from heat, stir in the cheese and a few dashes of hot sauce, and season to taste.
4. Spoon shrimp over grits and serve.

Variations:
• Fry a few slices of bacon until crisp, crumble, and set aside, then sauté the vegetables in the bacon fat instead of butter or oil. Stir the crumbled bacon into the cooked shrimp.
• Substitute ½ green bell pepper for the red bell pepper and add 2–3 chopped fresh or canned tomatoes when you sauté the vegetables. Cook for 5 minutes or so to thicken the sauce before adding the shrimp.

Blown Away in the Bahamas

It is unlucky to start a cruise on a Friday, the day Christ was crucified. In the 19th century, the British navy tried to dispel this superstition. The keel of a new ship was laid on a Friday, she was named HMS *Friday*, launched on a Friday, and finally sent to sea on a Friday. Neither the ship nor her crew were ever heard of again.

Robert Hendrickson, The Ocean Almanac, 1984

GIVEN THE UNPREDICTABILITY OF the sea, perhaps it's not surprising that mariners have always been a superstitious lot. *The Ocean Almanac,* a fascinating compendium of nautical lore that we keep handy on *Receta's* bookshelf, lists forty-four things I must or must not do to court good luck and avoid bad. Hand a flag to a sailor between the rungs of a ladder or lose a mop or bucket overboard, and bad luck is sure to follow. Ditto if you invite a priest aboard—but it's a good idea to have a naked woman (thought to have a calming effect on the sea, which is why so many ships once had bare-breasted figures on their bows); a clothed woman, however, makes the sea angry. At the very top of the *Almanac's* list of sea-going superstitions is the caution about starting out on a Friday.

With *Kairos* tied alongside us, we wait eleven nail-biting days in an anchorage at Key Biscayne, near Miami, for decent weather to cross to the Bahamas.

It's January; the days are warm and lazy. We go for long walks, catch up on boat jobs, share dinners, and, one afternoon, play with the manatees that have swum into our anchorage. These huge, slow-moving beasts that surface every few minutes to breathe are thought to be the basis of sailors' tales of mermaids. But only someone who had been at sea a very long time would divine a beautiful woman from these wrinkled, whiskery snouts and leathery elephant bodies covered with patches of algae and barnacles. Also called sea cows, manatees are, like their grazing namesakes, none too bright. They like to rest just below the surface, where they are often hit by speeding powerboats (whose drivers, some of them none too bright either, ignore the signs telling them to slow down in manatee zones), keeping these unfortunate mammals on the list of endangered species. (Their numbers were reduced well before powerboats, when they were hunted almost to extinction for their meat.) However, manatees haven't learned to fear boats or people, and they swim trustingly up to our dinghy and let the four of us scratch them. One big guy, all 10 feet and probably 1,000 pounds of him, rolls onto his back like a puppy to have his tummy scratched, his flippers up and his tongue lolling out.

Meanwhile, we're frustrated as hell. *Kairos* has been tied to us for so long that Steve has dubbed Todd and Belinda "the remoras," after the fish that attach themselves to ships, sharks, and other big fish to hitch rides and feast on food dropped by their obliging hosts. "Things could be worse," Todd says. "We could be someplace cold—and at work." The dreaded "W word," as it's called in cruising circles. He's right, of course, but the tourist board has convinced us it's better in the Bahamas. Besides, Belinda and I are *desperate* to get the crossing over with. Each day we're primed for it, pumped, filled with nervous energy, ready to go—and then we gradually deflate as we hear the weather reports and realize we won't be leaving. At the same time, we're also a teensy bit relieved that we've been granted yet another reprieve. Boaters do this crossing all the time, but for us it's a Big Deal—*our* first challenging passage—and the longer we wait, the more our minds blow it out of proportion.

It's not the distance that makes the crossing potentially difficult—only 47 miles separate Key Biscayne from Bimini, where we plan to land in the Bahamas—but rather the Gulf Stream: a 40-mile-wide river of warm water that flows northward past the coast of Florida at speeds of up to 4½ knots. We have to build it into our course, initially heading south rather than directly across to Bimini, to compensate for it sweeping us north. But even with a perfectly calculated course, the Gulf Stream can make the crossing miserable. When the wind is out of the northeast, north, or northwest, it collides with the north-flowing current and sets up white elephants—steep, square, often dangerous, and always stomach-churning waves. All the guidebooks agree: Don't cross the Gulf Stream until you have a weather window without any "north" in the forecast. Which is why we've been waiting eleven days at Key Biscayne.

Finally, it looks like a window is opening. On a *Friday*.

We go.

Perhaps that's why *Receta* snags a lobster trap on the way into Alicetown, Bimini. Of course, we don't know for sure that's what it is—just that we are entering a strange harbor, on a falling tide, in an unfavorable wind, with the current against us, a shallow sandbar on one side and rocks on the other, and suddenly it has become almost impossible to turn *Receta*'s wheel.

We had crept out of Key Biscayne in predawn darkness, *Receta* leading the way, *Kairos* (and a string of other boats) following—an arrangement that boosted my already-high anxiety level several notches. Before we even left the anchorage, my stomach had knotted up the way it used to thirty years earlier on the mornings of high school geometry tests. I couldn't imagine choking down breakfast and settled instead for a couple of seasickness pills.

Barely twenty minutes underway, with the lights of Key Biscayne alongside us, Steve, steering, misread a buoy and almost passed it on the wrong side, requiring a sharp, sudden change in direction. Looking behind us, I can see the procession of following boats make the same sharp jog one by one, like trusting players in some on-the-water game of Follow the Expert.

There was no mistaking the place where the Gulf Stream kicked in: The ocean suddenly felt friskier, the waves were bigger, and the line on the horizon where ocean meets sky turned jagged. I sensed some queasy hours ahead, but after that initial friskiness, the sea never got worse. The waves remained bearable, even comfortable, and Steve's plotting was perfect; although *Receta* was pointed in the wrong direction, the Gulf Stream took charge until—seven hours of fast, uneventful passage later—Bimini appeared in the distance, right where it should be. Ahead of us, like two distinct pieces of cloth joined by a seam, the ocean abruptly changed from dark cobalt to turquoise, at the precise spot where the deep Atlantic meets the shallow Bahama Banks. The Big Deal was almost over—and, to my amazement, it hadn't been such a big deal.

When we had planned our adventure back in Toronto, reaching the Bahamas was the first Really Big Goal; if we accomplished that and nothing else, the trip for me would have been a success. My confidence soared.

It was short-lived.

Steve is busy taking down the sails, the engine is on, and I am at the helm when the steering problem begins. Suddenly, the wheel is very stiff, the boat unresponsive. "The worst possible time for something to go wrong," I point out, quite unnecessarily, as we prepare to negotiate the harbor entrance. Steve has taken over the steering and is trying to hide from me exactly how much muscle he has to use to turn the boat even a tiny bit. In case we lose *all* steerage, he decides to err on the shallow sandbar side of the long entrance channel and farther from the rocks. We bump, bump, bottom-bump our way over the sand.

Once through the entrance, he manages to crank the helm far enough left to convince the reluctant *Receta* to head toward the dock, where we need to check in with Bahamian Customs and Immigration. And it's then that I see it: a thick yellow polypropylene rope streaming incriminatingly behind the boat, wedged against the rudder and preventing it from turning—a rope that most likely has a lobster trap attached to its other end. "All those miles down the Chesapeake without becoming tangled in a crab pot, and *now* we do it, our first day beyond the U.S.," I moan. If the trap had snagged on a rock or coral head as we dragged it along the bottom through the entrance channel, or does so now, on the way to the check-in dock, the rudder will most likely be ripped off before the heavy line gives way. *If we make it to the dock*, I tell myself, *at least we'll have fresh lobster for dinner to go with the champagne.* We'd been planning to uncork a bottle to celebrate finally arriving in the Bahamas.

Receta makes it to the dock. Once the check-in formalities are over, Steve rounds up Todd, several long poles, and a Bahamian dockhand who's offered to help, no doubt seeing the promise of some free line, a free lobster trap, and a couple of free floats. I, meanwhile, have unearthed our biggest pot from the depths of the aft cabin. To cook the lobster.

They jockey the line out from the rudder, haul in all 80 feet of it—the trap was in deep water—and hoist the heavy metal cage onto the dock with great expectation.

No lobsters. Inside the trap is just one 3-foot-long, pissed off green moray eel.

*   *   *

Perhaps our flagrant disregard for maritime superstitions—not only did we set out on a Friday, we had changed the boat's name—is also responsible for the weather.

"Get out of Bimini as soon as possible. Leave tonight." These encouraging words are delivered shortly after the moray is evicted by the trap's new owner, one very pleased Bahamian dockhand. *Leave tonight? When we've just arrived? When we're exhausted and ready to open the champagne?* But the advice comes from Herb, and one doesn't take what Herb says lightly. There's this little matter of a gale approaching, he tells me, and we need to be tucked away somewhere protected—which is *not* Bimini—by Sunday afternoon.

Shit. Shit. SHIT. But I just chirp, "Roger that," as protocol demands. Because Herb Hilgenberg, the cruiser's weather god, is telling me this via SSB—single sideband—radio. From the basement of his house in Burlington, a city on the Canadian shore of Lake Ontario, Herb transmits forecasts and advice to boats throughout the Atlantic and Caribbean, speaking with fifty to eighty individual boats seven days a week, while hundreds of others listen in and heed his advice. It is a herculean, almost unbelievable, volunteer job. Herb—everyone calls him by his first name only, even those who've never spoken with him, let alone met him—doesn't take weekends off. He works holidays, even Christmas and New Year's. Every day of the year, he spends hours compiling and interpreting weather data, works out the safest routes for his charges, and then is on the radio for three to four solid hours, without a break. He's routed boats around storms and taken them through hurricanes. He's saved lives. Herb's advice is so highly regarded that he's one of the few nonmilitary people with access to U.S. Navy weather data. Rumor has it he even tells the U.S. Navy how to interpret it.

Steve and I decided a couple of weeks ago that I would have the job on *Receta* of talking to Herb, because the word on the cruisers' grapevine is that he's a bit more tolerant, a tiny bit more patient, when the inexperienced voice at the other end of the microphone is female. And we need to cultivate every last bit of tolerance we can get. We are completely green at this—green at understanding offshore weather forecasts and green at using our new, bought-and-installed-in-Florida SSB radio. I know that in theory the single sideband will allow us to talk to people (including rescue services, if need be) far beyond the line-of-sight limits of our VHF radio, which is standard boat equipment. It will allow us to tune in news and weather services around the world, even receive weather fax charts by hooking our laptop to the radio. But in reality, there's a steep learning curve associated with using the SSB, and we're still at the very bottom.

Herb does not suffer fools gladly. In the three weeks we've been listening, I've already heard him deliver serious dressing-downs on air—for all the world to hear. Pity the boater who doesn't comprehend or decides to question Herb's forecast or recommendation.

When it comes my turn, I start the tape in my little recorder, so we can play back and transcribe Herb's advice afterward. I can't take notes, concentrate on using the new radio, and respond to Herb at the same time. I'm so nervous at first of the medium and the message that I'm positively doltish: One afternoon, I confuse the days of the week; the next day—horror of horrors—I forget to say thank you before signing off.

But crusty Herb also seems to have an uncanny ability to take the measure of the unknown person at the other end of the mike. As we waited and waited to leave Florida and each day he announced there was no weather window, it was as if he could sense my nervousness and my need to get the crossing over: "Relax, take advantage of the time," he told me one afternoon. "Go shopping." Herb clearly has my number.

Although they're few, he has his detractors—nobody's going to call the weather right 100 percent of the time—but we've had too many experienced cruisers tell us how he saved their bacon for us to ignore his advice. We decide to leave Bimini first thing in the morning.

By early Sunday afternoon, we're tied to a dock at Chub Cay, in the Berry Islands group of the Bahamas, at a pricey, protected marina—not the undeveloped, pristine (and free) anchorage where we expected to be staying. At the afternoon check-in, Herb approves our location. But the wind is light, the water a sparkling aquamarine jewel, and the anchorage around the corner—a gentle unprotected indentation in the island's shoreline—looks like the archetypal Bahamian beach scene of tourism brochures and guidebook covers. "Looks like we could have stayed in the anchorage and saved some money," Belinda says—*Kairos* is tied to the dock opposite us—and I agree. I'm beginning to doubt the words of the master.

At 3:30 A.M., the increased tempo of the spinning blades of the wind generator on *Receta*'s stern wakens us. The wind has started to pick up. By 9 A.M., boats that spent the night in the anchorage are streaming into the marina with reports of how unpleasant their night had been. Digging out extra lines that we've never had to use before, Steve spiderwebs *Receta* between the dock and the pilings, and lashes the sails in place so they can't unfurl in the wind. To reduce the boat's windage, we take down the canvas that protects our cockpit from sun and rain. "Put the cushions belowdecks too, and anything else that isn't tied down," Steve advises, not doubting Herb's warning one bit.

By noon, we have to yell directly into each other's ears. The wind is grabbing the words out of our mouths and flinging them out to sea. By nightfall, it's a sandblaster, driving grains from the beach a quarter mile away into our skin, our mouths, our eyes, and through the fine screens that cover the boat's tightly closed ports. By midnight, the howling is so loud I can't hear myself think—probably a good thing—and hard metallic sheets of rain are being riveted into *Receta*'s deck.

Until now, the most wind I'd experienced on a boat was, oh, maybe 25 knots. And I didn't like it. Steve switches on the boat's wind-speed indicator; the digital readout climbs to 45 knots—50 miles an hour—but another boat, with a taller mast (and its anemometer higher in the air), is on the radio reporting gusts to 70. I get down our cheery bookshelf friend *The Ocean Almanac*: On the Beaufort Scale, which measures wind velocity, winds of 45 knots are "strong gale," force 9; winds of 70 knots are force 12, hurricane force, top of the chart—or in Sir Francis Beaufort's words: "that which no canvas could withstand."

For the rest of the night, the wind shrieks through the rigging like a thousand banshees, and *Receta* is heeled over at the dock, straining at her lines, which at midnight Steve had crawled out to double and triple. Welcome to Paradise. It was never like this on the travel posters.

The next morning, the lone sailboat that had remained in the anchorage limps into the harbor, a piece of its stainless-steel rigging ripped from the deck and dangling like an overcooked noodle. The blades of the boat's wind generator had been spun off their mount by the relentless wind—a giant, knife-sharp propeller beanie lifted into the air and into the rigging. A Bahamian fishing boat is reported sunk; three of its crew swam safely to shore, but a fourth is missing. The captain of the *Heaven Sent*, a fishing boat safely in the harbor, is asked to go out and search. He refuses, saying he won't risk the lives of his crew.

Even boats tied up in the relative protection of the harbor have been damaged: a sail that unfurled and shredded, a canvas bimini top ripped from its supports and snatched skyward, a flipped and punctured dinghy.

"Hailstones the size of golfballs," says the captain of another commercial boat that arrives later in the day, while assuring me this is unheard of in the Bahamas. He also tells me the missing crewman has been found. Herb, meanwhile—and after last night, who would dream of doubting him?—says *another* gale system is right behind the first.

"We shouldn't have left on a Friday," I say to Belinda.

"I shouldn't have skipped church yesterday," she says back to me.

In fact, "the Christ child," El Niño in Spanish, is responsible: El Niño, the warm-water current that gets its name because it arrives off the coast of South America around Christmas. Every few years, El Niño's warming effect is stronger, lasts longer than usual, and has extensive meteorological effects well beyond the South American coast. Climatologists call these "El Niño years," and in this part of the world, an El Niño year translates into more, and more intense, storms stirred up across the eastern Gulf of Mexico and Florida, and then hurled into the Bahamas. This is not just any El Niño year—it's the strongest El Niño in a *hundred* years, ranked by the National Oceanic and Atmospheric Administration (NOAA) as one of the major climatic events of the century. It is not an easy year to be a nervous first-timer on a sailboat in the Bahamas. The only consolation as we sit trapped at Chub Cay waiting for the second gale system to arrive is that the fishing boats laden with fresh stone crab claws and conch have been driven into harbor by the weather too.

Thwack, thwack, thwack, THWACK. Belinda's thirty-fourth birthday, and the dinner party is on her boat. It will be more of a surprise that way, Elizabeth and I, the cooks, had reasoned earlier in the day. If we invite Belinda and Todd to one of *our* boats for dinner—Elizabeth and Don are on *Adriatica*, which left Key Biscayne on Friday when we did—Belinda will figure it's for her birthday. Much more fun if we don't say anything and just show up on *Kairos* with food and drinks and take over her galley. Todd happily agrees.

The only problem is, we've chosen conch as the main course, and it needs to be thoroughly tenderized or dinner will have the consistency of an inner tube. The weapon of choice is the conch hammer, the same sort of wooden or cast aluminum mallet used for tenderizing meat. So here we are, Elizabeth and I, beating the hell out of a dozen conch, spraying raw conchy bits all over Belinda's galley, all over ourselves, and all over the ceiling of her boat. "Pound until it's translucent, almost lacy," says Steve, reading from the recipe Elizabeth found in one of her cruising books. "When you hold it up, light should show through it." *Thwack, thwack, THWACK.* I beat the piece I'm working on a few more times for good measure, splurting a bit of conch juice onto Steve's glasses and Belinda's teak walls in the process. I'm so glad we decided to have the birthday dinner on her boat.

The queen conch—pronounced *conk* to rhyme with *bonk*—is a cornerstone of Bahamian cuisine, and the islands bear the proof: mounds of empty conch shells, the mottled cream and tan exteriors and pearly pink interiors bleaching white in the sun. The shells can be up to a foot long, though most are no bigger than eight or nine inches. Each one has a small telltale hole chiseled between its short blunt spikes—where a knife was inserted to sever the tendon so the tasty inhabitant could be pulled out.

Conch has been a popular food in the Bahamas as far back as the Arawaks, the islands' original inhabitants. People on remote cays have long depended on "hurricane ham": conch meat that's been flattened, tenderized, and hung in the sun to dry until it takes on the color and texture of its namesake. Cured this way, conch will apparently last without refrigeration for a year, handy during bad weather, when boats carrying provisions can't get to the islands and it's too rough to take to the water to fish. The fresh meat is sweet and mild—somewhere between clam and calamari in its taste and chewy texture—and widely acclaimed as an aphrodisiac.

Elizabeth and I are making cracked conch for the birthday dinner. The name of the dish has nothing to do with the pounding the main ingredient gets; it comes from the cracker meal—crushed crackers—with which the tenderized fresh conch is coated. It's then either deep-fried or panfried, which will allow us to add a nice coating of splattered grease to the conchy bits decorating Belinda's galley.

Conch live in water ranging from just a couple of feet to a hundred feet deep, sucking up algae, grasses, and other organic matter as they propel themselves—*very* slowly—across the bottom using a muscular foot. Catching them, we've been told, is easy: You just dive down and pluck them out of grassbeds and off the sand. *Finding* them is a bit trickier, since the ones in the shallow, easily accessible areas have long since been harvested. Mostly now, local conch divers have to work in deeper water, and off more remote cays, breathing through a long hose attached to an air compressor on the boat as they swim along the bottom stuffing the overgrown escargot into their net bags. The divers stay out for several days at a stretch, camping at night on deserted cays, until they have a full boatload to bring to market. To keep the conch alive, they thread them on ropes and leave them in shallow water, then stop on their way home to pick them up.

Steve and Todd bought the birthday party conch from a small Bahamian boat that had pulled into Chub Cay. Knowing the fishermen were unexpectedly stranded here by the weather too, they had taken along some beer to smooth the purchase. A dollar a conch, the appreciative divers tell Todd and Steve. "And it will make the dead rise," one of them remarks, grinning.

Deciding not to take the comment personally, they ask the men to show them how to clean the conch—"a practiced art best learned from another boater," our guidebook had warned. "Don't be surprised if you are not an expert on the first try. It takes some repetition to build up your conch-cleaning skills."

That would be an understatement. The fishermen hand Todd and Steve each a sturdy knife and let them practice—at least until their patience wears thin. "In the time it took Todd and I to extract and clean one conch apiece, the Bahamian guys had done maybe fifty," Steve says, overstating only slightly.

The process involves first knocking a hole in the shell at the highest point between its second and third rows of peaks, using a machete. For those not quite so confident of their aim, a mason's hammer will do the job without quite so much risk to the digits that are holding the shell. Then insert the knife through the hole and with a deft twist cut the tendon attaching the conch to the shell. If you've gone in at the right place—not as obvious to a neophyte as it sounds—you should now be able to pull the entire conch out of its shell in one piece, by reaching in the opening at the bottom and tugging on the black claw, or foot.

The whole animal is theoretically edible, if not exactly appealing, so the Bahamians next show them how to clean it so they're left with a solid hunk of white muscle, saving the other bits to use as bait. They pull out a gelatinous, wormlike bit of innard from the conch's stomach. "Very good for you," one of them says, popping it raw into his mouth and raising up his forearm at a right angle to his body, just in case there's any doubt about what "very good for you" means. Apparently, this part of the conch—a protein rod that helps the animal digest its food—is thought to be the prime repository of its aphrodisiacal power. A real treat, too, we are subsequently told, and we spot toddlers on other cays sucking them down raw, like fat translucent strands of spaghetti.

The fishermen then cut off the other unappetizing bits—the eye stalks and the trunklike snout—but warn Steve and Todd to leave the claw on until the very end: They'll need it for a handle while they pull away the conch's leathery, slime-coated skin, a task accomplished with the knife, pliers—or one's teeth. Now the conch is ready for pounding.

In the hands of a pro, the cleaning process takes maybe thirty seconds. Novices, however, are advised to set to work well before they want dinner.

The cracked conch is a huge hit, and the birthday girl pretends to ignore the devastation in her galley. We serve it in real Bahamian fashion, accompanied by hot sauce and the staple side dish, peas 'n' rice. By the time we finish the chocolate birthday cake, the stuffed sleepy looks around the table make it seem highly doubtful that anything will be rising on any of our boats tonight.

I'm not sure about this way of life I've bought into. Mother Nature is the keeper of the Day-Timers now, and there's not a thing I can do about it: We're trapped at Chub Cay for nine days before the wind lays down enough to let us leave.

And squalls and strong, blustery weather continue to torment us when we can finally move into the Exumas, the group of 365 mostly uninhabited islands and cays that stretch in a long necklace for 120 miles from Nassau to the Tropic of Cancer. At one cay, we anchor behind a big catamaran named *Penelope*. Everyone on board wears a T-shirt emblazoned: "*Penelope*—The El Niño Tour." It seems we've unwittingly signed on, too. At least there are no more gales.

Receta sits suspended in liquid air off Allan's Cay, casting a shadow on the sand 10 feet beneath us. The water is placid, soft, blazingly turquoise—a pool of melted gemstones that seduces us into forgetting the *other* days, when *Receta* was corralled at one cay or another, bucking in the waves.

We've come to Allan's Cay to see the rock iguanas, a threatened species that lives here, on two neighboring cays, and nowhere else in the world; only four to five hundred of the reptiles remain.

When we pull the dinghy up on the deserted beach, they slowly emerge from the scrub, having learned (from tour groups) the sound of an engine means the possibility of a handout: grapes presented on the ends of sticks, bits of lettuce, slices of cantaloupe. Soon the sand is littered with the 3-foot-long prehistoric-looking things. Though we offer them nothing, they stick around, their attitude somewhere between somnolent and watchful, their mouths set in permanent anticipatory grins.

The clear water makes it all too apparent there are no conch around the cay for easy picking. But it doesn't matter: Steve has spotted a local boat with shells piled in its bow, and he dinghies over. These conch are $1.50 apiece—but for that price the guys clean *and* pound them, for which I am grateful, since I'm cooking in my own galley tonight. And they throw in a couple of fillets from a grouper they've speared, gratis, as part of the deal.

Perry and Noel are their names, and along with the conch come more—unsolicited—stories of its power. "My wife glad when I go fishin' for a coupla days 'cause den she get a rest," Perry says. And Noel explains the effect of what he calls "coo-coo soup": If a woman cooks it for you and you eat it, you won't want to make love with anyone but her—not his words precisely, but that's the tamed translation Steve gives me when he returns. Unfortunately (from my point of view), they don't tell him how the soup is made, but they do provide instructions for preparing conch on the barbecue, topped with garlic, onion, sweet pepper, and tomato. "Taste just like lobster," Perry says, once again stressing, with appropriate hand gestures, the potent results.

It doesn't *really* taste like lobster—but it *is* delicious: as sweet and rich, but with a different texture and flavor. We scarf down five conch between us, and I can hardly wait to get my hands on more to make the recipe again.

Steve notices, uh, nothing different. Me neither. And he isn't throwing glances at other women (at least I don't catch him), even though I don't make him coo-coo soup. Despite checking every Bahamian cookbook I come across, I never find a recipe.

I was looking in the wrong spot, I discover much later. I needed to check a guide to Bahamian English, not a cookbook.

I eventually find the entry in *More Talkin' Bahamian* by Patricia Glinton-Meicholas: not coo-coo, but *cuckoo* soup, as in the bird that has a habit of laying its eggs in other birds' nests, from which comes the word "cuckold." "Talk has it," Glinton-Meicholas writes, "that if you are a man of the age of consent in The Bahamas, you tend to avoid dark, multi-ingredient soups . . . It might be cuckoo soup into which certain bodily fluids have been put to 'tame' you . . ." Her mother tells the story of a young man who throws a bowl of soup out the window, suspecting it is of the dreaded cuckoo variety. One of the family pigs eats it and within minutes is running around and shouting, "I want to get married, I want to get married."

Much later still, I have a chance to ask a trio of sophisticated, stylish Bahamian women for their opinion on the power of conch. Two of them dismiss it scornfully as just male rubbish. The third one smiles. "Anything you believe can work, can work," she says.

Norman's Cay, to the south of Allan's, is a long, skinny upside-down U of low-lying coral and sand covered with scrubby vegetation. Between the arms of the U, near its open end, a DC-3 lies three-quarters submerged in a few feet of water, a short snorkel from where *Receta* is anchored in a deeper portion of the cut. In the late seventies and early eighties, Norman's was a trans-shipment center for the Medellin cartel; the DC-3 was making a delivery, and didn't quite make it to the airstrip.

So much drug money passed through the cay in those years— $3 billion worth of cocaine, so the story goes—that the cash was weighed, not counted. The Bahamian government of the time was persuaded to turn a blind eye, and visitors were discouraged;

bullet holes from the discouragement are visible in the derelict, overgrown buildings near the water's edge.

Eventually, the DEA convinced the Bahamians to take action, the cartel was forced out, and the cay abandoned.

"We can't go in for a beer," Steve says with dismay. "We don't have any money." We're both staring at a minuscule, palm frond–roofed bar and a handful of pastel cottages that shimmer like a mirage in the afternoon heat on the supposedly deserted cay. A sign warns us to look both ways before crossing the old drug-runners' airstrip, which lies between us and the mirage. A couple of small planes—not at all mirage-like—are tethered on the scrub at the edge of its cracked concrete. On the other side, the overgrown vegetation turns abruptly into tended grounds, tropical plantings, and conch shell–lined walks; the open ocean glitters behind the buildings.

We've come to shore for an afternoon walk because once again the wind is blowing stink and *Receta* is hobbyhorsing on her anchor chain, making it less than comfy onboard. We're stiff from the previous night's sleep too—since we had to continually tense our muscles to keep from being tossed around in our berth like sacks of potatoes. To work out the kinks, we'd first gone on a snorkeling (and conching) expedition, but cut it short when the waves and current made it more work than fun. So we threw on dryish shorts and Ts, and ran the dinghy up on the beach to explore the deserted cay instead—without even a dollar in our pockets. Why would we bring money when our guidebooks assure us there's nothing at all here beyond the derelict, pock-marked vestiges of the drug-running era? And then, about a half-mile up the cay's cratered road, we stumble on this. "MacDuff's," a Scottie dog–shaped sign says.

The surreal watering hole is still there when we return late the next afternoon with cash. Inside, the blond, heavily tanned guy behind the bar wears a tank top and a tiny Speedo and grooves to

Jimmy Buffett. In fact, Dale Harshbarger even *looks* like Jimmy Buffett. Our request for Kaliks completely wipes out the supply of the Bahamian beer in his cooler. Business has been brisk recently, he says, and it's hard to calculate how much he'll need at his tiny, just-getting-going bar, when patrons must fly in on their own planes or sail in on their own boats and then happen upon the place.

Ponytailed and laidback all the way to the sixties, the bikini-clad Dale makes popcorn while I slowly extract his story, my old journalism antennae quivering. A pilot himself, he had been flying around in the early nineties—he mentions the words "midlife crisis" at this point—trying to find a piece of property with beach on one side and an airstrip on the other, when he spotted a little ad in an aviation magazine for this spot on Norman's Cay. He bought it and set to work turning it into an outpost of Margaritaville, fixing it up bit by bit while getting the word out to pilots that they'd no longer be greeted by guns if they landed. The bar opened just a couple of months back, and its spiritual inspiration, Jimmy Buffett himself, had already visited in the flesh, landing his plane on the weed-sprouting airstrip. Or so the sole other patron of the bar this afternoon—who, no surprise, is also a pilot—tells us when Dale wanders off.

"You didn't have to worry about not having money," he says. Dale is already accustomed to running chits for unsuspecting cruisers who come ashore and then stumble on the bar as we did, parched and penniless.

The next evening, MacDuff's is positively packed—granted, it takes only eight bodies to pack the place. Local pilots Mike and Mike, who occupy two of the stools, have done a run to Nassau in their plane and picked up a fresh supply of the desperately needed Kalik. They're introduced by their nicknames, which reflect what people here usually say to them: "I Need a This" and "I Need a That." They've also picked up a sack of groceries for

Mary and Scott, off the sailboat *Partner-Ship*, who occupy two more of the stools. They've been here before, and needed this and needed that and knew enough to ask. Yesterday's pilot is back again, this time with his wife, and they fill the other end of the bar. CNN Weather flickers on the satellite TV, and although the volume's turned way down—you don't interfere with the Buffett tunes—it still commands regular attention from this group of pilots and sailors.

Until, that is, the satellites cut out. The sky has blackened, and one of those regular squalls begins to hammer the building, rain dancing on the palm fronds and slanting through the screens. No windows that close in this bar. And in short order, water is pouring through the unfinished cupola at the center of the roof. The regulars calmly adjust their stools to avoid the deluge (mostly unsuccessfully), don the rain gear they've cleverly brought along, and continue to drink their beers. Dale continues to serve behind the bar—but with one hand now, since the other is holding a large open umbrella. "Your personal Mary Poppins," he says. "Louvers for the roof are on the list, but they're way behind a steady supply of Kalik."

I Need a This (or is it I Need a That?) launches into a tale of another storm, featuring fallen trees and downed power lines. But Dale's generator continues to crank without interruption—at least until, several Kaliks later, the rain slackens enough for Steve and me to trot the half-mile back across the airstrip and down the now deeply puddled road, past the shot-up buildings to the beach and our dinghy, me laughing—and weaving—the whole way.

Cracked Conch

This dish is well worth a bit of mess in the galley. Fresh conch is sometimes available in specialty fish markets and in some Asian grocery stores; ask your local fishmonger if he or she can order it for you.

SERVES 4

4 large conch, cleaned
4 limes
2 large eggs
½ cup water
Hot sauce
Salt and freshly ground black pepper
1 cup dried bread crumbs, cracker meal, finely crushed corn
    flakes, or matzoh meal
½ cup vegetable oil (approx.)

1. Slice conch lengthwise into thin slices and then pound the slices until they are almost translucent. Squeeze the juice from two of the limes over the sliced conch and allow to sit for a few minutes.
2. Mix eggs, water, a few dashes of hot sauce, and salt and pepper in a bowl.
3. Combine crumbs and more salt and pepper on a plate or in a plastic bag.
4. Dip a few pieces of prepared conch in the egg mixture, then in the crumbs. Shake off excess.
5. Heat a shallow layer of oil in a large skillet. Fry a few slices of the conch just until golden. Repeat with the remaining slices, adding more oil to the skillet as necessary.
6. Drain on paper towels. Serve with the remaining limes, cut into quarters, and hot sauce.

Tips:
- The cracked conch can be deep-fried if desired.
- Bahamians often dip and fry the whole conch without slicing it. Simply pound it until it is double its original size and then marinate it for an hour in lime juice and a bit of chopped hot pepper before cooking.

Perry and Noel's "Tastes Like Lobster" Conch

If you can't get fresh conch, try this recipe with monkfish. A firm-textured fish with a mild, sweet flavor, monkfish is sometimes called "poor man's lobster"—making it an appropriate choice for this dish. Monkfish will require about double the time on the grill.

SERVES 4

4 tablespoons butter
4 cloves garlic, thinly sliced
4 large conch, cleaned and tenderized
1 onion, thinly sliced
1 sweet green or red bell pepper, thinly sliced
1 tomato, diced
Salt and freshly ground black pepper
¼ cup white wine

1. Butter four large pieces of heavy aluminum foil. Sprinkle each with a little of the sliced garlic.
2. Put one of the cleaned and tenderized conch on each piece of foil. Top each with ¼ of the onion, pepper, and tomato, and the rest of the garlic. Dot with remaining butter, season with salt and pepper, and sprinkle with the white wine.
3. Tightly seal the packages and cook on a preheated barbecue for about 8–10 minutes.

Bahamian Peas 'n' Rice

"Every cook have his own recipe," one of the friendly young fishermen on the boat *Heaven Sent* said when he gave me the basics of his version of this staple side dish. The "peas" are the small speckled-brown pigeon peas grown in backyard gardens throughout the islands, closer to black-eyed peas in look and taste than the sweet green variety. They are mostly sold canned or dried.

SERVES 3–4

2 tablespoons vegetable oil
1 small onion, diced
¼ cup chopped celery
¼–½ small hot pepper, seeded and finely chopped (or to taste)
2 tablespoons tomato paste
1 cup cooked pigeon peas or black-eyed peas
1 teaspoon chopped fresh thyme or ½ teaspoon dried thyme
1 teaspoon salt
Freshly ground black pepper
1½ cups water
1 cup uncooked rice
Hot sauce

1. In a heavy pot, heat oil. Cook onion, celery, and hot pepper for a few minutes until softened but not browned.
2. Add tomato paste and cook for 2–3 minutes.
3. Stir in pigeon peas, thyme, salt, and pepper. Add water and bring mixture to a boil. Stir in rice, reduce heat, and cook, covered, over low heat until water is absorbed and rice is done to taste, about 20–25 minutes.
4. Remove from heat and allow to stand, covered, for about 10 minutes. Fluff rice with a fork, and serve with hot sauce.

Tip:

- Many peas 'n' rice recipes include some diced salt pork, which is fried until crisp. The onion, celery, and pepper are then cooked in the fat rendered from the pork.

Escape from
Chicken Harbor

I've seen countless cases of the fear of night sails leading a cruising couple into problems. . . . Far from being a scary enemy, the dark is more often than not the cruiser's friend.

   Bruce van Sant, The Gentleman's Guide to Passages South, 1996

. . . I have no desire to sail strange waters at night.

   Christopher Columbus in his ship's log, October 15, 1492,
   when he was exploring the southern Bahamas

CHRISTINE ROLLE IS LOOKING for a husband, and she's settled on Steve. A wiry Bahamian in her mid-sixties, she's dressed formally despite the heat: tan trousers and matching vest, long-sleeved oxford shirt buttoned to the neck, western-style string tie. I've arranged for Christine to take a few of us on a day trip around Great Exuma, the large island near the bottom of the Exuma chain. Before we start off, she serves us some sweet panfried cakes and a deep green tea she's brewed from avocado leaves—"very cooling in the hot summertime," she says, making it clear that this March day, with its temperature in the low eighties, doesn't come close to qualifying.

I make the mistake of asking how to make the yummy little cakes. "See, she doesn't even know how to cook," she says to Steve, pointedly ignoring me and my question.

Born and raised on Great Exuma, Christine is a bit of an island oddity: an unmarried female entrepreneur. She owns a general store in the settlement of Farmer's Hill, at the north end of the island overlooking the rugged windward coast. But she also manages property for absentee owners, has her own minibus taxi, runs a highly acclaimed tour service, and is a specialist in Bahamian bush medicine. Her search for a husband is part of her schtick, and I unwittingly play right into her hands.

"If you lived with me," she says to Steve, offering him another cake, "you could have these all the time." And with that pronouncement hanging in the air, she slides into the driver's seat and we're off.

A few minutes later, she pulls to the side of the road and leaves the minibus without a word, disappearing into the dry underbrush. "She's gone for a pee," says one of the female passengers, and the rest of us women nod knowingly. Perhaps—but she returns with an armload of greenery and dumps it at the front of the minibus before driving on. She repeats the process a few more times, until she's accumulated a small mountain of branches, vines, berries, and fruit behind the driver's seat. This, she eventually tells us between trips into the scrub, will be the basis of our bush-medicine lesson.

Before that, though, she intends to teach us a thing or two about the island's history, which revolves around Lord John Rolle, who imported cotton seeds here in the late eighteenth century. As was the custom, the slaves who worked his fields took their master's name, which is why Christine—and almost half the island's other 3,600 residents—have the surname Rolle. Two of the island's settlements are named for Lord John, too: Rolleville at the north, Rolletown at the south. By the early nineteenth century, however, Rolle's new crop was proving a failure, and with emancipation looming, he decided to deed his 2,300 acres to his about-to-be-freed slaves.

"That land, called generation land, was to remain common property for all Rolles, passed down through the generations. It can never be sold to outsiders." And with a pointed look at Steve in her rearview mirror, Christine adds, "If you want to become part owner of this land, you would have to get rid of your present wife and marry me. I've had no offers, so all I can think is that no one knows the value of this land, or the extent of my talents."

Which she soon begins to demonstrate with a "herb lesson." Pulling from her pile, she points out leaves that are boiled to make teas that ease toothache, cure dizziness, relieve fever, bring on labor, and soothe stomachache, back pain, and broken hearts. In the tough times, prickly pear leaves substitute for shampoo, she says, and the velvety leaves of the glove plant can be used to wash dishes: They make suds when rubbed in warm water. Sturdy featherback leaves are natural spoons—useful in "the back days when we had no silverware." She hands out small red berries that we're to rub on canker sores so they will heal more quickly, and divvies up branches of avocado leaves so we can brew our own cooling tea on our boats.

But her pièce de résistance is love vine, the bush medicine equivalent of conch. "For men with a weak spine," is how she tastefully puts it. You boil the vine and dose your lover with the resulting tea, "and he will hold to you as the love vine holds to the tree." She grabs a red-faced Steve to demonstrate. Love vine, like conch, is well established in Bahamian lore. "Makes Viagra seem like a Flintstone vitamin," another Bahamian—this one male—subsequently tells me.

Of twenty children born to her mother, Christine was one of only five to survive. She was orphaned at an early age, dropped out of school in fourth grade, and set to work. Eventually, she started driving a taxi because she saw the possibilities of tourism and liked meeting people. Her shiny air-conditioned minibus is a real sign of success on this island of dented rattletraps and dusty minibikes. Now, she's even put out a little book, a slender guide for visitors called *Bahamian Bush Medicine*.

At the end of the trip, she passes out homemade coconut candy—and mentions casually that the recipe is in the book. I can't resist, and we buy a copy. She hands our purchase straight to Steve, with a big smile. The book is inscribed "Love always, yours, Christine Rolle."

Steve is a popular guy here in George Town, the largest settlement in all the Exumas, and not just with Christine. Darry calls him "Sugarbunch," and Mom gives him a big hug every time she sees him. Darry is short, squat, and thirtyish, with a fabulous gap-toothed smile and coal-black hair that sticks out from her head in all directions, as if she's had an unfortunate encounter with an electric socket. She sits under a big pink-and-blue umbrella in the straw market, just down the road from where Christine parks her minibus. Truth be told, Darry calls out, "How ya doin', Sugarbunch?" to all her friends who pass and look like they might be enticed into a chat—and Steve never lets her down. The man who used to describe himself as antisocial loves to stop and buy a couple of tomatoes or a cucumber—she sells a bit of backyard-garden produce along with her embroidered baskets and placemats—so he can gossip with her for a few minutes, usually about her family or the weather.

Mom, on the other hand, is more reserved. Three days a week, her blindingly white late-model van rolls into George Town from the south end of the island and parks on the shoulder of the main street opposite the dinghy dock. A plumpish woman in her late sixties with a large gold cross hanging down her ample front, Mom unfolds herself from the van and settles into a chair next to it, ready for action. The back of the van is lined floor to ceiling with racks holding trays of her baked goods: white bread, soft and sweet; whole-wheat, just as soft but perhaps a touch less sweet; and, usually on Wednesdays, crusty (compared to the white and whole-wheat, anyway) French sticks. Then there are the sugary muffins, the glazed and filled sugar doughnuts, the cakelike coconut bread, and the overweight cinnamon crullers that drip sticky white icing.

Steve is always good for a loaf of bread and something sweeter, and Mom pulls herself to her feet and gives him a big hug along with the goodies. "Praise the Lord," she always says—at least once. Sometimes, too, she'll tuck a muffin in Steve's bag and wave off his attempt to pay. But Steve really isn't special: Mom hugs all her customers and their spouses. Though her van says "Mom's Bakery," everyone calls it the Hugmobile.

George Town's long, lovely Elizabeth Harbour is sandwiched between Great Exuma Island to the west and Stocking Island to the east. On the protected leeward side of Stocking, the shelling is superb. The water gently folds over on itself when it reaches the beach and recedes in sparkling half-moons, leaving a line of jewels behind. On its raw windward side, the surf chews up most of the shells and spits them onto the sand in slivers, but we head to this side to body surf and take long solitary beach walks. The shiny black rocks have been sculpted smooth by the waves, the scrub-covered sandy hills bitten away by tide and wind. At the island's eastern end, the sea surges through a narrow cut, exploding with a roar out of blowholes in the rock, sending salt-water geysers frothing into the air. There's a stretch of sand on the leeward side where the sociable swim, schmooze, and play volleyball, but elsewhere you can sit and stare at the ocean for hours scarcely seeing another soul. Across the harbor are the conveniences—such as they are—of George Town itself: a few stores, the straw market, a supermarket, a laundry, the telephone company where laptops can be plugged in to pick up e-mail, and a handful of restaurants.

It's no wonder that cruisers—in some years, as many as six

hundred boats—arrive here and stay for months. Which is also the drawback of this idyllic spot: At times it seems suspiciously like summer camp for the whole family, a sort of self-run Club Med, an endless round of organized activities and communal drinks and meals. Morning aerobics classes on the beach. Volleyball every afternoon. Organized beach walks. Seminars on everything from relationships to religion. "Who wants to beach walk in a crowd?" I crab in my journal. "And aerobics? In paradise?"

The VHF radio bleats incessantly as people organize yet more fun. I'm tempted just to turn it off—but of course I'm afraid I'll then miss something good.

Like an old-fashioned party-line phone, the VHF allows others to listen in. Cruisers call it "reading the mail." Since everyone knows there's always *somebody* eavesdropping, VHF conversations tend to be practical, and pretty tame. But it's taking me a while to remember that.

"I *desperately* need a bikini waxing," I lament on the radio one day to Belinda, announcing the fact to the entire anchorage. "I guess I'm going to have to use that do-it-yourself kit we bought in Florida. Have you tried yours yet? Over."

The next day on the beach, a woman I barely know looks me up and down and offers her own solution to my personal grooming woes.

Belinda eavesdropped one night on a conversation between two women, one asking the other if she had a can of corn, for a recipe already in progress. The answer was no. "*I* had a can of corn," Belinda told me the next day, "but if I broke in and said so, they would have *known* I was reading the mail." She was saved from her dilemma by yet another eavesdropper who broke in first.

Elizabeth Harbour may be beautiful, and protected from the violence of the ocean outside, but it's not calm. The winter weather pattern in the Bahamas is one of a progression of northers blowing through every four to six days, and they kick up the wave action even inside the harbor. In this El Niño year, the northers come more often, and more fiercely, and the water inside the anchorage rarely settles down. With his 6-hp Evinrude, little *Snack* simply isn't up to the task of powering over the waves—he just plows into them—and the half-mile trip from our anchorage to town is guaranteed to leave us and everything in the dinghy caked in salt and soaking wet. The trip back, when poor *Snack* is invariably weighed down with groceries and full jugs of fresh water or diesel fuel, is usually worse.

Although it's a sun-drenched morning, we stuff the laundry into a double layer of heavy-duty garbage bags and tie them tightly closed. (I wash the smaller, lighter stuff onboard in two buckets and hang it on the lifelines to dry, but in a nod to convenience and the local economy, we take towels and sheets to the laundry.) The laptop makes the trip to town first sealed in a big Ziploc freezer bag, which is then zipped into a carrying case, wrapped inside another heavy-duty garbage bag, and stuffed into a backpack, which Steve wears. We put on foul-weather jackets over our shorts and T-shirts. My own backpack contains several more garbage bags, to protect whatever we buy in town on the trip back. "Cruiser's luggage," the bags are called.

After town, we invariably need a shower to wash off the salt from the trip, but the routine is a swim first. Boris, however, has been getting in the way of routine.

Boris is a 3-foot-long barracuda who lives in the anchorage and has started appearing punctually every afternoon, just as I'm ready for my dip—as if he's punching in on his jobsite time clock. I get on the swim ladder, and Boris tucks his pointy nose out from behind the rudder. I know what the books say—he won't bother me if I don't wear any shiny jewelry and if there's no blood around—but Boris has the look of someone who doesn't go by the book. It's hard to convince myself he is benign when that big mouth full of teeth is so close to my tender tush.

But I finally settle on a plan: I make Steve go in the water first and keep watch.

We planned to stay in George Town two or three weeks. We stayed three months.

George Town is known as "Chicken Harbor." Many cruisers come this far, and decide it's far enough. From here on, if you're continuing south and into the Caribbean, the sailing gets harder, and the islands get a lot farther apart. No day-hopping from anchorage to anchorage anymore, skimming along the shallow Bahama Banks in sunlight, protected by the cays from open ocean. From here on, night passages are inescapable. From here on, you're heading almost directly into the incessant trade winds—on the nose, sailors call it—which means hammering endlessly headlong through waves. The island-hopping route from the Bahamas south to the heart of the Caribbean is called the "Thorny Path" for good reason. It's tough on the boat, tougher on the crew. With longer distances and more-off-the-beaten-path destinations, self-sufficiency also becomes more critical: an adequate supply of spare parts and the confidence to deal with boat breakdowns, emergencies—and each other.

In fact, by the time some couples get this far, relationships have started to fray, if not unravel, another reason to turn around and head north. Southern Florida is littered with fully equipped cruising boats for sale, their brand-new equipment scarcely used, the evidence of dreams gone sour. Most often, it's the woman who delivers the ultimatum—me or the boat—tired of taking orders from a partner who knows more (or thinks he does), tired of feeling incompetent, tired of discomfort and fear, missing home. And—this is a big one—tired of her spouse's company twenty-four hours a day.

For some, there's no decision to be made: Whether it's a once-in-a-lifetime cruise or an annual cycle, they never planned to go any farther than the Bahamas, and George Town is the turn-around spot. Others, planning to carry on, find one excuse or another to delay departure: one more potluck to attend, one more round of sundowners on the beach, one more piece of equipment to fix. They let one weather window slip by, and then another, until they finally turn north—homeward.

For us, George Town is where we need to decide if we want to continue cruising for a second year. It's late March; we left Toronto just seven months ago. But if this is to be only a one-year cruise for us, we're more than halfway through and it's time to turn around and start back. Thanks to El Niño, I feel like I've had only the barest taste of idyllic cruising life—and already I have to decide whether I'm ready to commit to more, and harder. Though neither Steve nor I will admit it as we mock the organized routines of Camp George Town ("let's organize a beach walk with scheduled stops for shell-collecting, aerobics, and a religious discussion"), stopping here has been a relief. By the time we arrived, we were ready for a rest, ready to settle into a routine, a word that hadn't been in our vocabulary since we left Toronto. And even though we've been here almost a month already, the time for decision-making and moving on still seems to have come much too soon. Dithering isn't an option: The coming of hurricane season demands a decision now; we have to be either much farther north or much farther south by the time it arrives in June. Steve is nervous but ready to go.

For all our cruising inexperience, Steve and I actually have an advantage: in the couple-relationship department. Keeping a boat running happily is, in many ways, like running a business, and we're used to working together. We already have years of experience negotiating disagreements and trading off strengths and weaknesses. (I'd learned years ago that it's embarrassing to cry in front of your coworkers.)

And so I revert to old form: I schedule a meeting. As the basis for discussion, I sit at the laptop and compose a 1,600-word memo setting out the pros and cons of continuing on versus turning north toward home. Very uncruiserlike, and downright radical behavior in a place so laidback one of the most popular T-shirts in the straw market reads: "Nobody move, nobody get hurt."

Our closest friends are going the other way. Elizabeth and Don are returning to home base in the Chesapeake; theirs was a one-year cruise, with the Bahamas the only goal. Belinda and Todd have long since decided to head north, to cruise the Eastern Seaboard and the coast of Maine. "The boat's not ready to go farther south, and neither are we," Todd says.

I'm not convinced we're ready either, but the meeting does the trick: We made it this far—despite my worries. Which, it seems, are the same old worries I had before we left Toronto. I'd be crazy to turn us back before our time is up.

The next week is a series of dinghy dashes from one of George Town's anchorages to another, following up radio calls from people looking to unload stuff that we will now need. We zip over to one boat to get sturdy jugs for the extra diesel fuel we'll be carrying on the longer passages ahead. Ed, their owner, waves off our attempts to pay with either cash or the bottle of rum I've brought as backup currency. "Just do something nice sometime to help out another cruiser," he says. "That's what this is all about." Another cruiser, an American heading home, sells us a brand-new life raft. Yet another boat, this one returning from the Caribbean, has all but three of the navigation charts we need. Steve has spare engine parts shipped in; I take the dinghy and go to Spanish lessons on the beach—to bolster my rusty college vocabulary with phrases such as: "*El motor no funciona*" (The engine won't run), "*Hay un mecánico diesel que hable inglés?*" (Is there a diesel mechanic who speaks English?), and "*Mi barco se está hundiendo*" (My boat is sinking).

* * *

Dear Belinda and Todd: It's been almost three weeks since you headed north, and we're still in George Town. In fact, we've tried three times already to leave, but three times things have gone wrong . . .

The first time, our engine died as we were threading our way out Elizabeth Harbour, leaving us—quite literally—between a rock and a hard place. We had to zigzag our way back and anchor under sail—a little tension-wracked, skill-building exercise, something we had never practiced together before leaving home. First, twenty quick tacks required to keep us in the narrow, twisting channel of safe water, marked only by subtle color changes and landmarks on shore. With reefs or rocks on both sides, the turns had to be tight, precise, and fast. Steve, at the helm, was uncharacteristically tight-lipped when he wasn't shouting instructions at me, and my knees were actually knocking as I waited for the next shout into action, knowing that I tended to be clumsy when I tried to be quick.

As he started each turn, Steve released the headsail, and as it blew across to the other side of the boat, I cranked it in on the winch, grinding it in with the speed of a woman possessed. "More, more," he yelled each time, and even though the sheet was already taut and groaning, I put all my weight behind the winch handle and muscled the sail in a few inches tighter. Every inch made a difference in how close to the wind Steve could point the boat, and the closer to the wind, the farther from the reefs.

Then came the act of anchoring—completely stopping the boat in a particular spot without having an engine to throw in reverse to act as a brake on *Receta*'s 23,000 pounds. As Steve steered her toward an empty area of the anchorage, I furled the headsail—again, using a winch; again, at a speed I didn't think I was capable of—to slow us down. He then ran forward to the bow to drop the 45-pound anchor, while I steered us directly, precisely into the wind, at which point the mainsail would be ineffective and *Receta* would essentially coast to a stop. Now to the reversing part, to put a backward pull on the anchor to set it in the sand. As Steve paid out the anchor chain, I backwinded the mainsail by putting my weight against the boom, which essentially started *Receta* coasting backward in the breeze. Pretty impressive stuff for a rank amateur, but once the hook was set and the adrenaline stopped flowing, I collapsed below for a 10 A.M. nap.

By the next day, Steve had the engine started, and we up-anchored to take *Receta* on a test spin—only to have to return under sail and anchor under sail again. Our anchorage neighbors told me they thought we were purists who just didn't believe in using an engine . . .

I can hear you laughing, Todd. Obviously these people didn't know me very well.

Although I was lighthearted with our friends, by now I was seriously demoralized. *Receta*'s engine is actually the source of some of my greatest "sailing" fears—and the fact that it had stopped working before we even started down the Thorny Path had me *really* worried. It's not just that the engine is old, and shoe-horned under the steps in a way that makes working on it difficult even for professionals; it's also that diesel mechanics aren't Steve's strong point. Completely confident in matters of sailing and navigation, he is learning as we go with "Mr. Engine, Sir," as I respectfully refer to the smelly red beast in its presence, hoping to placate it. Seeing capable, confident Steve worried and unsure fuels my own anxieties.

He tried one thing after another to coax it back into action—no luck—dinghying into shore between troubleshooting attempts to call a mechanic in Florida who had done routine maintenance on Mr. Engine, Sir, for advice on what to try next. I again began to question our decision to continue south. What if something like this happened in a more remote, less repair-friendly spot? I envied the boats where one-half of the cruising couple was a mechanic, or an engineer, or anything but a magazine and book designer, a career that had almost zero applicability in our current predicament.

Finally Steve diagnosed the problem—not the engine after all, but air in the fuel line from a cracked filter housing—and fixed it (luckily, he had another housing stowed in his spare parts bin), and we were nervously ready to leave again. This time, a phone call home revealed my father had been rushed into intensive care.

Dad recovered nicely, and a week later we were ready to leave again. Just twenty minutes outside the harbor, we got hit by a surprise squall—40 knots of wind, sideways-driving rain, daggers of lightning attacking the sea, huge steep waves that appeared out of nowhere. We'd never seen anything quite like it, except maybe on the cover of *Cruising World* magazine's "Safety at Sea" issue: "How three boats got pulverized and what they did wrong." The other boats that had left that morning realized the wisest course of action was to go back, to retreat to the safety of the anchorage. For us, there was no choice: I had become suddenly, violently seasick, completely incapacitated, leaving Steve to manage the boat in the squall by himself.

Strike three.

I don't know, Belinda. Maybe someone is trying to tell us something. Maybe we're not meant to go farther south. We're licking our wounds, reevaluating our plans. But in the meantime, everything bad holds something good. Our aborted leavetaking means that we are still in George Town when the Family Island Regatta begins.

The Family Island Regatta is a traditional event that's been held each April for more than forty-five years. The raceboats are tall-masted wooden Bahamian sloops, the kind once used as workboats in the islands. With bragging rights as well as cash at stake, supporters from each boat's home island pour into George Town as the regatta approaches, and the town is reclaimed by the Bahamians, completely transformed from its cruiser-centric winter-season self.

Every day we go out in *Snack* to watch the races. The start line appears placid, almost still, the sloops apparently asleep at anchor with their sails down. But when the gun sounds, they spring instantly to life, the sails blossoming in seconds, opening like enormous white flowers, so lovely they make my throat catch.

With their minimal keels, these boats need to counterbalance the force of the wind on the acreage of sail. As many as twelve of the crew clamber outboard astride long narrow boards—called pries—that extend perpendicular from the boat on the windward side, their weight providing leverage to help keep the over-canvased boat upright. When the boat turns at the mark (the course is a big triangle), the crew scrambles off the pries and onto ones flung into position on the opposite side of the boat. The penalty for being slow is a capsize or even a sinking, so agility and quick reflexes, coupled with a certain amount of beefiness (the more weight outboard, the more upright the boat will stay and the faster it will go), are prized crew characteristics. Nerves of steel don't hurt either—since all this is happening at high speed within inches of other boats.

Along with the other dinghies and powerboats that make up the regatta's "spectator fleet," we follow them from mark to mark. I'm driving, faster than I want to, so Steve can take photos. And when he has me position *Snack* just beyond the big orange float marking an end of the finish line, closer than I want to be, one of the racing sloops comes screaming right at us, a white bullet with a football field of sail above. It just about T-bones us before veering off nonchalantly at the last minute, the guys on the fore-deck laughing and waving. They were just playing, having a bit of fun after a good race. The photographer, his eye happily glued to the viewfinder, didn't flinch.

My heartbeat back to normal, we head into George Town. "You'd barely recognize it," I e-mail Belinda and Todd. "Wooden shacks have sprouted all along the point." Some are nothing more than serving counters, with yummy smells issuing from behind them; others have yummy smells *and* a handful of tables and chairs. Ribs, chicken, and snappers smoke away on long barbecues made from oil drums cut in half, while conch fritters—crunchy, deep-fried balls of dough with bits of conch hidden inside—bubble in big pots of oil, tended by oversized ladies. When the balls turn golden, they scoop them out, drain them for the briefest second, and pop them into brown paper bags that quickly become sodden with grease as we munch our way down the road. We feel duty-bound to try the fritters at two or three different spots, until we settle on our favorite, which has the highest conch-to-dough ratio.

Right at the water's edge, where some of the smaller racing boats have tied up for the night, an apron-covered man turns out conch salad. His place of business is even more bare bones than the shacks—just a rough wooden table with a pile of conch shells to one side and a half-dozen yellow buckets to the other. When you place your order, he picks up a shell, knocks a hole in it, and removes the mollusk with a quick twist of his knife. A few more swipes and he's got it cleaned, skinned, and dipped in one of his buckets to rinse off the slime. He then dices it finely with onion, tomato, green pepper, cucumber, and fiery goat pepper, adds a dash of Bahamian sea salt, and squeezes sour orange, sweet orange, and lime juice over the whole mixture, creating a briny/sweet, hot/cool, crunchy/chewy salad to go.

At another shack, a lethal mix of gin and coconut water is being ladled out of a Bahamian cocktail shaker (a five-gallon bucket). "Honey child, come go with me/Back to the West Indies/Baby can't you see/I lost my strength and my energy/What I need is gin and coconut water, gin and coconut water . . ." proclaims a traditional island song. Like the Baha Men, who perform a version of it, we're soon singing its praises.

Steve finds a fat wad of bills on the ground amidst the revelers dancing in the streets to the tunes that blare from speakers the size of Volkswagens. "It could belong to anyone," he says. "Let's give it to Mom." We head for the Hugmobile, parked in its usual spot, a bit removed from the heart of the regatta action. In Williamstown, where her bakery is located, Mom is known for her good deeds as well as her bread and crullers. "This is for your church work," Steve tells her, explaining he had just come upon the money in the road. "Praise the Lord," she says. "*Praise the Lord*." She gives him a big glazed doughnut—and a *very* big hug.

After sunset, the shacks really get going, serving up full dinners of barbecued chicken, jerked pork, fried snapper, cracked conch, and souse, a thick, meaty stewlike soup made from the parts of the animal that might otherwise go to waste: pig's feet, cow's stomach, or sheep's tongue. (I decline, though Steve pronounces it delicious.) The dinners are all accompanied by cole slaw, peas 'n' rice, and another light Bahamian side dish, mac and cheese, baked and cut into squares. After all this (and the fritter first course), I am absolutely, positively stuffed.

Not so Steve, who next drags me into Aunt Keva's Dessert Shack. Steve is downright runty these days, still working off calories faster than he can take them in. A couple of weeks ago, while he was off somewhere in *Snack*, I had searched the boat in vain for my favorite khaki shorts. We had each bought a pair in Florida—mine, a ladies' small; his, a men's medium. I became suspicious when I found the men's medium tucked in a drawer. Sure enough, when Steve returned from his excursion, I checked the label in the ones he was comfortably wearing: ladies' small.

Aunt Keva, a substantial woman, takes one look and decides he needs a double helping of her guava duff. Guava trees grow readily in the sandy soil of the Bahamas, and guava duff is perhaps the most popular incarnation of the juicy, sweet-tart fruit—it would be named the Bahamian national dessert, if there were such a thing. Each cook puts her own spin on this cake that's steamed or boiled rather than baked. Aunt Keva's version is more pudding than cake, kind of like a tropical Christmas plum pudding. She scoops a huge spoonful onto Steve's plate, puddles it with potent hard sauce, and then dollops on a whipped-cream topping. Runty Steve finishes every last bite.

"Let's just go sailing," Steve says. No plan, no decision. We'll just see what happens. But we both know that if we're hit by another problem—another breakdown, another squall, another family illness—it will be strike four and we'll almost certainly head north, toward home.

Conception Island is a small cay that rises out of the ocean where Exuma Sound meets the Atlantic, a 40-mile day sail from George Town—in the right direction if you're starting down the Thorny Path. We spot our first white-tailed tropicbirds soaring overhead, glorious unmistakable things with a 3-foot-long streamer of a tail. The sailing is serene—no engine problems, no sudden storms—and when we arrive at Conception, the anchorage is ours alone—that is, if you discount the two laughing gulls that persist in sitting on *Snack*, shitting copiously, and cackling uproariously at the gooey white mess we'll have to clean up when they depart. I swim naked before dinner, the water so deceptively clear that I'm sure my feet will touch sand if I stretch out my legs beneath me. *Receta*'s depth sounder tells us the water here is 14 feet deep.

Steve hands me two perfect sand dollars that he's spotted on the bottom framed by delicate ridges of sand. The fragile white discs are the skeletons of a close relative of the sea urchin, and if they break open, five perfect replicas of a dove spill out—the Doves of Peace, so the legend goes. The doves have a rational, scientific explanation: They are the five teeth the urchin used to eat algae. But knowing the science doesn't change the fact: The sand dollar, with its doves, is believed to bring good luck.

Let's just go sailing tomorrow and see if our good luck holds, we agree over dinner. To Rum Cay, 20 miles farther along the Thorny Path.

I've managed to avoid it for the first eight months of our travels, but now it's inevitable. After Rum Cay, the next stepping stone is Mayaguana Island, at the southernmost end of the Bahamas: 137 miles from Rum Cay, twenty-seven hours at *Receta*'s anticipated cruising speed of 5 knots, no easy place to stop between the two. No way around it: an overnight passage.

I agree to two-hour watches, and my first is the 10 to midnight shift. As Steve heads below to sleep, I clip myself to the boat with my safety harness, hoping desperately that I can keep my pride intact and my anxiety at bay and refrain from calling him before his two hours of naptime are up. At least there's a routine to keep me busy: Keep an eye on sail trim, boat speed, and course. Scan the horizon for the lights of other boats, then go below every fifteen minutes to check the radar screen. "Why do they appear on *my* watch?" I mutter nervously—but in fact the boats add more interest than worry to the night. I track them on the radar, as Steve's shown me, to make sure we won't cross anywhere near each other. On the hour, I note our latitude and longitude in the ship's log, and carefully plot our position on the chart. In between, I sing to myself—a catholic repertoire of Hebrew hymns I remember from my childhood, black spirituals, and rock-and-roll—write letters in my head, develop the plot of a mystery novel, and watch the night sky. An almost-full moon pours molten silver on the ocean, the surface so calm it looks like smoked glass. For a while, *Receta* is accompanied by giant fizzling sparklers: the bioluminescence of thousands—millions—of tiny marine organisms that the boat stirs up as she slides by. Mesmerizing. I realize that not only am I not terrified, I'm not even worried; I am actually *enjoying* myself, almost completely relaxed. I sleep well when it's my turn, and the night flies by. I don't even think once about waking Steve.

We're anchored off Mayaguana by 12:30 the next afternoon. Herb and the other forecasters tell us this is a weather window for the history books, a once-in-a-lifetime weather window, a weather window to the Caribbean as big as a barn door. Foolish to stop now, we agree. Let's just go sailing. If we leave Mayaguana this afternoon, a two-night passage will have us in the Dominican Republic just after dawn on the third day. What's a two-night passage after such a benign silver-lined first night?

We've escaped from Chicken Harbor at last.

Bahamian Mac and Cheese

I was never a particular fan of Kraft Dinner, but I adore the macaroni and cheese that's a standard side dish with Bahamian meals. It's kind of like a savory noodle kugel from a Jewish kitchen, the pasta bound together with eggs as well as cheese, then baked and cut into squares—solid, soothing comfort food.

Evaporated milk is de rigueur, and gives the mac and cheese a rich, velvety taste.

SERVES 6–8 AS A SIDE DISH
½ pound uncooked elbow macaroni
1 small onion, finely chopped
½ green bell pepper, finely chopped
1½ cups grated cheddar cheese
2 eggs
Salt and freshly ground black pepper
1 teaspoon paprika
Hot sauce
1½ cups evaporated milk (1 12-ounce can)

1. Cook the macaroni in a large quantity of boiling, salted water. When it is just al dente, add the onion and pepper to the pot and cook for a minute or so more, until the vegetables are softened.
2. Drain the macaroni and vegetables and return to the pot. Add half the cheese and stir until it is melted.
3. Beat the eggs with a couple healthy dashes of hot sauce, salt and pepper, and the paprika. Stir the eggs and the evaporated milk into the macaroni and cheese.
4. Spoon the mixture into a well-buttered 8-inch or 9-inch-square baking dish and sprinkle remaining grated cheese evenly over top.
5. Bake at 350°F for about 30 minutes until mac and cheese has set and is bubbling and brown around edges. Remove from oven and let stand for 10 minutes, then cut into squares and serve.

Part Two

The Delicious
Dominican Republic

June, too soon
July, stand by
August, come it must
September, remember
October, all over
       Traditional rhyme about the West Indian
                    hurricane season

THE SQUEAKING OF OARS in wooden oarlocks signals the arrival of Eddy and Freddy. Their open skiff, with its worn paint job and battered gunwales, has two 100-gallon drums perched bow and stern. If you need diesel fuel in Luperón, on the north coast of the Dominican Republic, Eddy and Freddy are how you get it: They row it out to your boat and then pump it—slowly, laboriously, their T-shirts stained with sweat and fuel—by hand into your tank.

Eddy and Freddy have been rowing and pumping diesel since dawn. We are their last delivery of the day. It is ninety degrees Fahrenheit without a breath of wind.

"*Refresco? Cerveza?*" I ask them when they pause to wipe their dripping faces. Soft drink? Beer?

"*Presidente?*" Eddy asks. We've only been in Luperón a few days, but you don't have to be here very long to make the acquaintance of the President. It's the popular local brew, and a *grande*—twenty-two ounces of beer—costs just over $1 in the small bars and *colmados* in town.

"*No, lo siento. Tengo solamente cerveza americana.*" No, I'm sorry, I tell them. I only have American beer.

"*No, gracias,*" Eddy replies sadly, and Freddy concurs with a negative shake of his head. "*Agua, por favor.*"

They'd rather drink water.

When you're used to a tall, amber bottle of Presidente, I guess a can of cheap American swill makes a poor substitute. Presidente has body. Presidente has flavor. And we still have a couple cases of Florida-bought Old Milwaukee stored in our bilge that need to be consumed before we can buy more beer. Yesterday, I caught Steve pouring the better part of a can overboard—Steve, who *never* wastes an ounce of beer.

Presidente isn't the only thing that tastes good on this island. Fruits and vegetables grow on the mountainsides and in the valleys with wild abandon, seductively good and embarrassingly cheap: Silken avocados that dissolve like pale green butter on our tongues. Papayas the size of footballs, with honeyed flesh. Tart, refreshing *limones*—key limes—and *mandarinos*, overgrown mandarin oranges that spew sweet juice when we break through the peel. Intensely flavored sun-ripened tomatoes, lavish bunches of cilantro. Coconuts, cocoa, rich dark-roast coffee for $2.60 a pound.

As we approached the Dominican Republic at dawn, after two uneventful nights—*two nights!*—at sea, I could *smell* the land before I could see it: 15 miles out, the smell of trees after a heavy rain, a fertile, rich, *green* smell, the smell of things growing. And then, as the sun gave a glow to the horizon, the island's mountains emerged, thick with vegetation, a thrilling sight after three months in the flat, dry, scrub-covered Bahamas—particularly thrilling when making it here is such a huge milestone, when we came so close to giving up and going the other way. I know that in the greater scheme of things this was a short offshore passage—people who cross the Atlantic or Pacific by sailboat might be away from land for a month—but *I* feel like an explorer reaching a new world. "We are *so* proud of you," Elizabeth says, when she contacts us on the SSB radio. She and Don are in Virginia, almost home, their trip just about over.

Luperón's harbor is a stubby ragged Y cut into the coast 14 miles west of the tourist town of Puerto Plata and 46 miles east of the Haitian border. The entrance is a narrow slit of navigable water at the base of the Y, with hull-crunching coral teeth set just below the surface on either side. "When you're just off the entrance, call another boat in the harbor," we'd been told in George Town, "and ask them to come out in their dinghy and lead you in." There's no margin for error here, and the trickiness quotient was upped recently: The red buoy marking the hard-to-see reef edge on one side went missing several weeks ago, and no one's got around to replacing it yet. A few green stakes, though, are apparently still there. "Do *not* trust the stakes," our guidebook says.

Carl and Kathleen motor out in their dinghy to be our guides, and we follow close behind them: through the narrow slit in the reef, through a sharp dogleg to the right, all the way past the green stakes. As soon as we are safely beyond the stem of the Y, I see why Luperón is called a "hurricane hole," a place to hide from hurricane-force winds. Dense mangroves enclose the harbor, their roots poking out of the dark water like gnarled witches' brooms, with the mountains rising up close behind them. Together, they create a protected, cushioned pond, where two-dozen boats float this morning, hanging lazily on their anchors. Very little breeze penetrates, and the air is close and still, not merely warm but boiling stinking baking roasting unbelievably hot—even for people who've had several months of acclimatization in the Bahamas. The wind generator on *Receta*'s stern, which provided all the power we needed to keep the boat's batteries fully charged there, scarcely turns here. And gone is the crystalline Bahamian water. The bottom of Luperón harbor is covered in thick, dark, gooey mangrove mud, and the water itself is a slurry of silt mixed with considerable sewage runoff from the town; you can't see more than a couple of inches—well, maybe an inch—below the surface. This is not the place to consider popping in for a cooling swim—though the local kids have no such reservations and even eat the oysters (raw) that they pry from rocks and pilings. I quickly learn to carry a package of antibacterial wet wipes to use on our hands after we tie *Snack*'s soggy painter to the sagging dinghy dock at the edge of town.

In the Bahamas, where 80 percent of the food is imported, we were happy we had thoroughly stocked *Receta*'s food lockers before we left Florida. In proper frugal-cruiser mode, we had loaded up not just on beer but also on canned stuff we would *never* buy at home: soft gray canned asparagus and waterlogged canned green beans; canned flaked white-meat chicken (the poultry version of canned tuna) and—worst of all—disgusting-looking cans of *whole* chicken. "About 15 servings," the label chirrups unbelievably, showing a badly photographed, pasty-looking miniature bird perched on a blue background that does nothing to improve its looks. "Home-style goodness."

The Dominican Republic makes a mockery of our Florida supermarket sweeps. We barely open a Florida can—except for the Old Milwaukee—the whole time we're here.

We tie *Snack* to the dinghy dock, disinfect our hands, and walk down the gravel jetty toward the small village that starts at the far end. Like the island as a whole, Luperón is a combination of third and first worlds. Chickens scratch along the dusty roadside and the occasional donkey or pig strolls by, but reliable e-mail and fax service is available at the phone-company-cum-souvenir-store on the main street—as long as the power doesn't go out, which it frequently does. There are places that will do our laundry—but it's then spread out to dry on curbside bushes, roofs, and barbed-wire fences, where it will be leisurely coated by thick dust stirred up by the *motorconchos* that blast along the main street. Salsas and merengues blare from open doorways, and mangy dogs slink through the shade at the edges of the concrete buildings—painted soft pastels mostly, though the headquarters of the Dominican Liberation Party is a startling combo of bright purple and canary yellow. (In fact, it's called the Purple Party, and displayed as such on ballots, the rainbow of political parties a nod to the high illiteracy rate.)

When substantial supplies are needed, we can go to Santiago, the island's second largest city, about 38 miles away, where the supermarkets are said to be just like the Florida big boxes. Except that the parking lots have guard towers, and security guards with sawed-off shotguns roam inside and out, protecting these pockets of affluence in the midst of an impoverished country. The class divide in the Dominican Republic is blatantly huge.

But Luperón's small, un-air-conditioned, dark (to keep them cool), and disorderly stores turn out to be surprisingly well stocked. "Go to Ana's on the main street for chicken," Kathleen had told us. "It's the best spot—she takes off the head and most of the feathers." "And she's got beer and rum," Carl jumps in, "very cheap." "But watch out for the cat at the *supermercado* across the road. She bites."

Our noses lead us down a side street to the *panadería*, where squat loaves of bread are cooling on racks lining the sidewalk. We buy a bag of warm rolls and dive into them the minute we're back on the street. Steve is a bit put out to discover the seeds sprinkled on the one he is about to bite into are moving. Ants. Inside the bag. Yummy rolls, though.

At Ana's, besides cheap chicken, Presidente, and the Dominican Republic's three Bs—Brugal, Bermudez, and Barceló rums—we discover the creamy thick Dominican drinking yogurt, sold in *cuartillo* bottles and gallon jugs, which tastes like a rich delicious milkshake. At the *supermercado*, the cat is as crotchety as advertised. ("Don't worry, she didn't break the skin," Steve assures me after his friendly overtures are soundly rebuffed.) She prowls the aisles for four-legged intruders in search of peanuts and beans that have spilled out of bins onto the wood floor. Cases of Presidente and gallon cans of cooking oil teeter at the ends of the aisles. The *supermercado* accepts Visa just like the supermarkets in Florida, but when I slide into the front seat of the pickup the store's owner commandeers to take us and our groceries back to the dock, the driver carefully removes the pistol stuck into the waistband of his trousers and lays it on the seat between his legs.

"Tengo hambre"—I'm hungry—the shoeshine kid says to me softly. You don't have to look very hard to see poverty, and when someone tells you he's hungry here, you don't doubt him. I learned this our first night in Luperón, when a very pretty, very young woman started to braid my very short hair in a restaurant. Before I could muster the Spanish to refuse, she had one braid finished, with two beads and a piece of foil from a cigarette pack hanging on the end. "*Basta*," I tell her, enough. "But I have four children," she replies. It seems impossible given her young age, but the restaurant owner quietly confirms her story—adding that she supports the children herself. We pay her lavishly for the single braid, and later spot her in a corner, wolfing down a plate of food that she's bought with the money.

Now I dig out some change for the shoeshine kid. He knows we're both wearing sandals, realizes he can't work for the money, but he sees I'm holding a map. "Where do you want to go?" he asks in Spanish.

"*El Museo del Jamón*," I tell him. The Ham Museum. He picks up his shoeshine stool, motions for us to follow, and leads the way.

We had taken the public bus—actually, a couple of buses—kitty-corner across the country to visit Santo Domingo, 120 miles away on the south coast, leaving *Receta* at anchor in Luperón. A young Israeli man was looking after her; partway through a solo sail around the world, he was happy to make a little money to replenish his cruising kitty. After living on a boat for months, our small, basic Santo Domingo hotel seems like five-star luxury. King-sized bed! Air-conditioning! Full-size shower with hot water! Cable TV! In between watching the NBA playoffs (and the Three Stooges) in Spanish, we've been walking our feet off exploring the historic capital, which was founded by Bartolomé Columbus, Chris's brother, in 1496.

The shoeshine kid ushers us importantly through the door of El Museo del Jamón and exchanges a few words in rapid Spanish with the man inside. "Is it true? Did he bring you here?" the man asks. "*Sí, sí.*" He goes to the cash register and gives the kid some change—a finder's fee, for bringing us in, his lucky day. I don't bother mentioning that we'd already rewarded him, or that we would have found El Museo ourselves without much trouble, as we were just steps from its door when he intervened.

El Museo del Jamón is a small tapas-style bar, where the Presidente is served so cold it's almost frozen and the ceiling is festooned with whole serrano hams dangling side by side, dozens of them, marching from one end of the room to the other. On its bottom, each ham wears a small, pointed white paper cup—the kind you'd find at a water cooler—to catch any greasy drips before they land on the patrons who are sitting at the bar or tables underneath, tucking into plates of the ham (sliced paper thin), spicy chorizo sausage, and other porcine offerings. Steve, to put it mildly, is in heaven.

"Serrano" means from the mountains, and these hams are

dry-cured in the cool mountain air of the island's interior by Dominicans who have been trained in Spain, in traditional methods. Steve is a porkophile who's been severely deprived since he started living with me: With my Jewish background, I never ate pork at all while I was growing up, I don't cook it, and I still avoid eating it in its most obvious forms, such as ham and bacon. He pronounces El Museo's ham the best he's ever had: delicate, almost sweet. "I read a story years ago," I tell him as I soak a hunk of crusty bread in the garlicky red oil that's pooled around my chorizo (which I do eat, with barely a pang of guilt). "It was about a young Spanish bullfighter, who carried a serrano ham with him as he traveled from town to town, and bullring to bullring. He'd hang it from the ceiling of each hotel room, so he could carve off a slice whenever he wanted. This was the ultimate luxury for someone who grew up poor without enough to eat and now was tasting success for the first time."

That image had long stuck in my brain, but sharing it with Steve is a big mistake. Now he desperately wants to buy a whole ham from El Museo, carry it back to Luperón on his lap on the crowded bus, and hang it from one of the handrails in *Receta*'s main cabin. He can picture himself on future night passages, ducking below to remove a delicate slice or two whenever he feels the urge for a snack. The ultimate luxury, he quotes back at me. I draw the line: A mezuzah at the entrance to the cabin, and a whole *jamón* swinging over the settee? I think not.

The whole ham would have been troublesome in any case on the packed sardine can of a minivan that is the second half of our trip back to Luperón two days later. A packed *guagua*, as the public minivans are called here, makes a crowded bus in Grenada look positively spacious. This one is so jammed that its conductor kid hangs outside the open door as the *guagua* rips along, with just his feet inside, his body dancing in the air to the salsa blasting from the van's speakers and his hands beating out the rhythm on the roof. There is no room for a spare chorizo in this picture, let alone a whole ham. At one stop, an ancient, not terribly clean, and mostly toothless lady climbs onto the *guagua* with a live chicken tucked under her arm. She somehow squeezes in next to Steve and settles the chicken on her lap. It rides contentedly back to Luperón with its head and beak on Steve's thigh, while the woman rides contentedly with her arm around his shoulders. I ride with visions of chicken mites and body lice dancing in my head.

"I always meet skippers kicking themselves all the way down island because they didn't make room to buy in the Dominican Republic," says our gospel cruising guide for this part of the world (the same one whose author sings the praises of night passages, and the perils of green stakes). Presidente aside—there's *still* too much Old Milwaukee in the bilge—we make no such mistake. We squirrel away twenty pounds of vacuum-packed Santo Domingo coffee and a full case of MasMas bars—locally made chocolate bars stuffed with raisins and nuts. The only other time I've bought a case of chocolate bars was at Halloween, and then I had no intention of eating them myself; but Steve has convinced me that in the absence of a swinging ham, these will be the second-most perfect snack during future night passages. We content ourselves with only a half-dozen jars of tiny green olives—packed in brine with giant caper berries, themselves the size of olives—and as addictive as peanuts with drinks. (We would have bought a case of those too—if only the jars didn't leak.) And several large globes of wax-covered Gouda-like cheese are tucked into the very bottom of the fridge.

The local cheesemaker plies his craft on the outskirts of Luperón, near the cockfighting ring, selling what he makes from an open-fronted wooden building identifiable from the road by its hanging scale. Behind the selling area, the floor is wet with whey.

Wearing rubber boots and a garbage bag as an apron, a man paddles curds in a big plastic bucket, while balls of nascent cheese bob in other buckets nearby. From a distance, a long wooden table at the far end looks like it's piled with monster ripe tomatoes, but on closer inspection, the tomatoes turn out to be cheese—coated in red wax but not yet labeled. They'll keep for months, we've been told. While the cheesemaker weighs a couple for us, I ask him about the long, white rectangular blocks resting on the counter. He cuts off a piece for us to try: a salty, fresh, unaged farmer's cheese still oozing whey. "*Queso de freir*," he says. Frying cheese. What a splendid idea: a cheese specifically designed to be made more gloriously, fat-oozingly delicious by frying it. Of course we buy some of it, too—though not nearly enough to suit Steve. "It's a fresh cheese," I argue. "It won't keep like the wax-coated ones."

It doesn't have to: We polish off most of what we buy that night. Sliced and fried in a little oil and butter, the cheese stays firm and develops a golden crust. But when you cut into it, the interior is molten, delicious smeared on bread. "Or," Steve adds, "with a delicate slice or two of serrano ham." No whole ham swings on *Receta*, but there's no way Steve was leaving Luperón without a few fridge-friendly packages of the stuff.

It's now almost the end of May and time for us to get a move on. Hurricane season officially starts on June 1, though everyone we talk to scoffs at the idea of a hurricane in the Caribbean in June, or even July. "The months of June, July and October only produce about one hurricane every three years for the whole western Atlantic," one of our books tells us, and that includes the Gulf of Mexico as well as the Caribbean Sea. Still, our boat insurance sets July 1 as the deadline for being outside "the box"—the area through which hurricanes are statistically most likely to track. In the box after that, and *Receta* isn't covered by insurance if she's damaged by a hurricane or other "named storm." And if the insurance company thinks there are *any* odds of a hurricane in July, that's good enough for me.

A few cruisers, like Carl and Kathleen, have decided they love Luperón so much they will trust its reputation as a hurricane hole and spend all of hurricane season here. But most of the cruisers who ventured beyond Chicken Harbor have already left. Only a couple of stragglers—like us—are still here. We need to start hustling south.

The top edge of the hurricane box is at 35° north, between Cape Hatteras and Cape Lookout, North Carolina; the bottom edge is at 12°40', in the Tobago Cays, part of the Caribbean nation of St. Vincent and the Grenadines. Luperón is squarely in the middle of the box, 865 nautical miles from statistical safety by the island-hopping route: east from the Dominican Republic to the south coast of Puerto Rico; east along the south coast of Puerto Rico to the U.S. Virgin Islands and the British Virgin Islands; east through the Virgin Islands to St. Martin, at the top of the Leeward Island chain; east and southeast through the Leewards and the Windwards till we're finally beyond the box. East, into the prevailing trade winds; east right down the middle of the Thorny Path.

The first thorn is the Mona Passage, the 60-mile gap between the eastern tip of the Dominican Republic and the western edge of Puerto Rico, and our gospel guidebook is full of optimistic advice. "Unpredictable currents everywhere," it warns. "Rough shoals." "Steep seas." The ocean bottom here is to blame: It drops from a comparatively shallow 150 feet to the second-deepest hole in the world, the 16,000-foot-deep Puerto Rican Trench. As massive volumes of water tumble across the uneven bottom in an underwater waterfall, the surface churns, setting up wild and conflicting currents. Even in benign weather, crossing this stretch from west to east is like booking passage inside a washing machine.

Add to that the long lines of thunderstorms that religiously roll off the coast of Puerto Rico each evening, when the heat that has risen off the land meets the cooler offshore air. "The fiercest I've seen in my life," says the guidebook's ever-reassuring author. "Sometimes they . . . charge like bulls." A crossing of the Mona is not to be taken lightly. The guidebook spends seven pages discussing strategy and timing. Obviously, it would be foolhardy to leave on anything less than a perfect forecast.

Once again, I start checking in daily with Herb, waiting for him to give our passage his blessing. Working on acquiring martyr points, I even send Steve to a potluck on shore one night—with the big dish of tortilla lasagna I've made (cruiser's trick: stale tortillas make a fine substitute for lasagna noodles)—and stay behind, hunched by the radio, hoping to hear the good news. Wait, Herb says.

The next night I cheat: I check in at the start of the Herb Show, go off to shore with Steve for a happy hour beer, and am back onboard the boat just before the time Herb has been calling me the last few days. But there's no pulling a fast one on Herb. "I tried to call you earlier," he says, "but you didn't respond." It's as if he can see what I've been up to; I feel like a teenager caught sneaking in after curfew from a date. But I get my punishment: The wind is still too strong for us to leave. As the days tick by, I get more and more antsy: We have a *lot* of miles to cover in a steadily decreasing amount of time.

"Let's get our *despacho* so at least we'll be ready to go," Steve says. In order to leave the Dominican Republic, we need a *despacho*, a clearance paper, which we get from the *comandante*, the Luperón port commander. The *comandante* and his translator came onboard *Receta* to check us into the country, but we must go to his headquarters, the *comandancia*, to check out.

Cruising tales, we've discovered, always become exaggerated in the telling and retelling, and things are never quite so bad (or so good) as others make them sound. The trip to the *comandancia* is the exception: It's actually far *worse* than the stories that preceded it, which were already heavily sprinkled with words like "awful" and "disgusting."

The dirt path that leads to the *comandancia* starts behind the *lavandería* and leads across a stream and up a hill on the other side. It's not until we pass the laundry-strewn bushes that we get our first look at the bridge. I try to weasel out: Surely my services as a translator won't be required when we know the *comandante* has his own? "Nice try," says Steve. "In fact, you go first—you've got a better sense of balance than me."

The bridge doesn't have very many planks between its two stringers, leaving open gaps and excellent views of the stream underneath. But this is only the start of its deficiencies: Some of its limited number of "planks" are just rough branches, and it has no handrails. Oh, yeah, and the "stream" it's crossing is actually a smelly conduit for raw sewage. This ribbon of sludge, which runs through Luperón and down to the harbor, is the reason we don't swim in the anchorage. Falling off this so-called bridge into this so-called stream would be truly horrifying. Besides, I'm carrying our most important documents, our passports and boat registration, in my backpack. I get down on all fours and start to crab my way across.

The bridge is alive, a wizard's balance beam. The branches roll, the planks shift. Most of them have been merely laid across the stringers, not nailed down—and if I don't put my weight in exactly the right place, they pop up on one side like a teeter-totter. I have to test each one for its balance point before I commit. Steve, meanwhile, is taking careful note of which branches move when I do, and has no intention of starting his crawl until I reach solid ground. Coward.

But neither of us falls in, and after brushing the dirt off our hands and knees, we follow the track the rest of the way up the hill to the modest cinder-block building with the national flag flying out front. After the bridge, getting the *despacho* is a comparative snap. A junior official types it—in triplicate—on a manual typewriter that was probably new in the year of my birth. Every time he bangs the carriage return to start another line, the carriage flies right out of the aged machine and has to be reinstalled before the paperwork can continue. It's a cartoon come to life, and Steve is biting his lip so hard I'm afraid it will bleed. But at least the *comandante*, who only arrived here a couple of weeks before we did, is doing things completely by the book. There's no attempt to extract a little something extra from us for unofficial pockets, as there was with the previous *comandante*, we've been told, before he was hauled off to jail.

That night, over happy hour Presidentes, we warn another *despacho*-seeking cruiser about the bridge. Someone who's been in Luperón much longer than we have chimes in. "The bridge is new. And it's a *big* improvement over the old system." Apparently, the old system involved pulling yourself across the stream hand over hand along a slimy rope while standing in a leaky rowboat with a few inches of sewage water in the bottom. "People used to wear plastic bags on their hands and feet when they went for their *despacho*." I don't think he's exaggerating one bit.

An unfortunate little fact: The word "nausea" comes via Latin from the Greek *nausia*, which comes from *naus*, which means ship.

A few hours earlier, we had ghosted out of Escondido Bay, with the barest breath of wind in the sails, in the company of two other straggler sailboats. We had left Luperón together the previous day, after finally getting Herb's go-ahead, and had reached this lovely fjordlike bay after an easy overnight sail east along the north coast—so calm we motored partway. But we only stayed long enough to get a few hours' sleep, pour fuel from the jerry cans on deck into our tank, and make a fresh Thermos of coffee before getting underway again, heading for the Mona Passage.

Despite the very light wind, we keep the engine off, to make it easier to hear Herb. "Be sure to ask him specifically about thunderstorms," Steve says. "I see some dark clouds ahead." Herb, looking at his computer screens 1,800 miles away, says he sees no "organized convection activity," the forecast euphemism for "big-time pissing and blowing, accompanied by shitloads of lightning and thunder."

"Organized" is the operative word. The storm cells created along this coast as the land cools at night are localized—not part of the overall weather picture. And soon all hell is breaking loose around us as we motorsail southeast close to the coastline. "You're going to be passing through a big squall," Ken on the boat ahead radios back. "Get ready for it." We scramble to put on full rain gear—pants, jackets, boots, caps, and hoods—and then Steve takes down the sails while I steer. Soon blinding forks of lightning are sizzling down from the night sky and stabbing the surface of the sea around us. I count the seconds between the flashes and the thunder—far too few, given that *Receta*'s mast is the tallest object for miles around. Rain beating on my face, I wrestle with the wheel, attempting to stay on course while the wind howls and the boat plunges up and down in the suddenly steep waves.

The flashes and thunder become simultaneous. Steve has gone below to consult the radar, where the squall shows up as a dense splotch of black dots, and plot a new course that will, I desperately hope, take us out from under it. But in the meantime, I am alone on deck—and, despite the compass, I momentarily lose my bearings and am unsure which direction is toward shore and danger. For the first time this trip, I am honestly frightened. The glorious serenity of my first night sails—even of last night's sail—vanishes. I know with absolute certainty that I was right to dread night passages.

"Steer 145 degrees!" Steve bellows the new heading out at me and I emerge from my confusion and get us on the new course. But as we come out from under the center of the squall and the wind lessens, we need to quickly get a sail back up to steady us in the waves. "Keep the boat pointed into the wind," Steve calls from the mast, where he's now trying to raise the mainsail. "I'm trying—but I can't," I shout back. "It's too rough." Every time the boat slews sideways on a wave, the wind catches the flogging sail and prevents Steve from raising it any higher. With the sky total blackness, I can't see the waves to anticipate when or how they'll hit us. Steve's tethered to the boat with his safety harness, but with each wave I'm afraid he'll be thrown to the deck as the boat pitches. Eventually, we just give up, sentencing ourselves to a rough, uncomfortable night of motoring. And we're not even in the Mona Passage proper yet.

By daybreak, when we are, Steve's entry in the log is short and to the point: "Nasty waves." They seem to come at us from all directions, causing the surface to slosh and churn. At least in daylight we can get the sails back up, which helps our movement a little. The squalls are gone, the wind is a modest 10–14 knots—we are crossing the Mona in almost perfect conditions. And still it feels like we're traveling in a soup bowl being carried by a marathon runner. My seasickness drugs are no match for the Mona, and I begin to feed the fishes. Unfortunately, I can't do what the British admiral Horatio Lord Nelson suggested as the remedy: If you're seasick, he said, sit under a tree. We're still a full day (and night) from our landfall. Now I know why it's called the Thorny Path, and I wish I were anywhere but on it.

I subsist for the next twenty-four hours on water and sourdough pretzels—they're the only thing my stomach will tolerate, and they don't require me to expend any effort other than reaching a hand into a bag—and remain lashed to the boat with my safety harness until we arrive in Boquerón, Puerto Rico. I don't miss a single one of my watches, day or night, though, and I'm very proud of it.

"Here, this is for you." Robert, off the sailboat *Jake*, hands me a paperback in Boquerón. *Jake* had crossed the Mona just a day ahead of us. The book looks like a trashy thriller, and the cover says, in lurid letters, "Can death be the only way out?" For a few hours, I felt like it was.

The paperback is entitled *Incident in the Mona Passage*. Like its namesake, it's *awful*.

Luperón Papaya Salsa

There is no such thing as a small papaya in Luperón. I created this salsa to take advantage of the half we regularly had left after breakfast. Serve it alongside grilled chicken or fish—or with cream cheese on crackers, as a happy hour snack.

SERVES 4

½ large ripe papaya, diced (about 2 cups)
½ cucumber, peeled, seeded, and diced
½ small red onion, thinly sliced and separated into rings, and
    rings cut in half
3 tablespoons finely chopped fresh cilantro
½–1 small hot red or green pepper, seeded and finely chopped (or
    to taste)
1 lime, juiced
3 tablespoons fruity olive oil
Salt and freshly ground black pepper

1. Combine the papaya, cucumber, onion, cilantro, and hot
   pepper. Set aside.

2. Whisk together the oil and half the lime juice, and season to taste with salt and pepper. Toss with papaya mixture.
3. Taste before serving and adjust flavor with additional lime juice.

Tips:
• This salsa works equally well with ripe mango, or a combination of mango and papaya.
• The red onion adds color, but you can use a mild-flavored yellow or white onion instead.

Cheesy Chicken with Avocado and Tomato Salsa

Avocados were in season when we arrived in the Dominican Republic, and we said fat and calories be damned and devoured them regularly. This recipe showcases them—and the delicious Dominican cheeses—beautifully.

SERVES 4
⅓ cup cornmeal
Salt and freshly ground black pepper
¼ teaspoon hot red pepper flakes
4 boneless chicken breasts
3 tablespoons olive oil
1 clove garlic, halved
½ lime
½ cup fresh or store-bought tomato salsa
1 avocado, peeled, pitted, and thickly sliced
4 slices mild melting cheese (such as Monterey Jack, mild cheddar, or *queso de freir*)
Fresh cilantro, chopped

1. Combine cornmeal, salt, pepper, and red pepper flakes. Dredge the chicken breasts in the mixture.
2. Heat olive oil in a large frying pan with a lid and gently sauté the garlic for a minute or so. Add the chicken breasts, and sauté until a golden-brown crust has formed on both sides and the breasts are almost done, about 5–7 minutes per side. Squeeze the lime over the chicken.
3. Top each breast with some salsa, a couple of slices of avocado, and a slice of cheese. Lower heat, cover, and cook a minute or two longer until the cheese has melted. Garnish with the cilantro and serve with rice and more sliced avocado and tomato on the side.

Tip:
• This recipe can be easily adapted for the barbecue: Marinate the chicken briefly in a mixture of lime juice, olive oil, chopped cilantro, red pepper flakes (or chopped hot pepper), chopped garlic, and salt and pepper. Grill over medium-high heat until the chicken is almost done, about 5 minutes per side. Top each breast with salsa, a couple of slices of avocado, and a slice of cheese. Cover the grill and cook a minute or two longer until the cheese has melted.

Not Quite Seasoned,
But
Very Well Salted

November Mike November gave me the good weather news
Told me I was going on an easy downwind cruise
Well I guess he got it wrong and that's hard to excuse
'Cause I'm tossing up my cookies, my body's one big bruise
I got the three days out forty-five knot wind blues . . .

From the song "Three Days Out Forty-five Knot Wind
Blues" by Canadian singer/songwriter and cruiser Eileen Quinn,
from her CD No Significant Features

O H, THE IRONY. We left home to escape deadlines and here
we are being driven by a deadline: I'm *convinced* we
absolutely have to be south of the hurricane box by
July 1, as if the weather gods use a Day-Timer and have
scheduled a hurricane for the very next day.

After the Mona Passage, we scurry along the south coast of
Puerto Rico. "Take at least 11 days," the gospel guidebook says;
but the weather holds and we cover it in four. Then we boogie
through the Virgin Islands—"don't worry, we'll spend more time
here on our way north," Steve says—then jump to St. Martin
across the Anegada Passage, another choppy, current-wracked
stretch of water, unaffectionately nicknamed the Oh-My-God-A

Passage. Anchor, sleep, sail. Anchor, sail. Sail, sail, sail. We move every day—and sometimes night—the weather lets us, mostly motorsailing now because we're heading east and almost directly into the trade winds. (A boat under sail can't point directly into the wind.) This "beating to windward" is brutal—exhausting and uncomfortable as we slam into wave after wave, the bow sometimes burying in the steep seas, our muscles tensed and our bodies braced for hours on end. It's even harder on poor *Receta*.

"More leaks," I report dejectedly when I return to the cockpit after one of my infrequent daylight trips below during the nineteen hours we're underway to St. Martin. Given our direction, the ocean is simply too lumpy to make spending time in the cabin enjoyable unless I'm lying down to sleep.

Steve has already rebedded one of our lovely deck prisms, the one over the chart table, to stop water from streaming in whenever a wave washes over the bow and down the sidedecks (which is frequently). But now the deck prism in the galley has started leaking—the one over the dry locker, meant for storing nonperishable food and now an utter oxymoron. "The forward hatch is leaking, too," I inform him, on the verge of tears. Some of my clothes bags are sitting on the wet cushions directly under the leak, having bounced off the shelves when we hit a wave. We store our navigation charts under the cushions, and they're now the filling in a nice soggy, salty sandwich. The collar at the mast isn't totally watertight anymore either, and seawater has entered there, too, splashing the floor of the main cabin. It's hardly noticeable, though, since there's already a salt slick all over the floor from when our salty selves have slid below off-watch, peeling off soaking foul-weather gear to instantly fall asleep on the cushions in the main cabin.

"Nothing goes to windward like a 747," is the oft-used saying when someone decides to meet a boat at its destination rather than go along for the (bouncy) ride. I can see their point. "I am really *really* ready for this beating to windward to end," I announce.

To make it end more quickly—especially since the days are ticking down to July 1—I agree to do the next stretch, from St. Martin to St. Lucia, without stopping: 292 miles, 52 hours. Straight.

"Dinner tonight was somewhat misguided," I note in my journal about the first night of that passage. "Couscous topped with cold sliced grilled chicken. Delicious—but the couscous is too light for these conditions, almost 20 knots of wind. Blows all over the damn cockpit." Pretty cavalier words from someone who, just a few weeks ago, was making passage meals out of pretzels. But I'm learning, adjusting: No couscous, and no chopped fresh herb garnishes. (Green bits everywhere.) Nothing, in fact, that requires more than a bowl and fork to eat. And nothing that can't be prepared entirely ahead and just quickly assembled at mealtime. If the seas kick up, the last thing I (and my stomach) want is to spend time in a rolling galley. One Thermos was filled with hot coffee and another with boiling water before we started this passage; the baskets that hang close to the bottom of the companionway were piled with grab-and-go snacks (including a handful of Steve's precious MasMas bars). A supply of seasickness pills was stashed in easy arm's reach from the cockpit.

Unfortunately, there's no avoiding belowdecks weather duty. At least three times each day while we're underway—no matter how rolly it is—I have to sit at the chart table and listen to the forecast on the SSB radio, writing it down word for word, so we have it for reference. Somehow, I've become responsible on *Receta* not only for talking to Herb, but also for getting *all* the weather forecasts, whether we're at anchor or on the move. The chore load is already weighted heavily toward Steve because there is so much I don't know how to do; when we installed the radio six months ago, it seemed only fair that I should take on a job that was new to both of us. Besides, the first forecast we need to hear is at 5:30 A.M.—not a time of day Steve is happily awake.

That first forecast is delivered by November Mike, as he's nicknamed, and he holds the dubious honor of making me cry from frustration more than once. He sounds (to me, at least) like Rocky and Bullwinkle's nemesis, Boris Badenov—but on Valium. November Mike—or "Metal Mikey," as another cruiser calls him—delivers the offshore forecasts in a dour monotone; his voice has no inflection, he jams his words together, and he pauses in all the wrong places, creating a run-on string of easily confusable numbers and compass directions. Did he say west of 68° winds east—or east of 68° winds west? Which side of 68° was going to have the slowly decreasing 8-foot seas? Or was that *in*creasing? To a newcomer unfamiliar with the format and idiosyncrasies of the offshore forecasts, he might as well be speaking Badenov's mother tongue. After my first few teary attempts to get it all down—sometimes further handicapped by less-than-perfect radio reception—I started taping November Mike and then transcribing him, playing back the forecast over and over, phrase by painful phrase. By now, however, I've developed a shorthand for taking it down directly.

November Mike is the computer-generated voice of the U.S. National Weather Service. He takes his name from the call sign of the radio frequency he's broadcast on: NMN or, in the phonetic alphabet, November Mike November. "Nosignificantfeatures," his synthesized voice frequently drones at the top of the forecast. Early on, I thought this meant good weather. I was mistaken. Frequently, so too is November Mike.

"November Mike says winds out of the east, 20 to 25 knots, seas to 8 feet," I read to Steve as I climb back into the cockpit on the second morning of the passage. "Misstine"—the call sign of the flesh-and-blood forecaster I tune in next (David Jones, based in the British Virgin Islands)—"says winds east to east-southeast, up to 15 knots, with the sea state decreasing to 3 to 5 feet." This kind of forecast disagreement is par for the course. So is my postforecast angsting: Who to believe, the one promising a delightful day's sail or the one villainously proclaiming a lumpy, brace-yourselves ride? Unfortunately, Herb won't weigh in like Solomon until late in the day, but based on his report yesterday, I'm afraid he'd side with Metal Mikey.

In fact, the seas are kicked up most of the way to St. Lucia, with the wind staying close to 20 knots, and both sails are reefed. "It got lumpy this afternoon," I note unhappily the second evening of the passage. "Forward hatch is still leaking like a son of a bitch. Belowdecks is looking like a slum. I've decided just to close my eyes to the chaos."

At least we're no longer heading directly into the trade winds, since we're now pointing as much south as east. When we're in the lee of the islands along the way—Statia, St. Kitts, Nevis, Montserrat, Guadeloupe, Dominica, and Martinique—we're protected and even need an assist from Mr. Engine, Sir. But between islands, the wind attacks, heeling us over on a fast, wet, exciting ride. Engine on; engine off. Ease out a bit of reefed jib; crank it back in. Lights visible on the horizon, go downstairs to check the radar. Down and up, down and up—there's a lot of commercial traffic on the route we're traveling—to make sure we're not on a collision course. I'm downright *busy* on watch tonight.

"Nosignificantfeatures," Metal Mikey drones at 5:30 the next morning. Meanwhile, we almost lost our little stern-rail barbecue during the night: The stainless-steel mount gave way from the stresses on the boat, and Steve turned around on one of his watches to see it dangling precariously by one last twisted bit of welding. And when he now checks to make sure *Snack* is still tied securely on the foredeck, he fishes two flying fish out from inside it, carried onboard in waves during the night. Waves are still washing regularly over the bow and their spray is routinely nailing us in the cockpit. "Nosignificantfeatures" indeed.

"Nosignificantfeatures," I've gradually realized, simply means no sign of approaching organized tropical weather: no tropical waves, tropical storms, or hurricanes. Steve says it's simply radioese for "you may be uncomfortable as hell but you probably won't die."

Although the sun is shining, we keep our full foul-weather gear on to stay dry, and it's by now coated with a thick, greasy film of salt. So is every inch of exposed skin. I long for a shower, but it would take more energy than I can muster in these conditions.

"Maybe we'll hear from Robert and he'll have the solution," Steve says, attempting to jolly me out of the foul mood that threatens to descend when I feel disgusting. We had run into Robert and his partner Annette on *Jake*—the same Robert who had presented me with *Incident in the Mona Passage*—in the British Virgin Islands. Over pizza and beer one night, he had drolly informed us that he had solved the problem of not being able to take a real shower underway. "I needed something I could spritz myself with that would leave me feeling fresh and clean," he explained, while miming himself happily spraying his pits and privates. "I think I've finally hit on a winner: cheap mouthwash. Very refreshing."

When we finally arrive in Rodney Bay, St. Lucia, we splurge on a marina and its ample supply of fresh water to facilitate desalinating ourselves, our clothing, our bedding, and our boat. It takes me two soapings under the shower to get rid of the salt caking my skin, encrusting my hair, and lining my ears. I can't imagine how much mouthwash would have been required.

Six weeks later, on my birthday, Steve presents me with a special gift: a tank T-shirt on which he's illustrated one of November Mike's forecasts. The background is a weather map, showing a hurricane in progress. In front, falling squarely across my chest, he's painted November Mike's favorite phrase in large letters. Cruisers think the shirt is hilarious; everyone else thinks my chest has No Significant Features.

Sometimes even when you want to hurry, you can't.

From St. Lucia, we're only three day-hops away from Grenada—beyond the bottom of the hurricane box—where we plan to stay put for a while. But the weather gods are going to toy with me a bit longer—let the days tick past our deadline—before they let us take off. Which is why we get to see Nelson Mandela dancing.

We'd stopped in a little bookstore a short bus ride from the Rodney Bay marina to supplement the reading material we pick up at cruiser book exchanges. But everyone lined up at the cash is buying not books or magazines, but little pink tickets. I've got to know.

"Tonight is the closing night of CARICOM," the sales clerk tells me, "with entertainment from all over the islands." CARICOM—which stands for Caribbean Community—has been in the paper every day since we arrived in St. Lucia: A conference of Caribbean leaders is underway in Castries, St. Lucia's capital. Nelson Mandela is the guest of honor.

Steve is reaching for his wallet before I can even spit out a question about where, exactly, the closing-night event is being held and if we can get there by public bus. The salesclerk assures me we won't have any trouble.

That evening the 1A bus—the one that stops at the marina—drops us off at the bus station in Castries. I don't have a clue which way we should head, so I ask two young women. "Follow us," one of the pair says.

After a few blocks, they stop. "We have to wait here for a friend," the one says. "Go with them," and she passes us on to another set of women. Lynette and Ruth lead us right to the park, where linebacker-sized, black-suited, earphone-wearing security men in dark Ray-Bans guard the gates. It seems very un-island-like—until they start to flirt outrageously with Lynette and Ruth. "We men in black," says one of them with a grin. "We *black* men in black," adds the other. And I notice the guys providing security for the leaders of the Caribbean nations are indeed wearing large buttons that officially identify them as Men in Black.

Lynette and Ruth take seats beside us in the bleachers and give us a running commentary of who's who as the Caribbean prime ministers and presidents file onstage. When Nelson Mandela arrives, the crowd explodes—standing, yelling, and waving flags for their hero. As the band launches into a song written in his honor, he starts to dance, grabbing the other prime ministers out of their chairs to join him. The feel of the soft night, the island music, and the sight of Mandela, almost eighty years old, joyfully dancing as fireworks burst overhead dull my memory of the long, salty passage. It was simply the price to be paid for rewards like this.

Midway through the event, after the speeches, when we've left the bleachers and have joined the crowd of thousands on the field for the entertainment, the first young woman who had led us partway to the grounds earlier in the evening approaches and asks if we are having a good time. "I'm amazed she could pick us out in this crowd," I say to Steve as she walks away.

"Look around," he says. We are two of just a handful of whites. Of course we were dead easy to recognize.

Castries has a reputation for being a tough town. So when we leave the stadium, I don't really want to walk the dark streets alone, back down to the bus station. I'm not even sure we can find the way. Almost immediately, though, we see a 1A bus and flag it down. The driver stops, but shakes his head as I start to climb on. The bus is empty, except for a young woman in the seat next to him. "I'm not goin' direct to deh station," he says, waving me off.

I press: "We don't mind if it's not direct." He shrugs, "Well, you can come along if you want."

What ensues is an amusement-park ride up the steep and narrow streets that wind mazelike above "downtown" Castries, accompanied by reggae at ear-splitting volume. Even with my limited mental map of the city, I know we are most definitely not heading anywhere near "deh station." Eventually, we pull over in front of a small house, the bus seemingly perched at a 45-degree angle at the side of the road, and the woman disappears inside. The driver leaves too, and we're alone in the hot humid darkness; in the middle of nowhere, in a purportedly dangerous city, in what I now realize is an off-duty bus. Above the booming reggae, we can hear voices in the shadows. We are a mugging waiting to happen.

But *nothing* happens. The girlfriend eventually returns with a small suitcase and the driver climbs back in and starts the motor. He shouts good-bye to his friends, and we head back down the winding streets, reggae still blasting. He pulls up in front of the bus station, where an on-duty 1A bus is waiting. "How much do we owe you?" Steve says. Once again, the driver shakes his head and waves us off. "Nothing. I didn't bring you direct to deh station."

Lambi and Lobster

Mammie was a great cook—the best . . . We didn't have to buy eggs or vegetables, only people who lived in town bought things like that. What you didn't have in your garden you got from your neighbors. If you needed to buy fish you would just stand in front of your house and listen out for the conch shell blowing.

Marguerite Sheriff, about her childhood in Grenada;
"A Ride on the Board Bus," *The Melibea Review*, March 1998

"WOULD YOU LIKE SOME mangoes?" a woman's voice sings out from across the road, as we stand and admire a tree that's positively *dripping* ripe fruit.

Steve and I are in the middle of a game we play whenever we go for a walk lately: Let's pretend we can buy a piece of property in Grenada; what would we choose? We have fallen in love with this island at 12 degrees north of the equator since arriving here a few weeks ago. Now south of the hurricane zone, south of the box, we're planning to stay put for a while, and I'm beginning to relax. We arrived ten days after the insurance company's deadline for being outside the box—a meaningful deadline only if a statistically challenged named storm had hit during that time, which (of course) it hadn't. In Toronto, missing a deadline by ten days would have seemed the end of the world. Now it seems a fine accomplishment.

This sweet little stretch of land, a sweat-breaking,

fifteen-minute hike up the steep, potholed road from the dock at the village of Lower Woburn, is a strong contender in our let's-buy-some-island-property game. Along with a sweeping view of Clarke's Court Bay and, beyond that, of Hog Island and *Receta* calmly at anchor, it promises more mangoes than we could possibly eat, as well as papayas, breadfruit, and coconuts.

We might have missed the accompanying house entirely, though, if not for the woman's call. Tucked back from the road, it's almost invisible behind the umbrellaed tops of the coconut palms and the long-fingered leaves of a breadfruit tree. But when we turn toward the sound, we see a bit of blue-green wall with a smiling middle-aged woman, her dark hair drawn back in a bun, framed in a window.

Although my hanging baskets back on board are overflowing with mangoes, it seems rude not to buy some from this woman with the lilting voice, after being caught drooling at her tree. So I call back, "Yes, please," and we puff our way across the road and up an almost-vertical drive—so steep it makes the road look flat. The climb is immediately complicated by the appearance of a rambunctious pothound of indeterminate bloodline, who seems intent on snapping at anything that moves—in this case, my heels, toes, and ankles. "Stinky, *come here*." The voice is musical even when it's angry.

The drive flattens out into a sort-of carport—corrugated metal roof, open sides—with bits of outboard and drying fishnets scattered underneath and chickens pecking at the far end. Beyond it is the wooden, one-storey house, raised a good 8 feet off the ground on cinder blocks. Up a flight of steps and through the open door, a young man sprawls on the floor, watching a small TV, the only furnishing visible in the room.

The smiling woman waits by the steps, already holding a bag of at least half a dozen ripe Julie mangoes, the local favorite. She wears a white T-shirt emblazoned with Michael Jackson's face, which she's paired with a long flowered skirt and the ubiquitous island footwear, rubber flip-flops.

I pull out my cruiser's wallet, a sandwich-sized Ziploc stuffed with small bills and change. "Nooooo." That enchanting voice again. "These are a gift. I don't sell mangoes."

We start to chat, and eventually learn that Evette *does* sell fish, lobster, and conch, although she doesn't have any today—and she's not really trying to sell us anything anyway. She introduces us to her daughter, Gennel, fourteen, a tall sturdy teenager with the most beautiful eyes, who is timid at first but gradually begins to chime into the conversation. We're also introduced to a tiny herd of alternately shy and giggling little girls, neighboring kids Evette watches while their mothers work. Alisha, Morrisa, Dessian, and Bria, all four almost the same age and size, all four with elaborately braided and baubled hair, all big eyes and big smiles and buckets of crayons. I try to keep them straight: Alisha, white hair baubles, red shorts—or is she red baubles, white shorts? Just when I think I've got it, they jump around and change places and I make a mistake—much to everyone's amusement. And we officially meet the aptly named Stinky, who is now finding the dangling straps of my backpack irresistible. As Evette swats him with a flip-flop, she gives us her phone number and we promise to return in a few days for some conch.

It feels *soooo* good to know we can linger on this island as long as we want, to be able to tell Evette we will return to her house in a few days, without qualifying it by adding, "unless the weather is good, in which case we'll have to head off." No more timetable for a while, no more leaving a place before we're ready, because we have to outrace the calendar. We had toasted our arrival here with a bottle of champagne purchased in St. Martin, as a double rainbow—a sure sign of good luck—arced overhead, one end disappearing into the luxuriant green hills that are Grenada in the rainy season, the other fading into a curve of creamy sand beach. We have been gone from Toronto 323 days—and 102 of them have been spent at least partially in transit, including a medal-worthy (for me) twelve nights underway.

When we next tackle the hill to Evette's house, I'm toting our insulated cooler bag. I'd managed to determine on the phone that, yes, today Evette has "lambi"—the Creole word for conch—although her musical accent is almost impenetrable without visual cues to help. Grenadians in general (and Evette even more so) lengthen and soften their vowels—"Ann" becomes *Ahhhhnnn*—and don't pronounce the "th" combination: "three" becomes *tree*, "the" becomes *deh*. Add in the Creole words, the singsong cadence, and the unaccustomed grammatical con-structions, and Ahhhhnnn havin' trouble on deh phone . . .

There's a lambi dish I want to make, but I don't even know where to start. A few days earlier, we'd eaten lunch at the Little Dipper, a five-table, almost entirely open-air restaurant tucked amidst the foliage beside the road about a quarter mile from Evette's house. The conch was stewed, rather than fried or cooked on the grill as we'd had it in the Bahamas. The sweet, tender meat floated in a fragrant brown sauce with a hint of curry, and it had none of the rubber-band chewiness of undertenderized or over-cooked conch.

Evette immediately knows the dish, and getting her to share the recipe with a stranger isn't a problem: It's just that there *isn't* a recipe. She cooks by feel, not exact quantities—which makes it tough for those unfamiliar with the ingredients, and the local language. How much is a "tip"? How can I tell "counter flour" from "baking flour"? What is the mystery herb that sounds like "siveantime"? Distracted by the ever-present Stinky, who today has focused on the straps of my sandals, and not wanting to impose with endless questions and admit either total ignorance or inability to understand Grenadian English, I don't ask. Still, I do positively confirm that I need to "wash" the lambi in lime juice to start, "burn" brown sugar to get the dark, rich sauce, and add "a tip" of curry powder for flavor. But I'm going to have to figure out for myself how to put it all together.

At least these conch are already out of their shells, thanks to Evette and Dwight, the twenty-something young man we had glimpsed on our first visit. Raised by Evette almost from birth, he's the one who dives for the seafood she sells to help support the family. But we still have to do the cleaning and pounding. I give the job to Steve—seems only fair, since I'm doing the cooking— and having seen the effect of the process in the Bahamas, he heads to the beach, armed with a plastic cutting board, freshly sharpened knife, aluminum meat mallet, and pliers for pulling off the conch's slimy skin. He returns more than an hour later in a foul mood. While he was working on the lambi's skin, the mosquitoes and no-see-ums were working on his—"at least where it wasn't covered in conch goo," he mutters.

Dinner puts him in better spirits. I stew the lambi as I think Evette suggested, with onion, pepper, and coconut milk, and serve it over rice, with steamed "spinach" on the side sprinkled with a bit of freshly grated Grenadian nutmeg. At least that was what the emerald-green, arrowhead-shaped leaves were called in the market. But they have a delicious smoky taste, quite unlike the North American vegetable. (Months later, I discover that "spinach" here is actually an entirely different species of leafy green.) The lambi, meanwhile, isn't exactly what we remember from the Little Dipper, but we agree it's mighty fine. The conch is tender, the sauce a deep brown . . . just rather more sweet than rich.

"You put *how* much in?" Evette asks. I tell her I put about a quarter cup of brown sugar in the lambi sauce. "I burned it, like you said, and added it to the lambi and the other seasonings."

She is aghast. "Noooooo." That captivating singsong voice. "You just want a bit—maybe a spoonful."

Great, but what size spoon? She indicates on her finger—probably between a teaspoon and a tablespoon. Hmmm. No *wonder* the sauce was a little sweet.

It's a couple of days later, and we've hiked back up to Evette's, this time with a package of walnut brownies I've baked as thanks for the mangoes, which have long since disappeared. (And which, since we know the season won't last forever, were quickly replaced in town by more.) We haven't seen brownies—or any chocolate baked goodies—in the island stores and I figure they'll be a novelty. They are, although Gennel recognizes them instantly. "Dere's a picture in my schoolbook," she says shyly, referring to the text she uses in home economics. "But I never ate one." Though cocoa is an important crop on Grenada, the dried and roasted beans are almost all exported to factories in Europe for further processing. The few that are left behind are ground until they're soft, and the mushy mixture is rolled by hand into sticks or balls. In this form, the chocolate isn't suitable for eating or baking—it's mostly grated to make hot drinks. *Real* chocolate, the kind we know, is imported and expensive, Evette explains.

This trip, I'm determined to ask all the questions I should have asked the first time around. When Evette rhymed off the ingredients for the lambi, she had included salt and pepper, as well as seasoning and a seasoning pepper. The seasoning pepper was easy: The bushes they grow on—Evette has one alongside her house—look like they've been decorated for Christmas, and the market tables in St. George's are full of the tiny green, red, and sometimes orange jewels. A Caribbean cross between a sweet pepper and a hot pepper, they add the flavor of a hot pepper when chopped and tossed into the stew pot—without nearly the bite. "But what do you mean by seasoning?" I ask.

"You know, seasoning salt," she replies. I picture a jar of a spice blend like Mrs. Dash, and make a note to pick some up next time we're in town. I had figured out the mystery herb "siveantime" on my own, during our last trip to market, when I spotted some green bunches on the tables: Sive, or cive, is West Indian chives, stronger-flavored than their North American counterpart, closer in size and taste to our green onions. They're used to season stews and curries, as is thyme, so the two are helpfully sold together—a few stalks of sive tied with string to a couple of branches of fresh thyme—and talked about in one breath, "siveandthyme."

Meanwhile, Evette tells us to call her by her "home name," Dingis—"I was a very small baby, and dingis are little boats"— and lets on that she has a reputation as a *very* good cook. Since I've made it clear by this point that I'm no slouch in this department back home, and that I'm very interested in learning Grenadian cooking, Dingis is keen to help. There's a strong subtext here, however, a reason she feels she *has* to help me with my cooking: Like Aunt Keva, Dingis has decided that my husband is very skinny. *Too* skinny. *Dangerously* skinny. Couple that with the fact that we are childless—a married woman of my age?—and Dingis smells trouble on the horizon. Whatever my cooking skills, Steve is obviously not being properly fed. Unless I learn how to cook good (read: island) food, I'm not going to be able to hold on to my man: I need to fatten him up to keep him happy. Even with her accent, even with the Creole words, I have no problem understanding this. The message is loud and clear.

"Do you know coo-coo?" This time Dingis tows me straight into her kitchen, which is under the house and mostly open-air to keep both cook and house cool. It's pretty basic—a few open wooden shelves with pots and plates, a couple of stools, a low wooden counter, a fridge, and a small four-burner stove hooked up to a propane tank. The most prominent appliance is the large, new chest freezer plugged into an outlet on the house. There's no water in the kitchen itself: The tap (cold water only) and the wash-up area are outside, overlooking the road. Even though we haven't been invited inside the house yet, it's obvious there's no direct access to the kitchen; you have to go outside, down the steps, and between the cinder-block pillars to stir the stew or get a snack.

Several blackened pots crowd the stovetop, and I'm hoping Perry and Noel's aphrodisiacal man-trapping soup, still a mystery to me at this point, will at last be revealed. But no, Dingis cuts several squares from a battered metal pan: This "coo-coo" (that's indeed the way it's spelled) is a Caribbean version of polenta. "You boil some coconut milk and then you put in your cornmeal, and you stir it, stir it, stir it," she sings. When it thickens, pour it out into a pan, allow it to cool, slice, and eat. Some versions include okra; this one is plain. Some are made with water, this one with coconut milk—*much* richer. "It's good fried, too, with a cup of hot cocoa tea," Dingis explains. Nothing like upping the fat quotient.

She gives us each a piece and then, in a long procession—Steve and I, Dingis, Gennel, the four girls, and Stinky (once again snapping at my backpack, once again being whacked, to no effect, by Dingis with her flip-flop)—all climb the hill behind the house to see the view. Along the way, Dingis identifies the trees we pass: sugar apple and golden apple, their fruits not yet ripe; a tamarind festooned with pods; grapefruit, and more mangoes. "Gennel's placenta buried dere," she says, pointing to the bottom of a tall, heavily laden coconut palm. We're not sure whether Gennel is embarrassed by her mother's openness, or this is normal island practice. But it must have been good fertilizer, given the size of the tree. Next up are some huge plastic barrels full of oil, which Dingis rendered from a shark caught a few days earlier. The barrels are destined for a pharmacy in town, she tells us, where it will be sold for its health benefits, the local answer to cod liver oil. The tour also takes in the scruffy tethered goats grazing on the scrubby hillside, which are destined for the stew pot; goats are kept solely for meat in this part of the world, not milk or cheese. At the top, Steve makes us pose for pictures. In one direction, we look out on ridge after ridge of mountains, the foliage only interrupted by an occasional white building and orange tiled roof, with the open ocean hazily visible in the farthest distance. On the other side, the hill drops away sharply to a glorious view of the bay, where we can see sailboats at anchor, including our own.

It's time to show our hospitality. "Come out to visit us on *Receta* on Sunday afternoon with the girls," I tell Dingis. "Steve will pick you up at the jetty." Because we're not sure *Snack* is up to carrying everyone, we ask if Dwight, the young fisherman and lobster diver in her household, can bring half the crew in his heavy wooden boat. Unlike some of the local fishing boats (including my favorite, *Mr. Pitiful*), Dwight's doesn't have a name, but it's a typical island workhorse: about 20 feet long, brightly painted, completely open except for a small bit of decking at the pointed bow, with a well-used outboard. It could easily carry everyone to *Receta*, but that wouldn't be nearly as much fun for the kids as a trip in *Snack*.

What to serve? I worry about this conundrum for days, more than if I were giving a fancy party in Toronto, and I finally decide to mix up *vats* of fruit punch and Tang, cut two watermelons into wedges, and bake *dozens* of chocolate chip cookies, which I'm certain will be as novel as the brownies. I'm pretty sure Pringles— we stocked up in Puerto Rico—and dip (made boat-style, using long-life UHT cream which doesn't require refrigeration, soured with a bit of vinegar) will be popular with the kids. And I've got plenty of the freshly roasted peanuts that are sold from a cart near the perimeter of the market. The peanut vendor has become a regular stop each time we go into St. George's. His little brown bags, about forty cents each, contain plain or honey-roasted nuts—or the nastily addictive ones that have been caramelized with slivers of fresh ginger. And when you buy a few bags, he's guaranteed to throw in an extra. Steve, however, has become a favored customer, buying ten or more bags at a time, and now the amiable vendor throws in a *handful* of extra bags for free.

The day before the party, Steve makes a special trip to town to purchase crayons and drawing pads so the little girls will have something to do onboard. He also rigs our canvas rain-catcher as a tent on the foredeck, where they can color out of the sun.

When the boats arrive, I'm glad there are lots of snacks because there are definitely lots of bodies. In addition to Dingis, Gennel, and the girls—I still can't keep straight who's who—there is Allan, who's maybe eleven and from Lower Woburn, and a nephew of Dingis's who's maybe fifteen and is visiting from "the country," the north end of the island where Dingis's parents live. Dwight also comes aboard briefly, before heading off again to join his friends.

While the girls take turns "steering" *Receta* and quietly coloring on the foredeck (green is particularly popular, as the residue in the deck's nonskid surface later attests), Allan fishes off the side with our handline, putting Steve to shame. This kid has extremely quick reflexes, and in the time it would have taken Steve to catch one or two, Allan has a bucket filled with tiny yellowtail snappers, each one barely four inches long. Steve had been using the ones he caught for bait, to attract grouper that we then eat for dinner. Nope—these little guys *are* dinner, Dingis tells us. She guts 'em and fries 'em. I can't imagine how long it would take to clean enough to make a meal. She can't imagine what I'm getting at— in her eyes, there's nothing to it. And when she leaves at the end of the afternoon, the tiny snappers go with her in plastic bags.

It's difficult returning generosity—we always seem a step behind here. For Dingis has brought us a gift: a large lobster, which Dwight had caught that morning. No doubt remembering my treatment of the lambi, she is leaving nothing to chance this time and has announced she is coming into the galley to *show* me how to prepare it; no sense having a perfectly good lobster ruined.

The temperature is in the low nineties, and the sun is baking *Receta*, as it does every day. I'm used to the heat by now, but I'm not used to cooking in the middle of the afternoon with three bodies (Dingis, Gennel, and myself) squeezed into the tiny galley and a cauldron of water bubbling on the stove. While our guests show no signs of being affected by the steamy heat, sweat is pouring down my face and my shirt is glued to my soaking back. Unsure of the niceties of West Indian entertaining in any case, I'm finding it hard to be a gracious hostess when I feel like I'm in a race with the lobster to see who gets boiled first.

Once the lobster is cool enough to handle, Dingis authoritatively goes to work, cracking it with a hammer and pulling out the tail meat. Setting the rest of the lobster aside, she chops the tail into bite-size pieces while calling out requests for ingredients. I pull things out of baskets and cupboards and madly scribble notes as she slices onion, chops seasoning pepper, grates garlic, pounds sive, squeezes lime, and shakes curry powder into the bowl with the steamed tail meat. "Do you have seasoning salt?" she asks, and I triumphantly produce my newly acquired Mrs. Dash. Dingis shakes her head sadly—the student has failed again. In truth, I had suspected an error when I saw the price at Foodland: way too much for something used regularly by local cooks. She promises to show me *real* seasoning salt when we next visit her house, and when I eventually read the ingredients on the label of the little plastic bag, the mystery is solved: The fine white powder is pure, unadulterated MSG.

She tosses everything together—adding "a tip" of ketchup, another ingredient popular with island cooks—until the tail meat is well coated, then hands me the bowl to refrigerate. "It's for your dinner tonight, after we go home." Right before we're ready to eat, she says, I'm to give the mixture a quick stir-fry in hot oil. Then she turns her attention to the rest of the lobster.

Caribbean lobsters are different from their northern cold-water cousins. They're spiny lobsters, genus *Panulirus*, characterized by prominent hard spines on the body and legs, very long, thick antennae, and—most importantly from an eater's point of view— the absence of the large, meaty claws of *Homarus americanus*. Most of the spiny lobster's meat is in its tail, although the whole lobster is edible and delicious. Pound for pound, it makes just as good and just as much eating as its northern counterpart, because a good-sized spiny lobster also has chunks of tender meat in its body, antennae, and legs.

Which is why Dingis now shows me how to make what she calls "broth" from the remaining lobster. Break the legs, body, head, and antennae into manageable pieces and boil them up with seasonings, potatoes, carrots, flour dumplings, and "young figs." I know I haven't seen figs, young or old, anywhere on the island, and the combo of lobster and fig doesn't somehow sound right. Having learned my lesson with the seasoning salt, I explain to Dingis what a fig is back home. Again, she looks at me with a combination of amusement and amazement at my ignorance. Here, she explains, a "fig" (I later also see it spelled "figue") is a small, plump, finger-long banana. Young (green) figs are boiled and eaten like a starchy vegetable. With the potatoes and dumplings, they make the lobster "broth" a substantial dish— more like a hearty seafood stew—and I love the notion of stretching a single lobster to make two meals for two. There's a wonderful economy here.

As we discover that night and the next, the two dishes also taste unbelievably good. The curried stir-fried tail becomes our favorite way to eat lobster. The spices set up the flavor of the meat but don't overpower it, and the meal doesn't have the overwhelming richness that comes when you dunk each chunk in melted butter.

However, I end up making lobster Dingis's way only when it's for the two of us. When we start having guests from back home, they invariably expect their lobster straight. Too bad.

Steve takes everyone but Dingis for a spin in the dinghy and a swim on the beach. Though the kids live at the edge of the sea, they don't get out on the water very often—never in this sort of inflatable dinghy—and they love it. Clutching *Snack*'s pontoons and each other, they scream as if they're on an amusement park ride when the dinghy bounces over its own wake, and reach out to grab the spray. Then when Steve beaches the dinghy on Hog Island, they run back and forth through the shallows, splashing, belly-flopping—and still screaming with delight.

Like many middle-aged and older island women, Dingis doesn't swim, hates riding in Dwight's boat—"he go tooooo fast"—and doesn't particularly like being out on the water in any case. She and I stay behind and chat, woman to woman. We talk cooking, of course, but she also tells me about her marriage, her parents, and Gennel's birth.

It was during the time of the American invasion in 1983. Maurice Bishop's socialist regime had taken over in a bloodless coup four years earlier and aligned itself with Fidel Castro, causing much concern in the United States. When Bishop was murdered by a hard-line Marxist faction in '83, the United States had seen enough, and a joint American–Caribbean force invaded to "liberate" the island. Because of the turmoil, few buses were running, and Dingis had to *walk* all the way from Lower Woburn to the hospital in St. George's to give birth, 5 hilly miles in the tropical heat. A staggering thought: I'd have trouble doing it not pregnant and in the peak of health. Much to my surprise, I learn she is just forty. She's had to work hard, and it shows in her face. But although money is always very tight in her household, "No one goes hungry here," she stresses. Like others we meet, she tells us they live with what the land and sea provide.

* * *

A couple of days later, Dwight whizzes by and plops another lobster on our deck. Again, as with the mangoes, I assume a purchase, and I scurry below for my cruiser's wallet. But, again, the money is waved off. "It's a gift," he says. "It's thanks for your friendship."

"I hope the noise didn't bother you on Sunday," Steve says apologetically to the guys at the bar on the Hog Island beach. The bar is just a shack, really: four rough walls with a counter outside under an extension of the palm-frond roof, and a couple of picnic coolers; no seating, unless you count the big rocks that people sometimes perch on. No set opening times, either, but when someone's here, you can get a cold locally brewed Carib beer or possibly a rum. On Sundays, the guys build a fire on the sand, lay a rack overtop, and barbecue chicken quarters and maybe a lobster or fish or two. It's an excuse for people in the anchorage to gather for a potluck, bringing salads and desserts to go with the barbecued chicken they buy for $5 EC (about $1.90) apiece. Every once in a great while, a couple of pan players set up their steel drums and the unmistakable sound of the pans drifts across the water, coaxing the remaining stay-at-homes to come to shore for, oh, maybe just one beer.

Today we rowed *Snack* to the beach—that is, Steve rowed while I provided encouragement from a comfy spot at the stern—so we can clean the bottom. Evicting sea critters from the underside of both *Receta* and *Snack* is a regular item on our chore list. Steve puts on a scuba tank to do *Receta*'s bottom (I'm responsible for the rest of the hull), but the easiest way to do *Snack* is to remove the outboard—we hoist it onto *Receta* using a simple pulley system—then row to shore, flip *Snack* over on the beach, and tackle the accumulated sea life with paint scrapers and scrub brushes. A fascinating little marine ecosystem develops between cleanings: tenacious barnacles, various shades and textures of evil-smelling green slime, seagrass, and, today, something new: flat, shimmering, jellylike disks that squirt at me when I try to dislodge them with my scraper.

Steve has walked over to the shack to get us each a Carib to drink as we work. It's also a good excuse for him to make sure he hadn't accidentally offended local sensibilities by introducing a gaggle of noisy, splashing kids into Sunday's laidback beach scene.

"No problem, mon," Phillip tells Steve as he rummages in the bottom of the cooler for the coldest beer. "Dey from our village, dey our friends. We hear you invite dem out to deh boat." It becomes clear that our hospitality was unusual enough to be talked about in the village and, as a result, Steve and I have been deemed "okay." Locals apparently don't get many invitations to foreign cruising boats.

Steve, meanwhile, has been eyeing some long sticks with wire loops at the end that are leaning against the shack. "What are those?"

"Lobsta sticks, mon. You need a lobsta stick? Come back tomorrow and I'll show you how to make one."

We haven't been completely dependent on gift lobsters; since lobster season opened, Steve has gone on a couple of expeditions with other cruisers and brought back dinner on the end of his five-foot-long aluminum pole spear. The complex of skills lobstering requires is *way* beyond my abilities. For starters, each hunting trip below the surface has to be done on a single breath of air, because it's illegal for visitors (although not residents) to use scuba tanks. Lungs filled, you have to dive down—usually a good 15 to 20 feet here—poke under rocks and coral ledges, find a likely dinner prospect, get off a shot, retrieve the spear with dinner on the end, and get back to the surface—all before you run out of breath. Since the water slows down the spear, you need to be very close to your prey, too, before you shoot: mere inches away. And the whole time, although your lungs are burning and every split second is important, you have to swim calmly and gently so as not to scare off dinner.

The pole spear, which is also used for shooting fish, works on a similar principle to a slingshot. On one end is the sharp spear tip; on the other, a loop of surgical tubing. With the tubing anchored in the crook between your thumb and index finger, you pull the pole back, stretching the tubing, and then release your grip when you're almost on top of your prey. *Sproing. Thwack.*

The locals, however, scorn spears. "Don' want shoot he with a speargun—deh hole let all deh flava' out, mon," Phillip tells Steve when he returns to the Hog Island beach the next day. "Dat's why you need a lobsta stick, mon. Dis way." And he leads Steve into the scrub behind the beach.

A "lobsta stick" is a 3- or 4-foot-long branch with a fine, stainless wire noose on the end that allows you to snare rather than spear your prey. Instead of shooting the lobster, you lasso it by one of its antennae. When you tug on the stick, the noose tightens. A fishing swivel between the stick and the noose allows the lobster to spin and flail its powerful (delicious) tail without snapping the wire. It's firmly captured live. No hole, full flava'.

"A female bush best," Phillip says, cutting a couple of thin, flexible branches with his cutlass. Before Steve can inquire about how to distinguish the gender of Hog Island's bushes, Phillip is on his way back to the beach to rig the sticks over a cold Carib.

"You need a groupa stick, too?" While Steve is still trying to work out what a "groupa stick" might be, Phillip assumes the answer will be yes and starts to trim one of the branches with his pocketknife so there's just a small fork at one end. This stick isn't for catching groupers, it turns out, but for holding the ones that are speared. It will allow Steve to keep the dead fish at a distance from his body as he swims back to the dinghy, in case a barracuda or shark smells blood and decides to investigate.

A couple of days later, dinner is on *Receta*. Steve has gone diving with two other cruisers, and they return with a decent haul: four good-sized spiny lobsters and one huge coral crab (also called a king crab, or a channel clinging crab, and the largest species of crab found on Caribbean reefs)—all with holes obvious in their shells, through which the flava' is no doubt rapidly escaping.

"The lobster stick requires more bottom time," Steve confesses. "And it takes a bit of finesse to get the noose properly tightened so the lobster can't slip away. Didn't want to risk losing dinner —so I stuck to the spear."

I'm the designated cook. By popular request (these North Americans!), I'll steam the lobsters right at dinnertime and crack them into pieces, so we can dip the succulent meat in melted butter. But one lobster I'll cook ahead: I have my heart set on a decadent side dish of lobster pizza.

In this part of the world, if you want pizza, you have to make it—from scratch—yourself. I set to work on a batch of dough. And of course we'll need appetizers to go with rum punch before dinner, so I also cook the crab ahead and pick out the meat for deep-fried crab toasts. And since I'll have the oil going, it's only logical to deep-fry some plantain "spiders" for appetizers too. (Unlike its close relative, the banana, the starchy plantain needs to be cooked to be consumed—and frying is our favorite way.) This snack gets its name because the shredded vegetable emerges from the hot oil looking a bit like some crispy brown multilegged critter.

Just one problem: When you're cooking for six in a space four feet square, a menu that involves boiling, baking, and deep-frying is a *little* ambitious, creating a lot of heat and a mountain of dirty pots and pans—without either a dishwasher for the cleanup or an endless supply of fresh water from the taps.

But tonight it doesn't matter. We eat in the cockpit, where the breeze is gentle and the air comparatively cool, leaving the mess out of sight below. The light is soft, a combination of an almost-full moon and the glow of our cockpit oil lamp. The piping frogs provide the background music. Time is flexible, expandable; I can take all day tomorrow for the cleanup, if I have to, catching water during the regular afternoon rainy-season downpour to replenish our tanks. And everyone agrees the food is fabulous. Especially the lobsters—despite the holes.

Dingis's Curried Lobster

This treatment showcases the flavor of the rich meat without overwhelming it with melted butter. Serve the lobster over rice.

SERVES 2

1 large lobster (about 2 pounds)
1 small onion, sliced thinly
1 large clove garlic, grated
1 small cubanelle or green bell pepper, thinly sliced
¼ teaspoon seeded and finely chopped hot pepper
Salt and freshly ground black pepper
1 green onion, smashed and chopped
2 teaspoons white vinegar or lime juice
1 teaspoon (approx.) curry powder
1 tablespoon ketchup
2 tablespoons vegetable oil

1. Cook the lobster in boiling water. When it is cool enough to handle, remove the tail meat (and claw meat, if you're using a clawed lobster) and cut into small chunks. (Reserve the rest of the lobster to make Lobster Broth; see below.)

2. Toss the rest of the ingredients, except the oil, with the lobster meat. Taste and adjust seasoning, adding a little more curry powder if necessary. (There should be just a hint of curry flavor.) Refrigerate for a couple of hours to allow flavors to blend.

3. When ready to serve, heat the oil in a heavy pan or wok until very hot. Stir-fry lobster mixture for a minute or two. Add about ½ cup water to create a bit of sauce and allow to cook for just a couple minutes longer. Serve over rice.

Tips:

• Dingis's Lobster Broth needs to be made with a large Caribbean spiny lobster, because the parts that remain after the tail is used still contain substantial meat. Break the remainder of the steamed lobster into pieces and put in a large pot. Add a couple of potatoes and carrots (and green figues, or half a plantain, if you like), cut into chunks. Season with salt and pepper, and add a tablespoon or two of butter or margarine and an inch of water or light fish stock. Bring to a boil, lower heat, cover pot, and simmer, stirring occasionally, for about 30 minutes or until vegetables are tender. After the broth is at a simmer, drop in dumplings, if desired. (To make dumplings, combine 1 cup all-purpose flour with 2 teaspoons baking powder and ¼ teaspoon salt. Cut in 2 tablespoons butter or shortening to make small pieces, then add ½ cup milk all at once. Stir to mix thoroughly and make a soft dough. Knead gently with floured hands about five times until smooth. With floured hands, shape dough into 1-inch balls and drop into hot broth. Cover pot and simmer 15 minutes. Don't peek during cooking.) Serve Lobster Broth in deep bowls.

• If you have access to a West Indian market, substitute sive (West Indian chives) for the green onion and a seasoning pepper for the cubanelle (or green bell pepper) and the hot pepper.

Lower Woburn Stewed Lambi (Conch)

The hardest part of making this dish (once you have the recipe) is getting the lambi out of their shells, cleaning and tenderizing them. So buy your conch cleaned—or pass the job on to someone else.

SERVES 4

4–5 conch, cleaned, tenderized, and cut into 1-inch (approx.) pieces

1 lime, cut in half

1 onion, chopped

1 cubanelle or green bell pepper, chopped

1 green onion, chopped

1 teaspoon chopped fresh thyme, or ½ teaspoon dried thyme

1 clove garlic, chopped

2 celery stalks, tops only

Salt and freshly ground black pepper

¼ teaspoon ground cloves

2 tablespoons vegetable oil

1½ tablespoons burnt-sugar syrup or browning (see Tip, below)

2 ½ tablespoons curry powder

1 cup thick coconut milk or coconut cream

1–2 teaspoons cornstarch (optional)

1. Squeeze the lime over the conch, and rub with the pithy halves. Toss the conch with the onion, pepper, green onion, thyme, garlic, celery tops, salt, black pepper, and cloves; refrigerate for a few hours.

2. In a large pot, heat the vegetable oil and add the burnt-sugar syrup or browning; cook, stirring, for a minute or so. Add the conch with its seasonings and sprinkle with curry powder. Stir to

coat conch thoroughly and cook, stirring, over medium-high heat for a couple of minutes.

3. Add coconut milk or cream, lower heat, cover, and allow to steam for about 20 minutes, stirring occasionally. If the sauce seems too thin, mix the cornstarch with a little cold water, stir in, and cook a few minutes longer until sauce has thickened. Serve hot with rice.

Tip

• The burnt-sugar syrup—also known as browning or caramel coloring—that's essential to the deep rich sauce is available in bottles or jars in West Indian grocery stores. It's also used when browning meats for stews. West Indian cooks often make up a large batch of their own to have on hand by cooking brown sugar with water until it loses its sweetness and is a very dark brown. (Not only did I add too much burnt sugar when I made my lambi the first time, but I also didn't cook the sugar nearly long enough for it to lose its sweetness.) If you can't get burnt-sugar syrup, substitute a teaspoon of a North American browning and gravy enhancer such as Kitchen Bouquet.

Coo-Coo (Caribbean Polenta)

This dish, which came to the islands from Africa ("coo-coo" means side dish in a number of African languages), is the Caribbean version of polenta. Serve it with cream of callaloo soup or saltfish fritters (see pages 277 and 300), or any fish or stew, or do as Dingis suggests and fry up slices of cooled coo-coo for a snack.

SERVES 6–8
3 cups coconut milk (approx.)
1 tablespoon butter
½ teaspoon salt
1 cup yellow cornmeal

1. In a large saucepan over medium heat, combine coconut milk, butter, and salt. Bring to a boil.
2. Gradually stir in cornmeal. Lower heat and cook for about 5–10 minutes, stirring constantly with a wooden spoon to prevent sticking, until the mixture thickens and leaves the sides of the pan. (If it becomes too thick, add a bit more coconut milk or water.)
3. Pour the mixture into a greased 8-by-8-inch pan. Allow to set for a couple of minutes, then cut into squares and serve warm.

Tips:
- Some versions include okra (though we prefer our coo-coo plain). If you want to include it, thinly slice 4 okras and cook in the coconut milk until soft, about 10 minutes, before adding the cornmeal.
- Slices of coo-coo are also excellent grilled. Brush them lightly with olive oil and set on the barbecue. Cook until lightly crisped on both sides.

Plantain Spiders

Sprinkled with lots of sea salt and served hot, these are positively addictive—better than French fries—and a real happy-hour treat. I've yet to make them for anyone who can eat just one.

Watch them carefully while they're frying, and take them out of the oil when they're just golden. If they cook too long, they'll become hard.

SERVES 4 AS A SNACK

2 large plantains, 1 green and 1 semiripe
2 tablespoons very thin slivers fresh ginger
2 tablespoons very thin slivers garlic
Salt
2 cups vegetable oil (approx.), for deep frying
Freshly ground black pepper

1. Peel the plantains and shred coarsely using the largest holes on a hand grater. (You should have about 1⅓ cups.)
2. Combine the plantain, ginger, and garlic in a mixing bowl with a little salt and toss well to combine.
3. Heat oil to 350°F in a deep, heavy pot, wok, or deep fryer. Using 2 forks or spoons, carefully drop tablespoons of the plantain mixture into the hot oil. (Don't compress the plantain shreds tightly—you want them to look "spidery" when they emerge from the pot.) Fry until golden on all sides, about 2 minutes total.
4. Using a slotted spoon, transfer to paper towels to drain. Sprinkle with salt and pepper and serve at once.

Tips:
• Don't crowd the pot—fry a few spiders at a time and let the oil return to 350°F between batches.

- Plantains, which look like overgrown, sharp-edged bananas, are available in North American supermarkets located where there are communities of West Indians. Judge their ripeness by their color: Green ones are unripe, yellowy-green to yellow ones are semiripe moving to ripe, and yellowy-black ones are very ripe.

Mango Crisp

The perfect dessert when you have an embarrassment of mangoes. (And when you don't, you can substitute berries—blueberries, raspberries, strawberries—for some of the mango.) Although not an option on *Receta* (our boat freezer wouldn't keep ice cream), the crisp is delicious with vanilla ice cream. Alternatively, serve with lightly whipped cream, lightly sweetened sour cream or yogurt, or crème fraîche. (See Tips, below.)

SERVES 8

For the topping
> ½ cup flour
> ¾ cup quick-cooking or old-fashioned oats
> ⅔ cup packed brown sugar
> ¼ teaspoon freshly grated nutmeg
> 2 tablespoons finely chopped crystallized ginger
> ⅓ cup cold butter

For the fruit
> 6 cups sliced ripe mango (about 3–4 mangoes, depending on size)
> 1½ tablespoons freshly squeezed lime juice
> ¼ cup packed brown sugar (approx.)
> 2 tablespoons flour

1. Preheat oven to 350°F. Butter a 2-quart (8-inch-square) baking dish.

2. Prepare the topping: In a large bowl, combine flour, oats, brown sugar, nutmeg, and crystallized ginger. Cut in cold butter until mixture resembles coarse crumbs. Set aside.

3. Toss the mango with the lime juice. Combine sugar and flour, and toss with fruit. Taste and adjust sweetness if desired. Spread fruit in the prepared dish.

4. Sprinkle topping evenly over fruit. Bake in preheated oven for about 40–50 minutes, until the fruit is bubbling and the topping is crisp and lightly browned. Serve warm.

Tips:

- For a nutty topping, toss about ½ cup slivered almonds with the topping mixture.

- To make crème fraîche, combine 2 cups whipping cream and 1 cup sour cream in a nonmetallic bowl, cover with plastic, and let stand at room temperature for 16–24 hours or until thickened. Refrigerate until serving.

- To make your own crystallized ginger, peel ginger, slice into ¼-inch-thick slices, and boil in cane syrup or sugar syrup (see page 185) for 20 minutes. Remove from syrup, drain, and roll in granulated sugar. Allow to air dry on a rack, then keep in a tightly closed jar.

That Demon Rum

One part sour,
Two parts sweet,
Three parts strong,
Four parts weak,
Five drops of bitters, and nutmeg spice,
Serve well chilled with lots of ice.

Traditional West Indian recipe for Rum Punch

ID-MORNING IN THE ANCHORAGE at Hog Island, and I hear the unmistakable sound of a visitor approaching: the buzz of a small outboard, first getting louder, then changing to a gentle *putt-putt-putt*, followed by a squeak as an inflatable dinghy bumps our hull. With this advance warning, I'm already up the companionway in my bathing suit—usual onboard attire these days—before the visitor has a chance to rap on the hull and shout hello.

It's Treesha, off the big catamaran from California called *New Tricks*, which she shares with her husband, Tim, and Bubba, a slender, well-coiffed standard poodle.

"You're invited to a rum tasting tonight. On *New Tricks*. Around five. Bring yourselves and a bottle of rum." Before roaring off to spread the word to the next boat, Treesha explains that "the Minister of Rum" is behind the tasting. He's asked *New Tricks* to host it "because our cockpit can hold more people than anybody else's in the anchorage."

We've heard tales about the self-styled Minister of Rum, and I'm curious to meet someone who's been clever enough to make a career out of sailing and drinking. "We'll be there," I tell her.

By the time we arrive at *New Tricks* that evening, a line of dinghies is already strung behind each of the catamaran's hulls and more than a dozen couples are lounging in the cockpit. We add our aged Brugal rum from Luperón to the two-dozen or so bottles already sitting on the cockpit table, presided over by a clean-cut, sober-looking man in his mid-forties with aviator-style glasses and a droopy mustache. His papaya-colored polo shirt bears a crest on the pocket: a rum cask with "Office of the Minister of Rum" embroidered beneath it. He is intently stirring a bit of amber liquid in a glass with a swizzle stick that actually *is* a stick: a twig that he's just finished trimming with a pocketknife so the end branches into a circle of spokes. His demeanor implies the gathering is not merely an excuse for a party. Edward Hamilton, the Minister of Rum, is clearly quite serious about the business of drinking at hand.

In fact, not wanting to depend on the taste of a bunch of un-educated strangers, the Minister has brought along a dozen bottles from his own collection—which consists of about sixty different types of rum from one end of the Caribbean to the other, stored aboard his 40-foot sloop, *Tafia*, whose name is a French word for (what else?) rum. I'm already getting the feeling this is a man possessed.

"If you've never had anything but a rum and Coke, I feel sorry for you," he begins as he moves the bottles around on the table like a kid arranging armies of toy soldiers. "Rum is the most varied spirit that is bottled. It ranges from pure white alcohol just out of the still to fine aged spirits that will rival the best cognac." I can see Steve raising an eyebrow: We've definitely had the fresh-out-of-the-still stuff—Nimrod's comes to mind—but neither of us has tasted a rum that would come close to rivaling *any* cognac, let alone the best.

The Minister is sorting the bottles by their place of origin, French islands on one side of the table, everywhere else on the other. Then, within each group, he clusters them by their dominant raw ingredient, "the most easily recognizable factor affecting a rum's taste," he explains. He then gets down to business, pouring, swirling, and sipping as he talks.

Rum is made either from fresh sugar cane juice—"this kind of rum is called *rhum agricole* and comes almost exclusively from the French islands"; from cane syrup—"which is cane juice boiled down to remove some of the water," much the way maple syrup is made from sap; or from molasses. "In the English-speaking islands, most rum is made from molasses, which is what's left after crystallized sugar is extracted from sugar cane juice." (In the French islands, molasses-based rum is called "*rhum industriel*," and the islanders export most of it to France; they drink the *rhum agricole* themselves.)

As we had learned at Nimrod's, aging (or lack thereof) is the next big determiner of taste. "It's a pretty nebulous term," the Minister says. "A rum can spend as little as three months in the barrel and be called aged. And rum doesn't get any better once it's in the bottle." In the French islands, to be called *rhum vieux*—old rum—a rum must spend at least three years in a barrel. But in Spanish islands such as the Dominican Republic, there is no requirement as to how old rum has to be for the distiller to put *añejo*—aged—on the bottle. As an example, Ed picks up the Brugal Añejo we brought along. It's probably been aged just a short while, he says. Its deep rich color comes from the addition of caramel rather than from barrel time. Perhaps the 45-peso price (about $3) should have given us a clue. "Even well-aged rums almost always have their color enhanced with caramel." Except for aged white rums, of course, which are filtered to remove any color imparted by time in the barrel.

"The question I'm most frequently asked," the Minister says, not waiting for anyone to ask it, "is what is my favorite rum? I have a lot of favorites. I haven't found one that I want to drink to the exclusion of others." Later, in private, he confesses he has a "shortlist" of twenty-five favorites, and if he *really* had to, he could pare it down to maybe sixteen.

"But I want you to taste each rum for yourself and not rely on me or anyone else to tell you what you like."

This is what the crowd's been waiting for. But before he turns us loose on his table, the Minister offers a final tip: Be sure to have a glass of water between drinks. Otherwise, don't expect sympathy from him for your killer headache.

We look at the labels like Ed has told us to, noting the alcohol content, the distiller, the place of origin, and any information about the age of the rum. We pour a small finger in a glass, hold it up to the light to judge the color, swirl it, sniff it deeply, analyze the smell, and then take a taste. At least that's what we do the first couple of times. Things get a little more, uh, haphazard once people have tried four or five rums. I distinctly remember, toward the end of the evening, one of the guests interviewing the rest of us to solicit our opinions on the various bottles, using a well-gnawed corncob as his microphone.

Ed has written several books on rum, and he's brought along copies of his most recent one, his self-published *Rums of the Eastern Caribbean*—a useful refresher in case any of the details of the tasting are a little foggy the next morning—but given the frugality that abounds in cruising circles, he doesn't have many takers. "I'd rather spend the money on rum," whispers one crusty old salt. But, in fact, the book is an island-by-island guide to distilleries and rum shops, stuffed with "visas" that entitle the bearer to discounts throughout the entire Caribbean. A "passport to rum," Ed calls it, and a determined cruiser could easily recover his investment in reading material by using the visas for a free drink here, and a half-price bottle there. There's even a visa for a free shot of rum at Nimrod's—not a big incentive for me, I'll tell you, but of course we buy the book to add to *Receta's* by now over-stuffed bookshelf. "Keep the wind behind you and your glass half full," Ed writes in the front. Steve senses an epiphany.

It had come out in conversation at the tasting that we had worked in publishing in the "real world," and Ed had asked if he could pick our brains. Sure enough, a few days later, he rows his wooden dinghy over to *Receta* at sunset, a couple of rum bottles tucked between his knees. Trade tastings for publishing advice? Sounds fair to us.

He immediately heads belowdecks to *Receta's* galley, to mix us each a 'ti punch to start things off. The before-dinner drink of choice in the French West Indies, 'ti punch has the same mystique there that the martini does in North America. In Martinique and Guadeloupe, it's said you can judge the quality of a restaurant by its 'ti punch. And, like the martini, it demands a glass all its own—a small, squat tumbler that often bears a colored decal advertising the brand of rum the drink contains. Ed is forced to make do with our standard acrylic boat glasses. He has brought us a proper swizzle stick, though: one of his trimmed twigs with its propeller-like end for stirring.

'Ti is a contraction of the French *petit*, he tells us, which refers to the size of the drink—just a couple of ounces over maybe one ice cube—*not* to the size of the punch it packs, which is decidedly *grand*. It's a deceptively simple combination of *rhum agricole*, freshly squeezed lime juice, and pure cane syrup; the trick is getting the proportions right, when "right" is a matter of personal taste. One 'ti punch can taste dramatically different from another, depending on the balance of sour, sweet, and strong, and, most importantly, the brand of strong you use.

A couple of sips and Steve has declared a mission: As soon as we get to Martinique—the first French island on our way up the island chain—*Receta* will acquire a set of proper 'ti punch glasses, and the *rhum agricole* and cane syrup to go with them. He can't wait to start experimenting.

We talk more about rum than publishing, but that seems fine with Ed: This is a man who *loves* to talk about what he does for a living and how he does it—a rarity among cruisers who are escaping the "W word"—and, besides, it gives him a reason to row back again the next night, with a different selection of bottles tucked between his knees.

Ed admits he started the Ministry of Rum and appointed himself minister as an excuse to keep sailing the Caribbean and visiting distilleries—but he also wanted to raise awareness, he says, of what he felt was an underappreciated form of alcohol. Sure, sure.

"When I started traveling around learning about rum, people started giving me rum. The more I learned, the more rum they gave me. And the better the rums were." During his ten trips up and down the island chain, he's been shown private stills, sampled rums that are older than he is, and been served special home brews in off-the-beaten-path rum shops.

"There is no substitute," he tells us, unequivocally, "for seeing how the rum is made. Going to the distilleries and meeting the people who make the spirits will enhance your enjoyment of their efforts."

We take his words to heart and start to use his book as he really intended: as a travel guide to the world of Caribbean rum.

The narrow dirt road is shaded by stately old mahoganies and "deh tourist tree," as islanders call the gumbo limbo, the tree with the red-orange peeling bark. The dust we kick up as we walk is sticking nicely to my sweaty legs. We had started out from *Receta* in the relative cool of early morning, but that was three tightly packed buses and more than two hours ago, and I'm now feeling anything but fresh. When we changed buses for the last time in the town of Grenville on the other side of the island, halfway up the coast, we had asked the driver to let us off at Dunfermline Estate.

"All the bus drivers know where to stop," Ed had assured us. "When you get off, take the left fork of the dirt road to the distillery." That we've done, but there are no signs, no buildings, and no people in sight. "I don't know about this," I say to Steve.

"Yeah, but just take a whiff," says he of the sensitive nose. "This is right."

A few moments later I pick it up, and the air soon becomes heavy with the scent of rum being made: a smell that's part burned sugar—from the pots of boiling cane juice and the burning sugar-cane stalks used to feed the boilers—and part sweet fermenting syrup.

Eventually the laneway opens up to reveal a collection of old stone and wood buildings with sugar cane, bananas, and cocoa growing on the cultivated hillsides behind them. Clearly, Dunfermline Estate doesn't get many tourists. There's nothing quite so obvious as a visitor center, store, or even an office, and as we debate which building to head for, a bone-skinny man in ragged pants and T-shirt heads toward us. Both his long hair and his even longer beard are styled in dreadlocks, and when he speaks, it's a strong mumbled patois. Not your typical tour guide. "Good day," says Steve. "Is it possible to see the distillery?" We don't understand a word of his response, but his body language indicates he's agreed to show us around.

For the next half-hour we follow him from one building to the next, and listen to him "explain" what we are seeing. Dunfermline is the third distillery we've visited, and by now we, as Ed puts it, "speak a little rum." Fortunately. Braided Beard points to something, mumbles incomprehensibly, and we respond as if we've understood perfectly. Yes, of course, the piles of *bagasse*, the sugar-cane stalks from which the juice has been pressed. Yes, the water-powered cane mill that does the pressing job and delivers the fresh juice to the stone boiling house, where the fires are fed by the *bagasse* from the first step of the process. Yes, I nod knowingly, the fermentation vats, where the "wash"—the cane juice mixed with water and yeast—sits until the distiller determines it's ready for the still. At Dunfermline, where the rum is fairly heavy-bodied, that's ten to twelve days, though light rums are fermented for as little as twenty-four hours. We even manage to ask appropriate questions (at least we think they are) at what we think is the appropriate time.

The highlight of the tour comes when Braided Beard swings open the door to the still house, to show us the yellowed sight glass used for determining the alcohol content of the raw rum. The simplest still—the type beloved by backyard bootleggers—is the pot still, which consists (in simplest form) of a kettle heated over a wood fire and attached to a condenser. It makes alcohol in batches, a kettle at a time, and is labor intensive. To increase production, most distilleries use a variation on the continuous distillation column, which is fed by a continuous stream of fermented wash, heated by steam. Not Dunfermline. It uses a copper pot still, as it always has. The doorway of the still house is low, the interior dim. I duck and follow our guide into the darkness. *Whup-whup-whup-whup-whup-whup-whup-whup*. An extended family of fruit bats brushes past me into the light as I stifle a scream.

Dunfermline has been in operation since 1797, and the facilities don't appear to have been cleaned very often in the intervening two centuries. But neither that, nor the dirt floors, nor the open vats, nor the bats hanging in the rafters give us any pause about the sanitary condition of the finished product. *Nothing* could survive in Dunfermline rum. It's bottled at 70 percent alcohol, which makes it 140 proof. "Strong rum," the locals call it, which officially means any brew that's more than 50 percent alcohol.

We've got a choice between adding a bottle of the regular Dunfermline—aged "up to six months"—or the comparatively ancient three-year-old "Spicy Jack" to our growing onboard collection. Jack gets the nod, and Braided Beard digs out a bottle from the boxes piled in a corner. Just in case the "70 percent alcohol" doesn't make the point, the laughing mule on its garish label reinforces that the stuff has a wicked kick.

Ed's book continues to give a focus to our land excursions for months to come, and a further excuse to explore beyond the beaten paths. Its inside back cover becomes plastered with a series of Post-it notes: a shrinking–expanding–ever-changing key to the location, taste, and preferred usage of the various bottles in *Receta*'s stash of spirits. "Macoucherie Dark: Top shelf under sink in head; for rum punch." "La Mauny: Forward can locker; white *rhum agricole*; for 'ti punch." "Rhum J.M.: Starboard aft locker; TOP-OF-THE-LINE AGED RUM—FOR SIPPING ONLY—DO NOT MIX UNDER PENALTY OF DEATH." Steve is serious about this one.

The ten-year-old J.M., from the J.M. Rhumerie on Martinique—the island with more distilleries than any other in the Eastern Caribbean—is the proof for Steve that rum can indeed "rival the best cognac." Could there be a better reason to drive all the way to the island's northernmost edge? The drive along the twisting road that cuts through spiky pineapple fields is spectacular, but one sip of the decade-old J.M. in the old stone tasting room is more spectacular still. The aging warehouse has row after row of oak barrels, each one clearly stamped "Kentucky" and formerly used for bourbon. Regulations requiring other liquor producers to use barrels only once ensure a steady supply of "once-used" barrels for the rum industry in the Caribbean, where they're kept in service for ten to fifteen years—or until they begin to leak, whichever comes first.

At the La Mauny Rhumerie, also in Martinique, we get not only *rhum agricole* but also—finally—our set of 'ti punch glasses. "I set a personal best here by sampling three *rhums* before 11 A.M.," I crow to my journal, although I do tack on: "Good Lord, what are things coming to?"

At Shillingford Estates, near Mero, Dominica, it's purely because of the name and the label that we opt to buy the Macoucherie Dark and the Macoucherie Elixir of Bois Bandé rather than the blandly named West Coast Rum. "Macoucherie," after all, is patois for "come into my bed." The Macoucherie Elixir of Bois Bandé is a blend of rum, spices, and an extract made from the bark of the locally grown bois bandé tree, yet another reputed aphrodisiac. The island's indigenous people are said to have discovered the uplifting effects of bois bandé ("hard wood," in patois) centuries ago. "To be consumed moderately," the label on the bottle advises, but whether this is to avoid exhaustion or drunkenness isn't specified. However, I never see another rum in the West Indies with a similar warning.

Shillingford Estates is home to one of the few water-driven wheels for crushing sugar cane remaining in the Caribbean—we'd seen another at Dunfermline—and the manager offers to show us around: "You know a little something about how rum is made?" he inquires. I should hope so; this is, after all, now Distillery Tour 7.

Ed has more than seventy recipes for various punches and cocktail concoctions in his book, but perhaps the most basic, and the easiest to remember, is this one, which he claims comes from Barbados, the first island to export rum: *One part sour/Two parts sweet/Three parts strong/Four parts weak/Five drops of bitters, and nutmeg spice/Serve well chilled with lots of ice.* Five liquid ingredients and a sprinkling of spice. "It is agreed, as much as anything in the islands is agreed," Ed writes in the book, "that the word *punch* comes from the Hindustani word for five—*panch*." The *strong*, of course, is rum. The *sour* is usually freshly squeezed lime juice, and the *sweet* is traditionally cane syrup, sold in bottles, though a simple sugar syrup can stand in. The *weak* can be fruit juice, water, or a combination.

In this part of the world, *bitters* can mean nothing but Angostura Bitters, made in Trinidad. This "unique blend of herbs and spices," as the small paper-wrapped bottle trumpets, is made from a secret formula developed in 1824 by the surgeon-general of Simón Bolívar's army, Dr. Johann Siegert, to improve the appetite and digestion of the soldiers. Only five living people are said to know the formula, and there are rumored to be only two written copies in existence: one in a bank vault in New York, and one hidden in Trinidad. Among the ingredients the potion apparently does *not* contain is the bitter bark of the angostura tree; it takes its name from the town of Angostura, a trading port on the Orinoco River in Venezuela, where the good doctor was based.

The nutmeg dusting the top of a well-made rum punch is indelibly associated with Grenada. The air even carries a hint of the sweet spice, especially in the countryside where the fruit trees grow. Local lore says a doctor who had lived in the East Indies imported the first nutmeg to the West Indies in the early nineteenth century—to enhance the taste of his planter's punch, of course. The trees came to Grenada in 1843 and proved well suited to the hilly terrain and volcanic soil. Nutmeg became so important to the island—Grenada produces one-third of the world's supply and is the largest single supplier—that it is depicted on the country's flag. In fact, it's the *only* object represented on the flag, besides seven stars, one for each of the country's parishes.

* * *

We have planned a hike to the Seven Sisters, a series of waterfalls in the Grand Etang Forest Reserve, a protected rain-forest area high up in Grenada's interior. Our guidebook says they are the country's best, most secluded falls—and the most difficult to get to. "You need a guide," it states unequivocally.

We know guides are readily available, that we can hire someone to pick us up at the dinghy dock, deliver us to the reserve, guide us along the trail, arrange a lunch, and deposit us back at the dock at the end of the day. That would be too easy. We decide to do it ourselves, with two other cruisers.

The bus that crosses the mountainous backbone of the island leaves from the waterfront in St. George's, opposite the fish market. It's one of the typical minivans but, unlike the always-crowded short-haul buses—such as the one we just rode into town from Lower Woburn—this bus takes a while to fill. *And she not leavin' 'til she full up.* More than full, actually. There's no way the driver is going to make the trip through the mountains until he's got enough passengers to make it worthwhile. That's okay. No one—including us—is in a rush. Island languor has seeped into our bones.

A half-hour after we finally leave the waterfront, we're bouncing along a narrow roller-coaster road, and the driver is working through the gears as the van strains up hills and careens around curves—some of them so tight that I'm sure we're going straight into a rock wall. The bus passes right by the entrance to the Grand Etang Forest Reserve, but we'd been told not to get off there, to keep going and watch for a tiny hand-painted sign with an arrow that says "trail to the waterfalls," on the roadside a couple of hills after the park entrance. "It's apparently a much easier hike if you start from there," said our source, who hadn't. We'd run into him and his wife outside Nimrod's late one afternoon. They'd just wobbled off the local bus, their legs encrusted with mud. They'd spent the day with the Seven Sisters.

Sure enough, the sign appears, Steve raps on the roof, and the bus pulls over. As we follow the arrow, a woman crosses the road to meet us. This "easier" trail starts on a private plantation, and she is collecting a very modest fee on behalf of the plantation owner. In exchange, she gives us bananas for a snack, tells us we can take anything we want that we find on the ground along the way, and points us toward an assortment of walking sticks leaning against a shack near a triangular red sign: "Notice On Your Own Risk to The Falls." She is working here to make money for her granddaughter's schoolbooks and uniform, the woman explains. We know from Dingis that although schooling is free, and mandatory up to age sixteen, books and uniforms must be purchased. This is a huge burden—and a deterrent to keeping kids in school—for families with limited means. It's clear this woman doesn't see a lot of business from hikers, and when our entrance fee is a scant $5 EC ($1.90 apiece) we know she can't be making very much. "I put my faith in God to provide," she says.

As we start walking through the plantation, we have to duck to avoid low-hanging hands of bananas and sidestep piles of fallen mangoes that are starting to ferment, making me almost dizzy with their sweet, intoxicating smell. As the foliage closes in, I realize that we are walking through a dense grove of nutmeg trees, their branches drooping with yellow-orange fruits that resemble plump overripe apricots. Many have burst open, revealing the nutmeg nestled inside.

Fresh off the tree, a nutmeg is an absolutely gorgeous thing, Nature's interpretation of a Fabergé egg. Framed in one half of the creamy fruit is the glossy brown shell that encases the nutmeg seed, the part we grate into cake batter and onto rum punch. But the nutmeg tree produces two spices: The glossy shell is covered with a delicate lacy red coat that looks as if it is made from shiny wax. Dried, this lacy coating is the spice mace, used in pumpkin pie and other desserts back home and in curries and cakes here.

It's hard to walk without stepping on the fragile jewels, thick as fallen apples in an autumn orchard up north. We stuff our pockets, pulling the nutmegs in their bright scarlet coats from the split fruits. The fruit—also called the pod or pericarp—isn't edible raw, but is made into jam, jelly, and a delicately flavored syrup that is a highly successful substitute for maple syrup on French toast and pancakes, or as the *sweet* in rum punch.

Farther ahead, a lone man harvests for the plantation owner: He methodically whacks the branches with a long stick, and gathers up the fallen nutmegs, pericarp and all, into a big canvas sack. Afterward, he will separate the mace from the nutmeg by hand, and the raw spices will be taken to one of the island's processing stations.

The plantation eventually gives way to dense rain forest—a crush of trees with pillow-sized leaves and thick twisted vines. Outrageous flowers—the kind of elaborate tropical blooms sold for a small fortune by high-end florists—poke through the greenery: wild purple and orange birds of paradise, tall elegant spikes of wild red ginger, yellow and red heliconia that look as if they're molded from plastic. When there's a small clearing, we grab vines and swing, hooting and hollering; forty-six years old and I'm playing Tarzan. Mostly, though, the trail is narrow, steep, overgrown, unmarked, and slippery. When it disappears, we backtrack until we pick it up again—rather, we backtrack until all four of us *agree* we've picked it up again. Yesterday's showers have mixed up a nice greasy batch of mud, and we pull ourselves and each other up the steepest, slickest sections using branches, vines, and the walking sticks. Steve is the first of our foursome to join the muddy-butt club.

Eventually, a vista opens, and a waterfall tumbles down the rock face ahead. I splash my arms and face and dunk my kerchief in the cold milky pool at the bottom before we head on to

Sister 2. Above the first falls, the trail begins to crisscross the stream, and we have to pick our way across on the slippery rocks. Eventually, I pull off my hiking shoes and wade.

Only three hours later—although it seems triple that—we're back at the Grand Etang roadside. My legs are aching and filthy, and I'm convinced there are at least thirteen vindictive sisters, not the paltry seven advertised. I pick the mud out of my fingernails so we can stop in St. George's on the way home for a very late roti lunch.

When you orchestrate your own outings, whether they're to a rum estate or a forest reserve, the discoveries are hard-won—but each discovery seems yours alone. Days later, I can still hear the huge stands of bamboo creaking, still smell the sticky fragrant gum that seeped from the rough-barked gommier trees, still see the determined lines of leaf-cutter ants carting home jagged pieces of leaves like outsized green umbrellas, to use as fertilizer to grow the mushrooms they will feed their young. And I still have the seeds I picked up on the forest floor, deep-brown polished things called "donkey eyes," as cool and smooth as river stones. And of course I have my nutmegs.

Back on board, we peel off the lacy red mace and put it in a flat pan to dry. A couple of hours later, I can crumble it with my fingers, and it's ready to use, its brilliant scarlet already faded to a soft yellow-orange. The nutmegs need to dry for about six to eight weeks in a warm, dry place, according to the wrinkled, pipe-smoking lady I had consulted at one of the processing stations. There, the shiny brown seeds are spread out to dry on flatbed wagons that can be rolled into the sun during the day and back inside at night or when it rains. I pop mine into the cupboard over *Receta*'s engine and forget about them.

At the processing station, the nutmegs go to cracking machines once they're dry, and workers then separate the kernels from the shells by hand. The kernels are dumped into water tanks to separate the floaters, which have a high oil content and are sold for processing, from the sinkers, which have less oil and are sold as spice. Some of the floaters are destined for the nutmeg oil refinery at the north end of the island. Commercially, the oil is used as a flavoring and in soaps and moisturizers; but locally, some of the nutmeg oil will be sold as a "condiment" to relieve rheumatism, arthritis, backaches, joint pain, and the congestion of coughs and colds.

More than six weeks later, I crack one of my nutmegs open with pliers and grate the seed onto our rum punch with a stainless-steel rasp. The warm woody flavor calls up a day in the mountains, sunlight filtering through thick green foliage, falling water, oversized leaves, outrageously painted flowers. And mud.

Steve's 'Ti Punch

Much experimentation was required before Steve achieved what he thinks is the perfect balance of strong, sour, and sweet. Judge for yourself.

MAKES 1 DRINK

1½ ounces *rhum agricole* (see Tips, below)

¼ ounce pure cane syrup (see Tips, below)

¼ ounce freshly squeezed lime juice

Combine the ingredients in a measuring cup. Stir with a swizzle stick and serve over 1 ice cube in a small glass.

Tips:

- To be perfectly authentic, a 'ti punch should be made with clear *rhum agricole*, which gives the drink a distinctive taste. However, in a pinch you can substitute any white rum.

- Cane syrup can be found throughout the West Indies, as well as in parts of the southern U.S. It too has a distinctive taste— imagine a light golden, slightly smoky molasses—but simple sugar syrup is an easily made substitute: Combine equal parts (by volume) of sugar and water in a saucepan. Bring to a boil and stir until the sugar goes into solution. Cool and store in the fridge.

Steve's Favorite Plantains
(A.K.A. FRIED PLANTAINS WITH NUTMEG AND RUM)

Fried ripe plantains sprinkled with just salt and pepper are a common Caribbean side dish. One day I added a squeeze of lime, a splash of rum, and some freshly grated nutmeg—and from then on, I never made them any other way.

I like serving these plantains with grilled chicken or chicken curry. But in Steve's eyes, they go with just about anything. He was also particularly fond of the version I made with my home-made spiced rum.

For this dish, you want really ripe (but not mushy) plantains. Plan on half a plantain per person—unless that person is Steve, in which case, a full plantain per person is barely adequate.

Ripe plantains
Vegetable oil, or a combination of oil and butter, for shallow
    frying
Salt and freshly ground black pepper
Freshly grated nutmeg
Fresh lime
Rum

1. Cut the plantains in half crosswise and peel. (See Tips, below.) Slice each half lengthwise into ¼-inch-thick slices.
2. Heat a few tablespoons of oil or a combination of oil and butter in a large, heavy skillet over medium heat. Sauté the plantain slices until golden on both sides, about 4 minutes per side, sprinkling each side with salt, pepper, and nutmeg.
3. When the plantains are almost done, squeeze a little lime juice over top and add a splash of plain or spiced rum. Serve hot.

Tips:

- Plantains are more difficult to peel than bananas. To do it most easily, trim the top and bottom off each plantain and cut the plantain crosswise in half. Then peel off the skin by hand.
- To make your own spiced rum, have a drink out of a bottle of light or white rum to make room for the spices. (Light rums will take on the flavor of the spices better than dark rums, which often have a more pronounced flavor to start with.) Add a cinnamon stick, a whole nutmeg out of its shell, a few cloves, and perhaps one or two slices of ginger. (I have also stuffed in pieces of whole mace—but don't use the ground stuff, which is the type you usually find in North American stores.) Although some patient types allow their spiced rum to steep for months, you only need to let a few weeks go by before trying it.

Mr. Butters, the Mysterious Breadfruit, and Monday Night Mas

No doubt our productivity would have been affected. . . . Probably, this week may have seen a great number of people taking the remaining work days to recover after consuming too much alcohol, or being fatigued from the constant long sleepless hours over the days of festivity.

Editorial entitled "Now The Carnival Over," *Grenada Informer: The Fearless Weekly That Tells It As It Is*, week ending Friday, August 14, 1998

THE BEACH ON THE MAINLAND side of the Hog Island anchorage—a tiny patch of sand by two derelict, half-submerged Cuban gunboats, relics from the 1983 invasion—is diagonally across from the Hog Island beach and a minuscule fraction of its size. If you squint away the rusted hulks as you approach, the scene is what winter-weary tourists dream they'll get when they book their Caribbean holiday: a little beach all their own with soft white sand, swaying palm trees, and brochure-blue water under a flawless sky.

We'd seen cruisers dinghying into shore there only to return an hour later with arms full of watermelon and bags protruding with eggplant and squash. To us, the new kids on the block, it was a mystery, there being no sign whatsoever of habitation near that beach; certainly no market or store. But soon, through the cruisers' grapevine, we learn of Mr. Butters.

"Pull up your dinghy on the sand and follow the path from there," Terry and Nancy tell me. We had got to know them in George Town, and their sailboat, *La Esmeralda*, had arrived at Hog Island about a week before *Receta*. "The path will lead you right to his shack."

Mr. Butters used to make rounds of the anchorages on this stretch of Grenada's coast by boat, they had been told, selling his fruit and vegetables. But no more: Now, if you want to buy his produce, you have to go to him. Mr. Butters (as everyone respectfully calls him) has been squatting on the hillside behind the beach for the last seventeen years and cultivating the soil—by hand, without benefit of tractor, rototiller, or harvester.

"Did they say turn right or left?" Steve says as we drag *Snack* up onto the beach. Expecting it to be obvious, I hadn't bothered to ask. Once we leave the sand, we're at the edge of an expanse of more-or-less cultivated fields, hidden from the anchorage by a stand of white cedars and Indian almond trees and stretching a hundred yards in each direction. What's lacking is a sign that says "Produce stand this way." Cows moo unseen somewhere on the hillside in front of us. "Rare steak," says Steve longingly. (He's learned the hard way that the words "chewable" and "steak" don't go together here.) We wander right; nothing. We wander left; nothing. We wander right again, by this time wishing we'd brought a water bottle, and finally spot an overgrown, sort-of track snaking through spiky sugar cane.

Five minutes along, a donkey tied to a tree flips his lips at us with disinterest. Beyond him stands a rickety wooden shack. Out front, an elderly man studiously washes eggplants in a bucket of water that's so muddy it's hard to imagine the vegetables aren't emerging dirtier than they go in. "Mr. Butters?" He gestures with an eggplant a little farther up the hillside, where a younger, wiry man in torn, mud-caked trousers is bent over a bed of lettuce plants.

"Mr. Butters?" I'd been picturing a table with a tidy assortment of carefully arranged vegetables like those the market ladies have in St. George's. But "tidy" is the last word that comes to mind here. Although stuff grows *everywhere*, it's difficult to tell what are vegetable plants and what is just vegetation. Partly hidden by all that greenery, discarded sacks, bottles, pieces of wood, and old tires dot the landscape around two more shacks. Aside from the heap of muddy eggplants and a pile of dirt-splotched watermelons, there doesn't appear to be anything that might be for sale, and I don't know quite how to initiate business. I decide to take the direct route: "Good morning, we'd like to buy some tomatoes." With a reticent, eye-averted "good morning," Mr. Butters gestures for me to follow him into the fields.

I get my tomatoes right off the vines, warm from the sun, along with a thick-skinned cantaloupe, a soccer ball–sized watermelon, and a beautiful bunch of escarole fresh out of the ground, dirt still clinging to its roots. Perhaps in his mid-forties, with a carefully trimmed salt-and-pepper beard and a baseball cap jammed on his head, Mr. Butters is taciturn as we move from row to row and he loads up my arms and my canvas bag (now definitely destined for the laundry bucket). Meanwhile, I try to keep up a steady patter, complimenting him on his stuff—you can *smell* the sweetness of the cantaloupe—and exclaiming at the eye-popping view. (From the top of Mr. Butters's hillside, the entire Hog Island anchorage is visible, right out to where the waves break over the reefs.) He's uncommunicative, but not unfriendly, and when I *oooh* over the aroma from a little patch of purple-leaf basil by the shack, he picks a handful for me to take along, gratis.

He becomes garrulous—it's all relative, of course—only when Steve points to the homemade signs hanging inside one of the sturdier-looking sheds. Like the others, it only has three walls, but one of them is cinder block and the roof is corrugated tin. The signs are pretty much the focus of the interior; the furnishings consist of a crude bench and a couple of rough boards banged into the walls as shelves, which hold a yellow cooler and a pile of smashed cardboard boxes.

Slogans are hand-printed on the cardboard signs: "Land is the basis of our independence. Preserve it." "Sugar cane industry abandoned for golf course and casino." "The Mt. Hartman deal. Under the table." This one is illustrated with a stick-figure drawing of a Grenadian sitting across from Uncle Sam, who wheedles in a speech bubble: "Forget agriculture. We will give you dollars." And, yes, both have their hands under the table.

"See deh bulldozer?" Mr. Butters points at a piece of machinery overgrown with foliage on the adjacent hillside. "Dey've sold my land for a golf course."

We've heard the rumor floating among boats in the anchorage: The government has sold the strip of mainland on this side of the anchorage and all of Hog Island on the other to the Ritz-Carlton chain, which plans to link them with a bridge and put in a luxury hotel and golf course. Mr. Butters and his farm are a casualty of the deal, and he's being forced to leave.

Like the other cruisers, we're horrified that this little piece of undeveloped paradise may disappear—especially since the rumors also suggest that freeloading cruising boats will no longer be welcome in the bay. But communal self-interest aside, this really is a pristine piece of Grenada; to turf off the Grenadians and turn it into just another foreign-owned hotel and golf course with questionable benefit to the local economy would be a sad ending. Still, without any physical activity onshore indicating the start of a development, and with Grenada's existing resorts not running at even close to capacity, the story had lacked believability on the cruisers' grapevine. But here is Mr. Butters saying he expects to be booted off his land any day now—which is why he cut back on how much he planted this season, and why there's not much for sale. "Dey offered me other land, but it's no good for growin' tings, not like dis."

He's had some press for this outrage and even found himself on TV: He may not own this piece of hillside, but he's cleared it, improved it, and worked it for seventeen years and, around here, that makes it as good as his. His indignation, though, has mostly faded to resignation by now. When we say good-bye to trudge back to the dinghy, I'm doubtful he'll be here the next time we come—even though the bulldozer is overgrown with foliage.

That night, I sauté a couple of cloves of garlic in olive oil, add Mr. Butters's escarole and some thin slices of smoked sausage, toss it all with penne, and grate some good Parmesan on top. (I've managed to keep a hunk of Reggiano in the fridge since Florida, always finding a place to buy more—at great expense—before there's nothing but rind left. It's one of the few back-home ingredients I can't bear to give up.) I chop the basil and sprinkle it on thick slices of the sun-ripened tomatoes, and christen the dinner Pasta and Salad from Mr. Butters's Garden. I sure hope he's there for more.

The path is ridiculously easy to find, of course, on our second trip, and Mr. Butters is still there, as laconic as last time. Which makes him positively chatty compared to his wife, who is cooking in one of the shacks today, deftly turning sizzling slices of eggplant in big blackened frying pans over a wood fire. She seems quite shy and, despite my practice with Dingis and Gennel, I'm not yet skilled enough in Grenadian English to understand the few words she offers up. When I lean in to ask her what she's making, a shimmering wall of heat almost knocks me over. No wonder she's not talking.

"Any news about the development?" Steve asks Mr. Butters.

"I have to leave, maybe tomorrow," he says morosely.

When you shop at Mr. Butters's, taking along a shopping list or planning to buy ingredients for a particular dish is a waste of time. After the delicious pasta, I'm looking forward to getting another big bunch of escarole. No luck. No escarole. The trick, then, is finding out what Mr. Butters *does* have, because he never *volunteers* the information. Instead, you play twenty questions, which is particularly difficult since we don't really know what-all he grows. "Do you have any eggplants today?" "Are there ripe tomatoes?" "Is there lettuce?" "How about mangoes?" Eventually, after he says "no" to three or four items, the rules of the game permit me to ask if he has *anything* else that's ready—at which point he might allow that, yes, there are cantaloupes or, yes, he has some squash.

One day, when I've reached the end of my questions almost empty-handed, he reveals that he has beets. After all that, he comes up with the one vegetable Steve won't go near. I explain, but he insists I take a couple along anyway, without charge, for me. Another visit, he offers up what he calls a "marsh melon." Its rind is exactly like a watermelon's, but it's perfectly round and when we cut it open back on the boat, the flesh is a dazzling lemon yellow. It's absolutely gorgeous . . . and tastes just like watermelon. Steve and I can entirely demolish one of Mr. Butters's watermelons, I'm embarrassed to admit, in a single afternoon. Whatever the color.

Unfortunately, one thing Mr. Butters never offers is breadfruit. We've been tantalized by them for weeks, as the bus whips by the pendulous trees on its way into St. George's. As we rocket around every curve, the pebbly skinned, cantaloupe-sized green globes hang almost within reach. Just try to buy one.

Even though the trees are laden with them, there are none visible in the market. And there are none up the hill at the Marketing & National Import Board, the set-price (no bargaining allowed), government-owned business that sells "food crops" purchased from local farmers. None for sale on the streets. I decide to ask the market lady who's been helping me learn my mangoes. "All gone," she says. "Come in the morning." It's barely midday at this point.

Next trip, I try again. It's about 9 a.m. "All gone," she says. "Come in the *early* morning." The odds of us getting from *Receta* to the market much earlier are kind of slim, no matter how badly I want to make my own breadfruit salad. Meanwhile, they continue to taunt us from every tree.

Breadfruit plants first came to the West Indies from the South Pacific in the late 1700s, carried by the infamous Captain William Bligh, the idea being that the fruit from these prolific trees would be used by the British to feed slaves cheaply on the sugar plantations. One story suggests that breadfruit was in fact responsible for the mutiny on the *Bounty*: When Bligh left Tahiti in 1789, he took more than 1,000 breadfruit plants on the ship with him. There was a water shortage on board, and after discovering the captain was using a secret supply of water on his precious breadfruit plants, the crew mutinied. In any event, Bligh and a second batch of plants reached St. Vincent after the mutiny, on another vessel, the *Providence*, in 1793. (A descendant of one of Bligh's breadfruit trees still grows in the St. Vincent Botanic Gardens.) The British, however, were thwarted in their cheap-food scheme: The slaves refused to eat the foreign food, and it only achieved acceptance in the Caribbean years after emancipation.

Beneath the breadfruit's tough, lime-green skin is a firm, white, starchy flesh, slightly porous and fibrous at the fruit's very center.

When boiled or roasted—it can't be eaten raw—it's reminiscent of soft, doughy, freshly baked white bread; hence, the name. After this initial cooking, it can be fried, stuffed, mashed, creamed, scalloped, turned into a salad, or eaten plain with butter. In fact, this filling, carbohydrate-laden fruit serves much the same culinary function here as white potatoes (called "Irish potatoes" in Grenada) do elsewhere.

Our persistence in the name of homemade breadfruit salad finally pays off: In the supermarket at nearby Grand Anse, a store not generally noted for a stellar selection of produce, I spot a bin of bright-green cannonballs one day. The problem is, every one of them is cannonball hard. Hefting one of the smallest (which means it's still pretty large—a breadfruit can weigh up to ten pounds), I home in on a middle-aged shopper and ask her if it's ripe. She shakes her head with some amusement. "When a breadfruit is ripe, it's garbage. You want it while it's green. And you don't want one that's soft." She hands me back my completely solid offering and says it's ready to cook that day. After they're picked breadfruit apparently turn in short order to a smelly, unpleasant, mayonnaise-like mush inside, which is why there are so many still on the trees and so few brought each day to market. Dingis later tells me that the *surest* way to choose a good one is to have the market lady cut it open for you, so you can inspect the solidity of the inside before you buy.

Get out the cleaver: Cutting and coring the one I've bought requires serious muscle—kind of like dealing with a particularly ornery turnip, only one with twice the usual diameter to push the knife through. Islanders sometimes cook them whole, either in the oven or outdoors in the coals of a hot fire, and I'm beginning to see why. Once I've wrestled it into pot-friendly pieces, I boil it until it's al dente, about fifteen to twenty minutes.

By the time it's drained and cooled, I realize I'm confronting quite the pile of breadfruit. I cut half of it into cubes and mix it with chopped onion, celery, dill pickle relish, and a mayo dressing for the long-awaited breadfruit salad. I have enough for an extended-family picnic and, when we taste it, we'd swear we are eating potato salad. The other half I panfry in oil with a little onion. We'd swear we are eating home fries—and I have enough to serve an entire diner during morning rush. Not that both aren't delicious, but it's an awful lot of fuss to end up eating potato salad and home-fried potatoes *for days*.

From now on, if we want breadfruit, we'll get it in a restaurant—which isn't exactly hard to do. Wedges of boiled or roasted breadfruit are usually part of "provision," an assortment of root vegetables that accompanies traditional West Indian meals: boiled yam, sweet potato, dasheen, and taro, and sometimes boiled green plantain and pumpkin as well. The name "provision," also referred to as "ground provisions," is a perfect description for these abundant, readily available, nutritious, cheap, and easily pre-pared root vegetables, which have long provided sustenance in tough times. Eaten as part of provision, breadfruit is kind of like white bread: bland and inoffensive, albeit a useful vehicle for sopping up sauce and filling up hungry customers.

But wouldn't you know it? Now that I've satisfied the urge to cook my own breadfruit, the next time I beach the dinghy by the derelict boats, walk the overgrown track, and play twenty questions, Mr. Butters volunteers: "I got breadfruit ready. How 'bout a nice breadfruit?"

The cruisers' grapevine has more than Mr. Butters and a rumored hotel development to keep it humming these days. Carnival is around the corner, and there are decisions to be made.

"Carnival" comes from the Latin *carne vale*, which means "farewell to the flesh." This annual revelry traditionally precedes Lent, and got its start in medieval Europe when the aristocracy held elaborate celebrations and gorged on meat before the fasting and restraint imposed by Lent began. It came to the Caribbean with the French in the seventeenth century, was picked up by their slaves, who began to mock their masters with their own pre-Lenten celebrations, and grew in exuberance from there.

But it's early August—six months before or after Lent, depending on which way you look at it, and Grenada is getting ready to celebrate Carnival. The connection to Lenten denial has lost out here to practicality. The reason is Trinidad, a scant 75 miles to the south and home to the third largest Carnival in the world (behind Rio and New Orleans). Grenada simply couldn't compete with Trinidad's pre-Lenten bacchanal, and therefore switched it to summer, when it would coincide with the August anniversary of the Emancipation Act. Ironically, Grenadians only have themselves to blame: They were the ones who introduced Carnival to Trinidad, when Grenada's French settlers moved there in the late eighteenth century, after Grenada was ceded to the British under the Treaty of Versailles.

For cruisers spending hurricane season in Grenada, the timing is perfect. By the beginning of August, posters in the shop windows in St. George's have started trumpeting the various events. Though the preliminaries and semifinals of the music competitions begin weeks ahead, the heart of Carnival is three days, starting with *Dimanche Gras*—French for "Big Sunday"; through *J'Ouvert*—French for "daybreak"—on Monday morning, when revellers spread mud, oil, and greasepaint all over themselves and onlookers; through to Monday Night Mas, an "everybody dere" street party; through to the big Carnival finale on Tuesday.

Nimrod's is full of chat about which band to join for Monday Night Mas.

"Carib deh best." This, from a local who's stopped in for a quick eighth of rum with Hugh.

"But they're not taking any more people." This, from Steve, who's already tried to sign us up for the Carib band.

"How 'bout Heineken den?"

"Yeah, I saw the sign in Arnold John's store. We get six beers apiece if we join that one, which sounds pretty good. Besides, it may be the only band left that will take us. And Ann doesn't want to be left out."

"Your wife nice. You don' want vex she."

Mas—pronounced "mahss"—is short for masquerade. The *real* mas bands have been at work for months, stitching sequins and feathers and sparkly bits of cloth into elaborate, sometimes overwhelmingly massive—and other times decidedly scanty—costumes that reflect the theme the band has chosen for this year. These mas bands are serious business, and they will strut their spectacular stuff first in a glittering pageant on Monday afternoon, and then in a parade through St. George's for Carnival's finale on Tuesday. We will be spectators for those parts; Monday night is when *everybody* gets to play mas and dance up and down the hills of St. George's—no sequins, feathers, or practice required. The costume part is usually just a shirt or maybe a cap advertising the band's sponsor.

And so about a week before the start of Carnival, Steve comes home from town toting two Heineken T-shirts and the fistful of beer tickets that came with them. "Terry and Nancy and some other people we know joined the Heineken band, too," he tells me. To our surprise, though, we've discovered that not all cruisers are as determined as we are to get involved in island culture. Some aren't only ignoring local events and music, they're still *eating* much as they did back home. "They've got bigger freezers and more money than we have," Steve says, "but I'll bet they're not having as much fun."

The auditorium at the Grenada Trade Centre is packed with well-heeled locals; a government minister is in the front row, and the seats next to me are filled by middle-aged ladies in summery evening-out dresses who chat sedately before the show begins. But once the first performer takes the stage, all semblance of sobriety evaporates and the ladies turn raucous. Soon they're slapping their thighs, elbowing each other, wiping tears from their faces, and generally killing themselves with laughter. I'm laughing too, though I have only the barest clue why.

This is a pre-Carnival calypso and soca concert headlined by the Mighty Sparrow, Grenadian by birth but long since adopted by Trinidadians as their own. Calypso, or *kaiso* as it's called in Creole, is social and political commentary, oral history, and just plain bawdy mischief set to music. It has its roots in African culture, and was brought to the Caribbean with slavery. Soca, born in the seventies, is a "rhythmically enhanced" form of calypso with an intricate bass and percussion line; the name is a combination of *so*ul and *ca*lypso. Much calypso these days is influenced by soca, and the division between the two musical forms is indistinct. Both, though, are lyrically driven—and when you're unfamiliar with local culture, politics, and players, still having trouble interpreting basic conversations, it's not likely you're going to get the innuendoes of a ribald, government-critical calypso.

It isn't until the third time through the chorus that I catch on that "Four Kings," sung by the very popular Beast—a member of the Royal Grenada Police Force when he's not savaging the government in song—is a double entendre; I must have been misled by the sedate ladies next to me, who unabashedly scream out, "Four King," every time Beast cues the audience in. The ladies also seem partial to "Deh Monkey," sung by a handsome young Grenadian named Randy Isaac: "My friend Deneva invite me home by she/She went and take out deh monkey from where it been/Put it under she dress . . ."

"Ah want to see deh monkey, Ah want to see deh monkey," the ladies belt out enthusiastically when it comes time for the chorus.

Much to my glee, when Mighty Sparrow takes the stage after

intermission, he addresses a question directly to one of our group, an I-know-more-than-you-do cruiser who had raised my anxiety level every time I was in his company from Florida, where we first bumped into him, south to the bottom of the box. Now, accompanied by his pale-skinned wife, both their faces tinged a shade of brilliant red, he's getting it back. "Do you eat white meat?" Mighty Sparrow asks him for all the audience to hear. Unfortunately (from my point of view), he understands what he's *really* being asked, and saves himself from further embarrassment by emphatically nodding yes. Mighty Sparrow makes things easy for outsiders by prefacing each of his calypsos with a little introduction, and he has just explained that the next number accuses the men in the audience—mostly black, of course—of lying when they don't admit to eating "white meat." This is accompanied by a dangerous throaty chuckle, and the song that follows is performed in a rich, powerful voice with amazing range and color, accompanied by incredibly sexy moves. The Mighty Sparrow is no spring chicken: Sixty-three years old, he's been performing for more than four decades. Some of his themes are serious—education, emancipation, a unified Caribbean—though there are also odes tonight to Billy Boy (his penis) and saltfish, the piscine term for white (and dark) meat. The audience knows all the numbers and sings right along.

As Carnival draws closer, we're singing right along too.

"Dey have deh bellee, dey have deh bellee." It issues from the speakers on the bus to town, from people walking along the street, and from the radio on *Receta* during the daily "Top 20 Carnival Countdown." A contender this year in *both* the National Calypso Monarch and the National Soca Monarch competitions that are part of Carnival, "Deh Bellee" has caught fire. "But tell dem I am here to help deh country out/And to stop me dey will have to put a handcuff on me mouth/Dey have deh bellee, dey have deh bellee . . ." Getting more airplay even than "Monica Lewinsky" ("Go tell your uncle, go tell deh judge/go tell deh prosecutor dat you and I made love"), "Deh Bellee" even makes it into one of the prime minister's speeches.

The week before Carnival just happens to include Fidel Castro's first-ever state visit to Grenada, a major and controversial event, with most of the population still able to recall firsthand the Cuban presence and the U.S. invasion. We go to Tanteen, the parade grounds in St. George's, where we are given little paper Grenadian and Cuban flags to wave as Prime Minister Keith Mitchell and Castro take the stage. Mitchell makes the formal introduction. Dr. Fidel Castro, he says, has shown during his forty years in power that he has "deh bellee." If you have "deh bellee," you have guts, stamina, nerve, *cojones*.

We need bellee to survive Carnival.

The printed schedule says the semifinals of the National Soca Monarch competition start at 10 P.M. Steve and I arrive right on time. The club is deserted, no equipment on stage. We're on our own tonight; even those cruisers who *are* interested in island music are put off by the hour—past everyone's usual bedtime, and requiring late-night reef-running dinghy rides to and from shore. And these are, after all, only the semifinals.

We wander around by ourselves in the over-air-conditioned room until someone takes up residence behind the bar at the far end. "Aren't the soca semifinals here tonight?" Steve asks him.

"Yeah, mon."

"What time do they start?"

"Jus' now."

With typical North American logic, we interpret that to mean in a couple of minutes. By 10:30, a few people have wandered in and a couple of guys have started to arrange some mikes and amps. By 11, the room has begun to get crowded. Still no performers, though. Finally, around 11:30—when we, and the entire room, are well lubricated—the first singer takes the stage. The judging is based not solely on the music—in fact, the backup bands are on tape—but also on the performance: how the singer incites the crowd to a dancing frenzy. By 1:30, when we call it a night because I can barely stand or breathe in the steamy gyrating crowd, the competition is barely half over. And this, by the way, is a weeknight.

Castro's speech had started "jus' now" too: Thousands of Grenadians (and us) had sweltered in the hot afternoon sun for *three hours* past the scheduled time before the prime minister took the stage with his honored guest. *Three hours.* Steve says the literal translation of "jus' now" is "jus' throw away the schedule." It is the perfect island phrase. We adopt each other.

The finals of the soca monarch competition are at Seamoon, a huge open field where rallies, conventions, concerts, and sports events are held. A pavilion and stage are at one end and covered bleachers at the other, where we sit with Terry and Nancy from *La Esmeralda.* Like us, they jump at the chance to check out local happenings; Terry had taken charge of this outing and organized the transportation to Seamoon, more than midway up the island in St. Andrew's parish. "Bleachas deaaaddddddddd," shouts the emcee on the stage. And, comparatively speaking, I suppose we are. Most of the crowd—thousands of people—is on the field, dancing deliriously, jumping, waving flags, shirts, towels, rags in the air, a churning mob in the darkness, dancing, madly dancing, crowding the stage, backlit by the lights. "Stay calm, stay calm, *staaaaaayyy* caaaalm," the emcee exhorts the crowd, in tones intended to build the riotous excitement. Every few minutes, a flame shoots skyward from between the flags and rags, when someone ignites the spray from an aerosol can—hair spray, I think—throwing part of the spectacle into vivid silhouette and imprinting the ecstatically dancing figures on my eyeballs. We had been told we couldn't bring bottles inside the grounds; flame-throwers, obviously, are a different matter.

The competition started jus' now and will go till dawn; we finally depart around 2 A.M. I fall instantly asleep in the van, but awaken suddenly when it slows, squinting at the watch I've put on especially tonight: An hour has passed, we're in the center of St. George's, and we're surrounded by music—the sound of a full orchestra—and light so bright it's as if we've been flung into the middle of the next day. A pan band—a hundred or more players, some of them with five or six steel drums apiece—is practicing for the Carnival pan competition the following evening. At 3 A.M., in the middle of the street. "Why not?" shrugs the woman I later ask about this surreal practice session. "Dis way, no one know what deh band gonna play." I can feel the music pulsing inside me, such a powerful complexity of melody and rhythm it's impossible to believe it comes from instruments that are essentially oil drums. Then the van moves forward, the music recedes, and I am sure the brightly lit scene was an island dream.

Monday Night Mas. The gathering place for the Heineken band is in the parking lot of the supermarket on the lagoon across from the Carenage. "Do not pass your truck, *do not pass your truck*." The order booms into the night air from a 10-foot wall of speakers on the back of the truck that we are not supposed to pass. There's another truck, too—no speakers on this one, just coolers and kegs of Heineken. Hundreds of Grenadians and maybe a dozen cruisers mill around the trucks, clutching plastic cups of beer and wearing Heineken T-shirts. When the sound truck pulls out into the road, the DJ on the truck starts the music and we all fall in behind; the beer truck brings up the rear.

Perhaps a dozen bands like ours—Carib, Coca-Cola, Brydens (a liquor distributor, among other things)—are gathering in the steamy dusk along Lagoon Road, each with a truck equipped with a wall of speakers and a DJ. The DJ chooses the soca hits, the speakers blare them out at deafening volume, and soon we chippin' and winin' into town.

"Chipping," a rhythmic, foot-shuffling walk, allows one to save one's energy for "wining," a style of dance that involves rotating one's pelvis in a suggestive, arousing figure-eight movement. The name comes from "winding," which nicely sums up the pelvic rotation. Wonderful to watch—and impossible for most of us middle-aged outsiders to do, though we try our best and though the people around us are more than pleased to demonstrate. At one point, I'm sure Steve has got the motion, as he's gyrating behind me, making subtle contact in a most appealing manner— Steve, who is the first to admit he's no dancer even when the steps are more conventional. Then I notice Steve is standing *next* to me, and it's *someone else's pelvis* gyrating against my tush. "Dat boy could wine we, eh?" one of my other dancing neighbors comments, grinning with approval.

The lyrics of one song demand that the band "Reverse, reverse." The Heineken mob begins moving *backward* as one— except for the cruisers, who are still running the lyrics through our internal translation devices. I'm rammed into Steve and give him a beer bath, taking one myself from the cruiser klutz in front of me. We chip to the beer truck at the back of the band to refill our cups.

Whenever we approach one of the multiple judging stations along the route, the dancing reaches fever pitch. "Wave deh rags, wave deh rags," the DJ yells over the music, and a sea of towels, kerchiefs, flags, and other bits of sweat-soaked cloth pulses over-head. The judges will select a Road March Band and a Road March Monarch, the creator of whichever song is played most frequently during Carnival.

Not surprisingly, "Inspector" is crowned Road March Monarch . . . for his song "Deh Bellee." Not surprisingly, the

Heineken band isn't crowned anything. I figure the cruiser contingent, with our pitiful dancing and gradually waning energy, was a serious detriment, although our still-dancing neighbors assure me otherwise. But by midnight, we chippin' and winin' *very* slow; my calves are aching—five hours of nonstop dancing up and down hills—and my head is threatening to. I've used up all six of my beer tickets—though, in my defense, I spilled the better part of several cups.

When we get home, we undress in the cockpit. Our clothes stink of beer and sweat, and I refuse to allow them into the cabin below; in fact, I consider burning them. According to the newspaper reports the next week, 35,000 people—a third of the island's population—were in St. George's tonight. I never felt the least bit threatened in that sexy, drunken, gyrating crowd.

"I would even cross the Mona Passage again if it meant getting to Grenada for Carnival," I say to Steve as my head hits the pillow. There is no higher praise.

Post-Carnival the radio airplay changes, moves on to other songs, more reggae and rapso than soca and calypso. But we're not ready to move on—we can't get the Carnival hits out of our heads. We *need* to hear them. We need to visit Doc.

Doc is an imposing man with the build of an NBA center and a fondness for gold jewelry: several immense rings, a heavy link bracelet, and a thick chain around his neck from which dangles a pendant the size of a saucer. Doc is no shrinking violet.

He's the proprietor of Music City Record Centre, and a fixture of the St. George's music scene. The first time we visited his shop, on the second floor of a building near the fish market, was a few days after the Mighty Sparrow concert. "Let's try to get the new Sparrow CD," Steve had said, "and maybe one by that young guy with the dreadlocks and the fabulous voice. Do you remember his name?"

"Ajumal, I think." He'd been a standout of the performance, a crowd favorite, obviously one of the island's stars.

The entrance to the Music Centre had a metal gate locked across it. "When does it open?" Steve asked a guy in a nearby store. "Jus' now," he replied.

After hitting the bank, dropping off film for developing, having a late breakfast, and browsing in an art gallery, we returned to the Music Centre. Still locked. Off to the market, a handicraft shop, and a bookstore. Finally, around noon, we return to find the gate has been pulled back, and we walk up two flights of narrow steps into a dim, un-air-conditioned, barren space. The display cases are almost empty—just a few flags and kerchiefs—and the only music that appears to be for sale is on vinyl: old record albums hanging on one pegboard wall. It's so unpromising and so uncomfortable—I'm already dripping with sweat up here right under the tiled roof—that I'm tempted to turn around and go back down the steps. But by then a commanding presence has appeared behind the counter, and turning on our heels would seem rude.

"Good day, do you have any CDs by Ajumal?" I ask, trying to sound knowledgeable. "Ajamu," the commanding presence says. "No, but I'll call him at home. Maybe he can bring some over." Steve and I exchange glances, picturing the manager of Sam Goody's on the phone. "Hey, Mick, sorry to bother you, but got any *Bridges to Babylon* on hand? Customer here wants one."

Ajamu can't help, but Doc—he's introduced himself—promises he'll bring us back an Ajamu CD from his forthcoming trip to New York, and the new Mighty Sparrow CD, too. Meanwhile, he'll play something else for us, and give us a crash course on Carnival and the Grenada music business. Because of the country's high duties on CDs, he explains, he can't afford to keep a lot in stock, and the musicians can't afford to bring many back into the country when they're manufactured abroad. Tapes are a

AN EMBARRASSMENT OF MANGOES

different story—those can be whipped up right on the premises. Copyright doesn't seem to be an issue.

From then on, we make Doc's a regular stop on our trips to St. George's—or as regular a stop as his irregular hours will allow. Doc's is also a rum shop, with live music at night, which explains the erratic opening hours. We get our Ajamu CDs—jus' now—after going away empty-handed on a couple of trips; and we get the complete Carnival schedule Doc promised us—also jus' now—after he eventually piles us into his car, drives to the Carnival office in another part of the city, and goes inside himself to pick it up.

"Doc," Steve says, on our post-Carnival visit, "is there a collection of this year's Carnival hits we can buy?"

"No problem, mon," says Doc. He'll just put a tape together for us. Exactly which hits did we want?

"'Bellee,' 'Deh Monkey,' 'Four Kings,' 'Jumbie,' 'Stamp Up,' 'Aroun' deh Town' . . ."

"Don't have dat one yet. Radio station has deh only tape. But Elvis"—creator of "Aroun' deh Town"—"gettin' me a copy soon."

Creator-sanctioned bootleg tapes. We order up one for us and one for Nancy and Terry on *La Esmeralda*. Doc tells us when they'll be ready.

I return on the appointed day to pick them up. Good thing Doc's is also a rum shop. I can have a drink, read my book, and wait. My order will be ready jus' now, the young man running the tape machine tells me.

Pasta from Mr. Butters's Garden

Quick, easy, and tasty. Serve the pasta with crusty bread and sliced tomatoes drizzled with olive oil and sprinkled with chopped basil. The tomatoes provide a lovely contrast to the green pasta sauce.

SERVES 3–4, DEPENDING ON HOW HUNGRY THE CREW IS

½ **pound smoked sausage, sliced thin, or fresh sausage, casings removed**
2 **tablespoons olive oil**
2 **cloves garlic, chopped**
1 **bunch escarole, roughly chopped (about 10 cups)**
Salt and freshly ground black pepper
Splash white wine (optional)
½ **pound penne or other pasta**
Parmesan cheese, freshly grated

1. In a large frying pan, cook the smoked sausage for a few minutes until it releases its fat, or cook fresh sausage, breaking it up with a fork, until lightly browned. Remove meat from pan and set aside. Drain fat from pan.
2. In the same pan, heat olive oil and gently sauté garlic. Add the escarole a bit at a time, adding more as the first batch begins to wilt, and sauté until it is all wilted. Season with lots of black pepper and a little salt. Add a splash of wine or some of the pasta-cooking water if it seems dry and cook a minute or so longer. Return the sausage to the pan and toss all together.
3. Meanwhile, cook the penne and drain. Combine with the escarole mixture and serve with Parmesan sprinkled on top.

Furious Georges

For several hundred years, many hurricanes in the West Indies were named after the particular saint's day on which the hurricane occurred. . . . In 1953 . . . the nation's weather services began using female names for storms. The practice of naming hurricanes solely after women came to an end in 1978.

National Weather Service, National Oceanic
and Atmospheric Administration

GRENADA HAS NOT BEEN hit by a hurricane since 1955. But furious Georges is not behaving as he's supposed to, and the cruisers at Hog Island are worried.

Mid-September is the dangerous heart of hurricane season—*September, remember*—and tropical waves are rolling off the coast of Africa with nerve-wracking regularity. In fact, three of them are marching across the Atlantic at the moment. By itself, a tropical wave isn't really something for us to get worked up about, although they bring wind and "convection activity," that lovely forecast euphemism for clouds, squalls, rain, thunderstorms, and other such unpleasantries. The real problem comes when a tropical wave starts to become "organized" and develops a low-pressure cell to become a tropical depression; which can become further organized and start to spin around the area of low pressure, developing into a tropical storm; which can then grow into a hurricane; which is exactly what Georges has done.

The storm started life last Wednesday as a tropical depression off the coast of Senegal. By Thursday morning, he had started to show some "rotary circulation" and wind speeds above 39 miles per hour, and was upgraded by the National Hurricane Center in Miami to a tropical storm. At this point, he was assigned the name Georges. The World Meteorological Organization has six alphabetical lists of names, which are used in rotation, one list a year. Georges is the seventh named storm in the Atlantic in 1998. We start plotting his position and projected path in grease pencil on our hurricane tracking chart, a $2 piece of erasable plastic I had hoped we'd never have to use. Every eight hours we tune in the National Weather Service on the SSB radio to get the latest "tropical storm advisory" and update the chart. By Thursday night, Georges has been upgraded to a hurricane, which means winds of 74 mph or more. He is at 41 degrees west longitude, 1,300 miles directly east of the West Indies.

I've learned enough about weather in the last year to know that as storms move westward off the coast of Africa, they tend to track northward, and if they move far enough north fast enough, they peter out harmlessly at sea. However, if a storm passes 40 degrees west longitude without a significant curve to the north, watch out. Georges isn't showing any inclination toward curving north and is already being discussed in the forecasts as a serious threat. In fact, unless Georges decides to change direction in a hurry, he is going to slam the Eastern Caribbean in three days.

The next morning's forecast has him entering the Eastern Caribbean just 170 nautical miles north of us, midway between Martinique and Dominica. We are *way* too close for comfort.

On the current track, Grenada won't be in the most dangerous semicircle, to the north of the hurricane. But we will be in the southern semicircle of Georges's sphere of influence. "Be prepared for strong winds and seas from the northwest and southwest," says David Jones (a.k.a. Misstine), the British Virgin Islands–based forecaster. Our lovely Hog Island anchorage is open to the south. Winds at the center of the system are forecast to reach 126 mph in the gusts, with wave heights reaching 25 to 30 feet. If Georges sticks to the projected path, we could experience dangerous storm surge. And if Georges decides to take even the slightest jog to the south—not usual hurricane behavior, but not impossible, given he's already showing signs of not acting like a "typical" hurricane—we'd be in *very* serious trouble.

"At the moment, there are no signs of a swing to the north, but it's always a possibility." David's voice has an entirely different gravity than I've heard before.

"This isn't supposed to be happening," I moan stupidly. We lived up to our part of the bargain—we got our asses outside the hurricane zone. I am saved from Steve's refresher course on statistical probability by our need to make some quick decisions.

"What do you think we should do?"

"I don't know, what do you think we should do?"

Staying right where we are isn't necessarily a bad idea: We've been at Hog Island long enough to know our anchor is well set. We're positioned well, with plenty of space around us, and sheltered by the reefs and the hills. But this isn't a hurricane hole, and a storm surge could well make Hog's protective reefs about as efficient at stopping the ocean as a chain-link fence.

A couple of miles to the west of Hog Island is an almost completely enclosed lagoon surrounded by mangroves. Undeniably, we'd be *much* better protected there—if we could get in. The narrow reef-lined entrance will be tricky with the sea already starting to kick up and, more importantly, the protected portion is small and we don't know how many boats have already staked out spots. If we leave to find out, our pretty-good space here will be scooped up in a nanosecond, as boats are already flooding in from islands to the north, seeking protection.

We decide to stay with the devil we know—at least through

one more forecast; if Georges swings even a *tiny* bit to the north, we will be just fine. Terry and Nancy on *La Esmeralda*—new, like us, to Caribbean hurricanes—decide to leave for the totally protected bay. "We'll call you when we get there," Nancy says, "and let you know what it looks like." Meanwhile, we put out a second anchor and then a third to give us extra holding power. Otherwise, there's not a lot of activity here, and Hog Island is its usual sleepy afternoon self. Old hands like Ed, the Minister of Rum, appear unconcerned.

"We got in okay," Nancy reports when she radioes as promised. "But if you're coming, better come now. It's gonna be tough when the waves get higher."

"Roger that. I think we'll stay put."

Late in the day, we dinghy to the dock at Lower Woburn and walk up to Island View, the largest restaurant and bar in the village. It has great fries, and you can play dominoes on the patio while you wait for your food. But tonight the big attraction is the bar's satellite TV. On the wide expanse of Clarke's Court Bay the rising wind is noticeable. On shore, the goats *maa* nervously and the seed pods of the trees called mother-in-law's tongues clack noisily. Inside, the crowd at the bar is jittery, waiting for the latest update on the Weather Channel.

At the word "Georges," the room falls silent. It is projected to become an extremely dangerous Category 4 hurricane, close to a Category 5—the highest category of any storm—with winds of 140 miles per hour. But the course has changed: It has finally started to track northwest instead of due west.

A collective whoosh of relief, big easy swallows of beer, and again a buzz of conversation. But no one's really jubilant. Grenada won't get slammed, but someone else surely will—and soon. All of us— cruisers and locals—have friends or family on other islands.

As it happens, Georges enters the Eastern Caribbean on Sunday night, 290 miles north of us, passing directly over

Antigua. He vents his fury in turn on St. Kitts, Nevis, Statia, Saba, St. Martin, the Virgin Islands, Puerto Rico, the Dominican Republic, Haiti, the Bahamas, Cuba, the Florida Keys, and the Gulf Coast of the United States.

Receta barely rocks at anchor as we listen to ham operators hunkered down and broadcasting from the hurricane zone—to what is first a trickle and then a flood of damage reports. We're praying the friends who decided to spend hurricane season in unprotected spots had time to run for shelter. An 85-foot yacht has been tossed out of the water and onto an airport runway on St. Martin; the huge steel-and-concrete cruise-ship dock on St. Kitts reduced to toothpicks and thrown out to sea; the airport on Saba totally destroyed and power knocked out on the entire island and not expected to be restored for two months; the Virgin Islands, clobbered. The worst savagery is on Puerto Rico and the Dominican Republic, where the unrelenting rainfall leads to mudslides that wipe out entire towns. But our beloved Luperón, we hear, sheltered more than sixty boats, and sheltered them well. Our friends spiderwebbed deep into the mangroves there are fine.

At one point, we picked up a man transmitting out of St. Croix, in the U.S. Virgin Islands, just after the calm at the eye of the hurricane passed overhead. "The eye is gone and now we're getting the rest. I've got 20 knots, gusting 30. Now it's 30, steady. Now I've got 40 knots and gusting. Now I've got . . ." And he faded out.

Seventeen days, seven landfalls, 602 fatalities, and $5.9 billion in property damage. When a hurricane is unusually destructive, its name is retired "for reasons of sensitivity" and never used again. Only forty hurricane names have been retired since 1954. Georges is one of them.

A few days after the hurricane scare, Ed invites us over for dinner, to help him consume a new rum that's come his way and a mess of kingfish he's bought cheap at the market. As Steve and I are belowdecks putting a few things into a carry bag to take to dinner, we hear voices, close.

We both bound into the cockpit. It's just after dark and a light is flickering off to our port side—where a powerboat is hanging off the float that marks the position of one of the extra anchors we put out before the hurricane and haven't lifted yet. "They must have snagged their prop on our float line," Steve says. "I'd better go see if I can help." And he hops in *Snack* and heads off.

A few minutes later, I can hear *Snack* slowly returning. Steve is towing the powerboat back to *Receta*. It's the local Coast Guard boat. Whoops.

Steve ties it off to our stern and pulls himself alongside the cockpit. "Are they seriously pissed off at us?" I ask him softly. "Are we in deep shit?"

"No, it has nothing to do with us. They didn't run into our line. They just grabbed the anchor float to stop themselves from drifting onto the reef when their engine died." This, in itself, is almost amusing; Steve, who has no conception of time anymore, thinks it's hilarious.

"What happens now?" I ask, eyeing the boat strung out behind *Receta* and knowing that, even by island time, we're going to be *very* late for dinner at the Minister's.

"They can't seem to get it restarted—I think they may have flooded it at this point. The head guy says they radioed another boat to come and get them, but he asked if I would mind running him into the Hog Island beach. I couldn't say no—it'll only take another five minutes." And with that, he starts *Snack*'s engine and heads back to the powerboat. I go below to radio Ed to let him know we're going to be more than a few minutes late. "We'll explain why when we get there." "Roger that," he says. I figure it would be impolitic to discuss a Coast Guard breakdown on the open airwaves. More than impolitic, as it turns out.

Steve, meanwhile, putts gently to the transom of the Coast Guard boat to pick up his passenger. But before he's even stopped the dinghy, two Coast Guard guys jump in without a word. They aren't dressed for your average walk on the beach. Both are wearing camouflage fatigues, with life jackets on top, and military-issue black leather boots. The head guy is carrying an automatic rifle, and the other, a zillion-watt searchlight, turned off.

Not knowing what else to do—*they* are the Coast Guard, after all, and *we* are visitors in *their* country—Steve just switches on his light and turns toward the beach.

"No lights, please," says the head guy, exceedingly polite, but leaving no room for disagreement. "And can you go around that way, please?" He draws a curve in the air that winds between other anchored cruisers and ends up at the far end of the beach, away from the usual landing spot.

It's very dark, and the requested route to shore takes further advantage of the darkness around the anchored boats that don't have lights on. When *Snack* reaches the knee-deep water about 40 feet off the beach, the head guy announces, "Stand off here, please, and wait for us." Steve cuts the engine, and the two of them leap out of the dinghy and run full blast for the beach— "kind of like a two-man version of the landing at Normandy," Steve relates. "Then faster than you can say marijuana, they have their huge searchlight on, and the one with the gun is lining up some of the local guys against the wall of the beach lean-to." He and *Snack* have been commandeered for a raid—a drug bust, which the recalcitrant engine on the Coast Guard boat had threatened to spoil.

We really *like* the local guys on the beach. Steve knows most of them by now, thanks to Phillip, his "lobsta stick" mentor. "Dis mah friend Steve," he says every time Steve shows up at the shack now, taking him around for introductions and the bumped-fist handshakes that are the greeting between younger local men. "He know deh families in deh village." Steve is *horrified*—first, that he might be helping to get these guys in trouble with the law, and second, that they might find out exactly *how* the Coast Guard got to the beach.

A valid concern, since a fishing boat carrying two more local guys has just pulled straight up to the beach and the driver is panning the water with his flashlight. "Where's your boat? How'd you get here?" he angrily asks the Coast Guarders—who were waiting for this boat and now have the gun trained on it. Steve, meanwhile, ducks low in the dinghy and shields his face when the new arrival's light arcs in *Snack*'s direction.

"Turn out deh light." The rifle is quite persuasive, and the flashlight disappears.

The bust, however, is a bust: The guys are apparently all clean. They disperse rapidly, the local boats roaring off the beach— luckily not near where Steve waits—and the two Coast Guarders eventually wade back out to their landing craft.

"When I drop them back at their boat, the head guy tells me he'll be coming by with a check to compensate me for my help." He shudders at the thought. "I told him politely that he *absolutely* didn't need to bother." At this point, two Coast Guard boats are tied behind *Receta*, the second having arrived to help the first. "And we're not telling *anyone* what happened tonight."

Except the Minister of Rum, of course: You need a good excuse when you're more than an hour late for a dinner invitation, and being conscripted to aid and abet the Coast Guard in a bust works just fine.

Ed, who's visited more than one illegal still in the course of his rum research, can be trusted to keep quiet. And, besides, he knows all the local scuttlebutt. Sure, people do occasionally whip up to St. Vincent, where grass is grown, and then buzz back down to Grenada after dark, but it's no surprise to Ed that nobody got caught tonight. "The local guys would have been warned something was up," he explains while he fries the kingfish and we sip 'ti punches. "So they wouldn't have made a run. Besides, they always post somebody on the point with a light to signal, just in case."

A couple of days later, a smaller Coast Guard boat pulls up to *Receta* in the middle of the day. We hope no one on the beach is watching. The head Coast Guard guy from the other night is on board, just come to say thank you. To our relief, he doesn't offer up a check. But we get the feeling that for the rest of our stay in Grenada, we're safe from the Coast Guard inspections that foreign cruising boats are periodically given.

Mango season is waning. The perfumed piles in the market have shrunk and the price has grown. The real sign, though, is that there are none at all at the Marketing & National Import Board, where the bins reflect what the local growers currently have in abundance. A few weeks ago, one wall was lined with baskets of mangoes: Julies, Ceylons, Calivignys, and Peach mangoes. Now, we console ourselves with the voluptuous avocados that have replaced them.

Back home, food is divorced from the seasons, every fruit and vegetable imported from *somewhere* year-round. Here, we eat what comes ripe, and the reward is the taste. Before this, I don't think we knew what an avocado should taste like. The bananas have an almost forgotten banana flavor; the silky papayas expose the ones back home as dull imposters; the greens have un-expectedly strong, assertive personalities.

On my most recent trip to Mr. Butters's, I had again been hoping to get some of his pungent escarole to turn into topping for pasta, but again his escarole beds are picked clean. Instead, I leave with a bunch of callaloo.

Steve watches me dubiously as I chop up the heart-shaped

leaves. "We've only seen it served as soup," he points out. Callaloo—the thick green soup is called by the same name as its main ingredient—is ubiquitous throughout the West Indies. Every cook has their own version: some with crab, some with salt pork or beef, some with okra, some with coconut milk, some with evaporated cow's milk, some without any milk at all.

"It's a leafy green vegetable, same as escarole—I'm sure it will work just fine on the pasta," I reply.

While I'm transferring the chopped callaloo from the cutting board to the pan where the garlic is sautéing, I drop a piece on the floor. And just as I would do at home, I pick it up without thinking and pop it in my mouth.

The effect is almost immediate. My throat is on fire, and it's a worse fire than the one caused by Nimrod's rum: I'm being poked from the inside out by a million little glass slivers. I gulp water, then beer, to no effect. Steve's ready to hustle me into the dinghy to go to shore, and a doctor, but behind the pain is a dim recollection. "Check the cruising guide," I croak.

Our guide for this part of the world includes a few pages about island food at the back—and there it is, read once a long time ago and forgotten: Callaloo should *never* be eaten raw or under-cooked. The leaves contain calcium oxalate crystals, which cause "discomfort," as the book calls it; a bit understated, I'd say, when I feel like I've swallowed a fistful of nettles. The effect is temporary, though, the guide goes on to explain, and there is no permanent damage. "To use callaloo as a vegetable, boil it with a little salt for at least 30 minutes."

I turn up the heat and cook it so thoroughly it becomes a pool of green-brown sludge.

The "christophene saltfish cakes" that the market ladies told me how to make are a *much* more successful attempt at using local ingredients than callaloo pasta sauce. "Write the recipe down,"

Steve tells me while devouring a plate of the crispy fried cakes. "*Right now*, before you forget what you did."

He's been telling me to write a lot of things down lately, as I attempt local dishes and substitute island fruits and vegetables in the ones I cooked back home. I make latkes with grated plantains instead of potatoes, and serve them with mango salsa instead of applesauce. (No apple trees in this part of the world.) I use christophene instead of zucchini in my zucchini bread recipe, and papaya in my banana muffins. The muffins are fruit-sweet and moist and, as a bonus, a lovely color. "Write it down, write it down, *write it down*." Steve hasn't exactly been keeping quiet about my galley adventures and the interesting stuff he's been eating, and sometimes I find myself fielding questions from other cruisers like some culinary advice columnist. Unfortunately, I'm hardly an expert.

Dingis had already given me a lesson on making "regular" salt-fish cakes, but the "christophene saltfish cakes" the market ladies had suggested were new to me. "Saltfish" once meant salted cod almost exclusively. For New England and Nova Scotia, the Caribbean was a low-end market, a place to unload their second-rate salted-and-dried cod, where it provided cheap food for the slaves on the sugar plantations. In fact, "West India" became the commercial name for the lowest grade of saltfish. These days, it's no longer the cheap food it once was, thanks to the decline of the North Atlantic cod fishery, but it's still a popular ingredient in Caribbean cooking.

"Buy a nice tick piece of it," Dingis had told me. "Not deh little ones—dey boney." In Grenada, some locally caught and salted fish—shark, mostly—now shares space on store shelves with a variety of saltfish imported from Europe.

Christophene, meanwhile, had become a staple on *Receta* months back in the Dominican Republic, where it's called *tayota*. The pale-green squash-like vegetable is available in North

American supermarkets—it goes by a variety of names including chayote, chayote squash, vegetable pear, cho-cho, and mirliton (especially in Louisiana)—but I had never really appreciated it until I became a cruiser. It's the perfect onboard vegetable: cheap, available year-round, and hardy. (It keeps extremely well just slung in a hammock without refrigeration, a real bonus on a cruising boat.) Because of its delicate flavor, christophene is also versatile: It can be sliced raw into salads for crunch (even the almond-like seed in the center makes good eating); boiled, baked, stuffed or sautéed; added to stews, stir fries, and curries; and turned into soup. "Good for deh stomach," one of the market ladies tells me, patting her ample midsection approvingly. Another cruiser swears it can be used to make a mock apple pie.

But how do I turn it into those christophene saltfish cakes? Just grate some christophene and some onion, the ladies tell me— "maybe carrot too," one of them interjects—add chopped seasoning pepper, garlic, and sive and thyme. Mix in a little "counter flour"—this is coarse flour, I've by now figured out, rather than the more finely ground flour used in baking—and a "tick" of baking powder (which is, I think, a smaller unit of measurement than a "tip"). Then fry them in hot oil.

"And what do I do with the saltfish?" They shake their heads pityingly and laugh: "Dere no saltfish, girl." Okay, I get it: Christophene saltfish cakes are good for deh budget, too. They're made with christophene *instead* of saltfish.

Papaya-Banana Muffins

This recipe is a solution to the problem of too much ripe tropical fruit. These muffins have lovely color and flavor, and are nice and moist.

MAKES 1 DOZEN
1⅔ cups flour
1 teaspoon baking powder
1 teaspoon baking soda
¼ teaspoon freshly grated nutmeg
1 egg
⅓ cup oil
¾ cup sugar
1 cup mashed ripe papaya
½ cup mashed ripe banana (1 large banana)
¼ cup chopped walnuts (optional)

1. Preheat oven to 375°F and grease a medium-sized muffin pan or line it with muffin papers.
2. Combine dry ingredients and set aside.
3. Beat egg with oil, sugar, and mashed papaya and banana in a large bowl.
4. Mix in dry ingredients and walnuts (if using). Scoop mixture into prepared muffin pan. Bake in preheated oven for 18–23 minutes, until toothpick inserted in the middle of a muffin comes out clean.

Tips:
- If the papaya is quite ripe, it will yield a lot of liquid when mashed. Drain off this excess liquid before adding the fruit.
- You can make the muffins entirely with papaya if you like; just increase the quantity to 1½ cups. The muffins will have a slightly moister texture and a flatter top.

Christophene Quick Bread

Christophene makes an incredibly moist quick bread. It mixes up in minutes, and is great for snack or teatime.

MAKES 1 LOAF

1½ cups flour

1 teaspoon baking soda

1¼ teaspoons baking powder

¾ teaspoon cinnamon

½ teaspoon freshly grated nutmeg

¼ teaspoon salt

⅔ cup vegetable oil

¾ cup sugar

2 eggs

1 teaspoon vanilla

1 cup grated christophene, well drained (about 1 medium christophene)

½ cup grated carrot (about 1 medium)

1. Preheat oven to 350°F and grease an 8½-by-4½-inch loaf pan.
2. Combine dry ingredients. Set aside.
3. Beat oil and sugar together in a large bowl using a whisk or wooden spoon. Add eggs and beat until batter is creamy. Add vanilla, then grated christophene and carrot. Mix well.
4. Stir dry ingredients into christophene mixture and mix well. Spread in the prepared pan and bake for 50–60 minutes, or until a toothpick inserted in center comes out clean.

Stuffed Christophene au Gratin

These are a bit fiddly to make on a boat, since you have to use (and thus wash) two pots and a baking pan—but they make a great meatless dinner.

SERVES 2–3 AS A MAIN COURSE, 4–6 AS A SIDE DISH
2–3 large christophenes
2 tablespoons butter or oil
1 onion, finely chopped
2 cloves garlic, minced
¼–½ hot pepper, seeded and minced (or to taste)
1 stalk celery with leaves, chopped (optional)
1 green onion, chopped
1½ teaspoons chopped fresh thyme or ½ teaspoon dried thyme
1 cup grated cheddar cheese
¼ cup Parmesan cheese, grated
Salt and freshly ground black pepper
2 tablespoons dried breadcrumbs

1. Cut the christophenes in half lengthwise and remove the seed from each. Place the halves in a large saucepan and cover with water. Bring to a boil, and cook for 20–30 minutes, until the christophenes are slightly soft. (You should be able to pierce them easily with a skewer.) Remove and cool.
2. Carefully scoop the pulp out of each half, leaving about ¼" of shell intact. Chop the pulp and place in a strainer to drain; reserve the shells.
3. Heat the butter or oil in a frying pan and add the onion, garlic, hot pepper, celery, and green onion. Sprinkle with thyme. Cook until onion is soft and translucent, about 5 minutes. Add christophene pulp and cook gently for about 5 minutes. Stir in half the grated cheddar and half the Parmesan. Season to taste with salt and pepper.

4. Place the reserved shells on a baking sheet. Fill them with the christophene mixture. Combine the remaining cheddar and Parmesan with the breadcrumbs and sprinkle on top.

5. Bake at 375°F for about 20 minutes, until cheese has melted and filling is lightly browned on top.

Feelin' Trini
to deh Bone

Oh, merciful Father, in this bacchanal season
Where some men will lose their reason
But most of us just want to wine and have a good time
While we looking for a lime, Because we feeling fine,

> Lord . . . amen.

And as we jump up and down in this crazy town
Send us some music for some healing . . . amen.

> From the song "High Mas" by Trinidadian Calypsonian
> and Soca Star David Michael Rudder

TRINIDAD HAS ONE OF THE highest public holiday counts in the world. One of our guidebooks says that when Columbus "discovered" the island, he stumbled onto a big party. Another gives a short glossary of frequently heard Trini words—almost all of which have to do with partying and having a good time. *Fete, bacchanal, jump-up, lime*—they're all variations on the fun-loving theme.

At 11:30 on a Wednesday night in November, things are just getting going at the Mas Camp Pub in Port of Spain, Trinidad's capital. The room is packed not with college kids or twenty-something clubbers, but with middle-class, close-to-our-own-age Trinis. "Don't these people have to go to work tomorrow?" I shout at Steve over the music and laughter of the crowd.

Feeling a bit like Dorothy, we have been dropped into the heart of the Trini music scene—but we feel no urge to go home.

Wednesday night is Calypso Night here, a far cry from Movie Night, Wednesday's regular activity back at the cruiser compound in Chaguaramas, the "suburb" of Port of Spain where *Receta* is docked. The performer on the Mas Camp Pub's stage, a young up-and-comer, has just realized that Gypsy, the reigning king of extempo, is in the audience. "Extempo" comes from *extempore* and refers to spur-of-the-moment calypso: Each singer tries to outdo his rivals in improvised, unrehearsed rhyming song-duels set to standard melodic lines. And so the up-and-comer starts razzing the king—in extempo, of course—implying that he's afraid to come up onstage for a friendly little round of song. Gypsy rises to the bait, and the two duel it out at the mike, heads close together, to the crowd's glee. The up-and-comer gets the final shot: "I'm being paid," he sings, "while I got Gypsy to perform for free."

Now the Trini soca star Superblue takes the stage, and midway through his act, he also invites a number of well-known musicians in the audience to join him. In an abrupt change of mood and music, they link arms and break into Bob Marley's "One Love." Even we, newcomers to the island, know what's going on: It's an elegy to Kim Sabeeney, the "queenmaker," the organizer of Trinidad's beauty pageants. Her death a few days ago has been headline news, the papers full of stories about her contributions to the country and analysis of what her death will mean for Trinidad's place in worldwide beauty competitions. This is a country that takes its beauty pageants seriously—the reigning Miss Universe is a Trini—but then again, this is a country that has a lot of raw material to work with.

I'd caught Steve staring open-mouthed like a lovestruck (lust-struck?) teenager at the women in Veni Mangé, the restaurant where we'd had dinner earlier tonight. But who could blame him?

To a woman, they were absolutely gorgeous—and, besides, I had made the mistake of telling him how attractive I find the Trini men. Like the guy in the boatyard.

I had been working on earning more martyr points during the afternoon, scrubbing the accumulated burned crud off all the bits and pieces of *Receta*'s little stern-rail barbecue, when the voice snuck up behind me at the outdoor water tap. It belonged to one of the workers in the yard, where *Receta* has been hauled onto dry land to have her well-barnacled bottom scraped and painted. "We be havin' barbecue today?" he inquired. The "we" in his question was ambiguous, but it *begged* interpretation as meaning him and me, and I was ready to run in the 100-degree heat to the supermarket to grab a couple of steaks to throw on the 'cue. It was more than his looks—though they certainly didn't hurt; I've fallen in love with the soft, musical, lilting, smiling, flirtatious, seductive, downright sexy, melt-your-heart Trini voice. It was enough to make me forget I was covered in grease and sweat. It made me feel delicious.

Maybe *this* was what Dingis meant about Trinidad being dangerous.

"Ooooh. It *very* dangerous." Dingis shakes her head disapprovingly. We've hiked up the Lower Woburn hill—it's still much easier to do a thirty-minute sweaty round-trip walk than attempt communication by phone—to tell her we're leaving for a month or two: We're off to Trinidad, Grenada's neighbor to the south.

It's not the thought of us sailing 75 miles overnight that has Dingis worried. "She people not friendly, like we," she says. There's something of a love/hate, envy/scorn, country cousin/city slicker relationship between the two islands. Compared with Grenada, Trinidad is big, bustling, urban: 1.3 million people to Grenada's 102,000. Trinidad has a thriving economy, thanks to its oil and gas fields, and Port of Spain—home to 350,000 of the island's people—is one of the major commercial centers of the Caribbean. Many of Grenada's consumer goods are imported from Trinidad, and the few Grenadians who can afford it go to Port of Spain to shop. Trini music and foods flow north and threaten to drown Grenadian culture.

One of the hit songs of Grenada's Carnival this year was a many-versed calypso lament about how the culture of "TNT"— Trinidad is the larger, more influential part of the two-island nation of Trinidad and Tobago—is overtaking Grenada. "Supermarket have it bad/Everything from Trinidad/We lost local appetite/And we laugh and say we bright," sang its creator, Smallies, dressed in an outfit made from the Trini flag.

And the crowd would pick up the refrain: "Port of Spain, Port of Spain/There is no St. George's again."

"Be careful no one tiefs you," Dingis warns us glumly when she sees she's not going to dissuade us from the journey. We promise her we'll watch out for the pickpockets, muggers, and other un-savory types she's sure we'll find in Port of Spain, give her a hug, and tell her we'll see her soon.

From *Receta*'s bow, Steve hauls up the anchor a foot at a time, while I sit in the dinghy wearing my yellow Rubbermaid dish gloves and armed with a hammer and a toilet brush. While we have been parked at Hog Island for almost three months, assorted marine life has taken up residence on the anchor chain, and to avoid the smell of putrefaction in our anchor locker, the heavy ⅜-inch galvanized chain has to be scrubbed before it comes aboard—all 100 feet of it, one link at a time. The hammer is for the tenacious barnacles, which maintain their hold with a water-proof adhesive that's one of the world's strongest known glues, the envy of dentists. Steve pulls and I whack and scrub; despite my strong aversion to toilet brushes and other house-cleaning paraphernalia back home, I don't even mind the job.

I don't mind the night sail either. Anxiety and fear are noticeably absent—just a bit of nervous excitement at getting underway again after so long in one place. "It was an easy, uneventful overnight passage," I e-mail Belinda and Todd after the trip, eighteen hours from the time we lift anchor in Grenada until we're tied to the Customs and Immigration dock at Chaguaramas, the center of the island's recreational boating community. "Can you believe I can now actually refer to an overnight passage as easy?"

In fact, it's a lovely night, with a wind that tends to be too light rather than too heavy. The boat requires little attention, so I can stand watch—what a misnomer, since I'm curled up comfortably on the cockpit cushions, a coffee and a Dominican MasMas chocolate bar close at hand—lost in my own thoughts under the almost-full moon. Steve and I disagree about the moon and night passages. He likes to travel on no-moon nights; the darkness, he says, makes it easier to pick up the lights of other vessels. I, un-surprisingly, prefer a full or close-to-full moon; light is comforting, makes the night less ominous. I made my first night passages under a benevolent full moon, and from then on, I've loved the way moonlight makes the water sparkle. The bioluminescence—"living light" of tiny marine creatures—is usually best around the full moon, too, and tonight is no exception. In a sailing account I'm reading, I came across a traditional Irish nursery rhyme recited upon seeing the new moon; it has no sailing connection, but sounds as if it should, and I love saying it to myself as *Receta* glides through the night and the water glimmers: "I see the moon, the moon sees me/God bless the moon and God bless me/There's grace in the cabin and grace in the hall/And the grace of God is over us all."

The moon has importance to me now, in a way it never used to. I can tell you its phase, something I rarely noticed two years ago, more easily these days than I can tell you the daily headlines.

That tossed-off phrase "once in a blue moon" has come to have real meaning, too. A blue moon has nothing to do with color, but refers to the second full moon in a month—for me, a bonus—and a phenomenon that occurs on average only about once every three years. The coming year will have two blue moons, rarer still, and an even bigger bonus. (There won't be another year with two blue moons until 2018.)

Just two weeks ago was Rosh Hashanah, the Jewish New Year. As I said prayers privately, in a country without a synagogue, I knew that Rosh Hashanah coincides with the new moon. "Sound the Shofar on the new moon"—I had read it in the Rosh Hashanah prayerbook every year since my childhood. But the words were devoid of a connection to nature. Now they *meant* something: I already knew there would be a slim crescent hanging above *Receta* low in the western sky that night.

I've realized how disconnected my daily life had been from the natural world. The weather, the wind, the moon, even the seasons—and the attendant plants, insects, birds, and animals—came and went. But I was removed, at a distance. So what if the moon was new or the sky was pissing rain? I still had to go to the office. The natural world—in all its forms—is so much more immediate now. It forces me to pay attention.

After three months at bucolic Hog Island, Trinidad is overwhelming: the heat, the size, the pace, the number of boats, the number of people, and the sheer number of choices of things to do each day. And night. The cruisers' morning VHF radio net buzzes with activities, a hundred times worse than George Town. Dominoes Night, Movie Night, Trivia Night, organized taxi trips to the Port of Spain market, fabric-shopping excursions, happy hours, buffet dinners, potluck dinners, group outings to musical performances, festivals, and bazaars. Merengue lessons are Wednesday night, the Bathing Suit Lady comes on Thursday morning (she'll custom-make any sort of swimsuit you want from whatever fabric you purchase on the fabric-shopping excursion), the Veggie Truck arrives on Friday, and the Roti Van rolls in at about eleven almost every morning of the week. Once we get our Trini land legs, start scouring the newspapers for interesting happenings, and begin to explore on our own, things get even worse. Steve catches me digging out a mildewed day diary to keep track of everything we want to do and accuses me of backsliding. Perhaps *this* is what Dingis meant about Trinidad being dangerous.

Veni Mangé—"Come Eat"—is a pleasure to look at, and not just because of its gorgeous women. The art on the walls, the table settings, the menus, the clothing on the staff, and the food have all been chosen by someone with a real eye. Located in a Creole-style house, this one-night-a-week restaurant serves Creole-style cuisine, prepared by a Cordon Bleu–trained chef, one of two Trini sisters who own the place. The dishes are simple, but perfectly executed: grilled whole snapper with a ginger-lime-rum-butter sauce; battered flying fish with tamarind salsa. Midway through our first course—callaloo soup for me, saltfish fritters (sans christophene) for Steve—Rosemary, the front-of-house sister, sweeps in and begins rearranging table settings and juggling the seating, as if this were a dinner party she was hosting in her own home. And in a way it is: The room fills up, everybody knows everybody else, and even we are made to feel like old friends. "Come back on Friday," she says when she swings by our table to chat. "That's when we have a lime."

Trinis have perfected the art of "liming"—spending time relaxing, laughing, talking, drinking, enjoying music, taking it easy. A lime is any informal gathering for the purpose of having fun. Call it hanging out, or call it a party. "The perfect start to a great lime," says the advertising for Veni Mangé. "Bona fide fishermen only.

No liming here," reads a sign on the fishing cooperative on the road outside Port of Spain. The etymology of the word is hazy. According to one account, it was coined during World War II, when the nightclubs and dance halls of Port of Spain were frequented by foreign servicemen. The Americans appeared to have endless amounts of money to spend, but the less-well-off British were often forced to listen to the music from outside, watching the Americans inside dance with all the girls. Local schoolboys, who also used to stand outside listening, coined the verb "to lime"—meaning to stand outside a dance hall or party as the "Limeys" were doing.

According to another story that dates to the same time, the sour taste of limes is behind the term: If you weren't invited to a party, you would go to the house where it was being held anyway, but just stand outside and feel sour. This was called "sucking lime." Other friends might join you, and you'd all stand around outside talking. This was called "bussin' a lime"—which became shortened to "liming."

Someone dinghies by, sees us in *Receta*'s cockpit, detours over, and spends the next half hour hanging on to our stern ladder and chatting. I used to call this wasting time. Now it's "liming," an acceptable—even required—part of our day. I've learned I don't have to be frantically, productively busy every waking minute as I once was. I've taken to liming with a vengeance.

I spot the ad in the Friday-morning paper: "Friday Afterwork Stress Cooler" at the panyard of the Amoco Renegades, one of the country's top-ranked steel bands. Denyse Plummer, last year's Calypso Queen, is making a guest appearance. And the mas band associated with the Renegades will be launching its Carnival theme. Though Carnival is the ultimate Trini party, the celebrations start months ahead with big limes, some of them at panyards, the outdoor spaces where the pan bands practice. The mas bands present their new Carnival costume designs and sign up participants, the pan bands play, and everyone drinks and dances. Late fall is also the time for *parang*, the Spanish-based Christmas music that originated in Venezuela and features tiny four-string guitars called *cuatros*, which give it a distinctive sweet tinkling sound. Parang has been wholly adopted by the Trinis; there's even a subgenre with a dance beat known as soca parang. Along with the live pan, live calypso, and live soca, the Friday lime at the Renegades panyard will feature live parang.

"We *have* to go," Steve says immediately when I casually point out the ad. "You know how much work stress we've been under lately."

"But it says strictly by invitation."

"Well, you've got until this afternoon to figure out how to get us two."

Steve and I stand out at local limes. We don't look like locals—despite our deep tans, and despite wearing jeans as the Trinis do (in the 100-degree heat), in an attempt to blend in. I think we'll be unusual enough that we can talk our way into the panyard—but I don't want to risk having to deal with Steve's disappointment. Just in case, I make a call to the distillery that makes White Magic rum, which appears to be an event sponsor. "No problem," the guy I finally reach tells me. "Jus' come."

We arrive two hours after the starting time—"jus' now" is a Trini concept too—and the live music is jus' beginning. Of course no one asks to see an invitation. People are getting their stress cooled pretty quickly at the tables along one side of the panyard, where various exotic mixed drinks made with White Magic rum are being offered. I hand over $2 TT, which is the princely sum of 33 cents, and the woman behind the table ladles out a large cup of Moka Magic. It consists of iced coffee, cocoa, and condensed milk, blended with a killer quantity of high-test rum. One is enough to put a small-sized human on her ear.

White Magic clearly has the edge. At the next booth, Carib is

$7 TT a bottle. "White Magic posssaaaaaaay," comes the shout from the stage, and the crowd cheers wildly for the sponsor. A "possaaaaaaay"—posse—is a group of supporters. We'd become accustomed to the calls for various "possaaaaaaays" in Grenada, where emcees would goad the crowd by calling for people from each of the island's parishes. Once the local possibilities were exhausted, they moved on to other islands. One night, during a Carnival performance, there was even a call for "Toronto possaaaaaaay." Just about the only voice, I screamed myself silly, while my Grenadian neighbors—and Steve—looked on with much amusement.

We'd arranged for a taxi to pick us up at 10—that's when the ad said the event was over—but at 10 the Amoco Renegades are just getting ready to play. We send the taxi away.

A full-sized pan band, one hundred pannists playing their hearts out, is like no other sound in the world. A "divine frenzy," someone called it. "Righteous thunder." It's a sound that gets inside you, goes right to your core, so your heart beats to the rhythm and, no matter what, you can't keep yourself still.

We've heard full pan orchestras in competitions, both here and in Grenada. Competitions require a certain formality, and we sat in a grandstand, with the acre of pan players a distance from us on the stadium field below. Tonight, the Renegades are playing for their friends—in the midst of them, in fact, since the band has set up on the ground, not on the outdoor stage, as the other acts had. They are into the music, in a way that gives new meaning to that pat phrase. As we stand not six feet from the tenor pans, the sound reaches out and grabs us, takes us under its control, and demands that we participate in the divine frenzy.

When we finally leave, in the wee hours, the Renegades are still playing. We go home on another high.

You can't lime without getting hungry. And the food here—like the politics, the music, and the rest of the culture—strongly reflects Trinidad's blend of East Indian and West Indian. Columbus sighted the island in 1498, claimed it for Spain, and named it to honor the blessed Trinity. Spain kept control for three centuries—until it was seized by the British, who essentially kept it in one form or another until it gained independence in 1962. During their reign, the British needed cheap labor to work the plantations after emancipation; indentured servants from India filled the bill and flooded into the country. Today, 40 percent of the population traces its roots to Africa and 40 percent to India. West Indian cooking meets East Indian cuisine, and vice versa.

Pelau or *pilau*, a popular Trinidadian main dish made with shrimp, goat, beef, or chicken, is a Creolized East Indian pilaf; roti is an East Indian flatbread wrapped around West Indian fillings—and Trinis maintain they first did the wrapping. Channa—the East Indian word for chickpeas—are ubiquitous: They're served roasted with hot West Indian peppers and shadow benny to be munched, like peanuts, by the handful; and they're made into a West Indian–style curry. "Doubles" are one of the most popular Trini snacks: two pieces of roti-like bread with curried channa, hot pepper sauce, and kuchela, a spicy East Indian mango relish, sandwiched in between. They're sold from stalls at the market, vendors on the street, and, we've discovered, during intermission at concerts. When performances start late and go later, everyone is ravenous by intermission. Steve always goes for the doubles, but I search out the guys with the oil drum of hot corn soup, thick with dumplings and chunks of corn on the cob. Swirl in some shadow benny sauce—like a cilantro pesto—and shake in some fiery hot pepper, and you've got the perfect late-night food.

Roti vans prowl the streets of Port of Spain, the local equivalent of the chip truck or the hot-dog cart. Often here, the dinner plate–sized breads have *dhal puri*, East Indian spicy mashed split peas, rolled into them. Up and down the island chain the rotis are different: The filling can be dry or drippy; the bread can be slightly thick or very thin, flecked with dark toasted patches from the griddle or an all-over tan; some have chickpeas, some have more potatoes than meat. But if the filling of a true island roti is chicken or goat, you can be pretty well assured of one thing: It's going to have bones.

"*Lot* of bones," Basil had said dubiously the first time Steve ordered the goat roti at Pyramid, a tiny storefront restaurant in St. George's. Just up the hill from the Marketing Board, Pyramid had no printed menu, just a scrawled sign in the window that listed what was available that day. It became Steve's favorite lunchtime haunt, and after the first one or two visits, Basil, the bearded owner (as well as the only server, and the bartender), had an icy Carib sliding across the table at him before he had even dropped his backpack on a seat. "I *like* the bones," Steve said, and Basil broke into a smile. "Dey add flavor, but some people don't like 'em." He clearly means tourists. We discover, in fact, that restaurants frequented by tourists offer two types of chicken roti: a more expensive, boneless one, for the tourists, and one with bones, for the locals. I make a point of ordering the one with bones.

Perhaps Trinidad's most famous snack food, however, is the shark-and-bake, also called the bake-and-shark. Although you can get them all over the island, the kingdom of the shark-and-bake is Maracas Beach on the north coast. I am determined to make a pilgrimage.

I like my beaches wild—empty, lonely, and strewn with shells instead of people—which Maracas, Trinidad's most popular beach, is not. But, oh, the shark-and-bake. Every local has his or her favorite among the vendors that line the mile-long beach, but "Richard's deh best," said the person we consulted, and so

Richard's is the stall we're standing in front of. Pieces of flour-dusted shark sizzle in hot oil, and flat disks of dough, the "bakes," turn into golden, deep-fried puffs. The man behind the counter scoops them out, lets them drain for just a second, slits them open, and stuffs in the shark. We're then on our own to dress the sandwiches from the array of sauces and salads nearby: hot pepper sauce, garlic sauce, shadow benny sauce, onions, lettuce, tomatoes, chutney. The result is a gourmet-heaven filet-o-fish, the shark fresh and flaky when I bite in, the hot pepper and shadow benny sauces adding bite and a cool vinegary herb freshness, everything neatly (and sinfully) contained in the pocket of the bake.

Bakes are a mystery to me, their name belying their fried deliciousness; these bakes have been nowhere near an oven. "Those are really floats," I'm told, when I finally decide to inquire. "Because they float in the hot oil when they're deep-fried. So what you had was really a shark-and-float."

But no other bake I encounter is baked either, though some—like the ones Dingis makes—are shallow-fried. She's more semantically accurate about them, too: She cooks them in a skillet in a "tip of lard"—and calls them "fried bakes."

I'm assured they *are* sometimes baked, but you sure couldn't prove it by me: Every time I ask for a bake, I get something fried. Maybe there's something in my look that says to vendors up and down the island chain, "this woman loves crunchy, greasy, artery-clogging, straight-from-the-sizzling-oil food." And they'd be right.

Port of Spain "Stress Cooler"

This is my interpretation of the Moka Magic served at the Afterwork Stress Cooler (a.k.a. big outdoor party with live music and lots to drink). The original recipe came from the Caroni Distillery, the maker of White Magic rum.

MAKES 3 DRINKS

6 ounces white rum
1 teaspoon instant espresso powder
1½ teaspoons cocoa powder
1 ounce golden syrup or corn syrup
6 ounces evaporated milk
1–2 ounces sweetened condensed milk (approx.)
Freshly grated nutmeg

1. Combine a couple of tablespoons of the rum with the espresso and cocoa powders and stir until smooth.
2. Add the rest of the rum, the syrup, and the evaporated milk. Sweeten to taste with condensed milk.
3. Serve over crushed ice, with freshly grated nutmeg on top.

Chicken Pelau

This Trinidadian version of rice pilaf is a popular one-pot dinner on *Receta*, accompanied by kuchela—a spicy green-mango relish sold in jars—or mango chutney, and a salad. The crispy layer that forms on the bottom of the pot is called "bun-bun," and some people think it's the best part.

SERVES 6

1 tablespoon chopped fresh thyme or 1 teaspoon dried thyme
¼ teaspoon ground allspice
1 teaspoon freshly ground black pepper
½ teaspoon salt
3 cloves garlic
4 pounds bone-in chicken pieces
3–4 tablespoons oil
1 onion, chopped
1 red bell pepper, chopped
½–1 hot pepper, seeded and finely chopped (or to taste)
¼ teaspoon turmeric
2 cups uncooked rice
3 cups chicken stock
3 fresh or canned tomatoes, chopped
¼ cup roughly chopped roasted peanuts

1. Combine the thyme, allspice, black pepper, salt, and 1 clove of the garlic, finely chopped. Rub the chicken pieces with the mixture and refrigerate, covered, for a couple of hours or overnight.
2. Heat 3 tablespoons of the oil in a large pot. Fry the chicken pieces in batches, adding more oil as necessary, until they are golden brown on both sides. Remove from pot.
3. Finely chop the remaining garlic cloves and add to the pot

with the onion, red pepper, and hot pepper. Cook until softened but not browned. Sprinkle with the turmeric and stir. Add the rice to the pan and stir until the grains are coated with the onion mixture.

4. Add the chicken stock and the tomatoes. Return chicken pieces to pan, cover, and bring to a boil. Lower heat and simmer, covered, for about 20–30 minutes. Check the pot occasionally and stir. The pelau is ready when the chicken is cooked and the rice has absorbed all the liquid and is tender. (Add more stock or water if the liquid is absorbed and the rice is not yet tender.)

5. Sprinkle with the chopped peanuts and serve.

Return to Sweet Grenada

*F*OR SOMEONE WHO HAD followed the same hairdresser from salon to salon around Toronto for years to be assured a certain look, getting haircuts while cruising has required a bit of an adjustment.

During the early going, in the United States, I'd peer in shop windows, scrutinizing the cutters and their clients for signs of stylish proficiency. I'd ask other well-coifed cruisers, of course, who usually would tell me about the great cut they got in a port several hundred miles in the wrong direction. In Charleston, I even chased a woman and her teenaged daughter—total strangers—down the street. "Excuse me," I said when I finally caught up. "Your hair is fabulous. Where do you get it done?" "In Tennessee," said the woman. "We're tourists."

Beyond the United States, some cruisers let their spouses do the job. Even though I promised never to say a word whatever the results, and even tried to bribe him by letting him off dish-drying duty, Steve flat-out refused.

By the time we had reached Boquerón, Puerto Rico, a cut was long overdue. Eight of us piled into Raoul's van to be driven to nearby Mayaguez, the official port of entry, to check into the country. Afterward, Raoul dropped us at the Mayaguez Mall for the shopping spree he was certain all newly arrived cruisers would want. Not me. I bypassed the Wal-Mart and made a beeline for Rita's "Centro de Belleza." Could the beauty center cut my hair *ahora mismo*? Right now? "*No hay problema, señora.*"

No problem, except this "family hair-care center" resembled the beauty parlor my mother had frequented in the beehived sixties. No problem, except my Spanish wasn't up to the challenge of telling the hairdresser what I wanted. And his English didn't extend beyond, "You like?" which, as his work progressed, I was sure I wouldn't. By the time he washed, cut, moussed, dried, styled, and sprayed my hair firmly in place, I had a perky bouffant number that made me look like I was on my way to the prom, circa 1968. "My, you're brave," the other women commented when I returned to the van. Somehow I don't think that was a compliment.

In Trinidad, I don't have to worry about mousse, hairspray, or blowdryers. Margot simply plunks me down in a folding deck chair, wraps me in a smock, wets my hair with a spray bottle, and sets to snipping.

Before she and her mechanic husband gave up their jobs to sail south, Margot had been a hairdresser in North Carolina and, for a modest $10, she's happy to give cruisers cuts. To set up an appointment, you simply call her on the VHF and ask for a "session"—never a haircut—then arrange a time and an inconspicuous place to meet on shore. On most islands, including Trinidad, visitors aren't supposed to work, so she needs to be discreet. (A cut on the boat itself is a really bad idea . . . unless you want to spend a week cleaning up afterward.)

Fifteen minutes after she starts, I'm on my way again—perfectly satisfied. No hair hanging in my eyes or leaving sweat trails down my neck? Thanks, Margot. I schedule sessions in both Grenada and Trinidad.

When I next need a haircut, Steve and I are in Bequia, and Margot and her husband are still in Trinidad—150 miles away. "Go see Joelle," I'm told. "She cuts the hair of everyone in the island's ex-pat community." Joelle is an attractive, stylish Frenchwoman, who came to Bequia via Jamaica, and her "salon" is the living room of her house, overlooking the harbor. Before she starts, she holds up a mirror so I can see the back of my head—a refinement missing from my dockside cuts—and points out a very weird spot where a large, V-shaped chunk has been removed. "Someone must have slipped with the scissors," she says. I never noticed.

Cruising is a lifestyle, not a vacation.

I constantly have to remind myself of this the week we're living on the hard—on land, on *Receta*—in the boatyard in Trinidad. *Receta* was lifted from the water in slings and now sits supported on jackstands, her keel and bottom exposed and awaiting scrapers and rollers. She was not meant to be lived on out of the water. We can use neither our seawater-cooled fridge nor our seawater-flushed toilet, which means room-temperature drinks during the day and a bucket at night. (During the day, I can climb down the 10-foot ladder and visit the boatyard bathrooms.) Removed from the water, in the unshaded yard, *Receta* is a bake oven. Like every other cruiser on the hard, we rent an air-conditioner; it works only intermittently. Inside the bake oven, stripped down to my panties and a teensy top, I'm cleaning and refinishing *Receta*'s teak, inch by sweaty inch, a bit each day. To add insult to injury, I'm losing my underwear: The elastic has simply rotted from too much time in the sun and salt air. Life is not all rum and mangoes.

Maintenance on a boat in the tropics is constant. Having the bottom scraped and freshly painted will mean less scrubbing for us to do, but sea life doesn't restrict itself to a boat's bottom. An unpleasant smell occasionally wafts up through the drains in the galley's double sink: the aroma of dying organisms that had moved into the drain hoses. Sea life takes up residence in the fridge filters, too: itty-bitty shrimp, fingernail-sized crabs, worms, seagrass, and the occasional smaller-than-a-guppy fish; plus sand. Neglect the filters for a week—sometimes less—and the fridge will stop. We have to clean things here I never thought of cleaning on land.

And then there's the toilet, where the consequences of even a little neglect are truly gruesome. Over time, minerals calcify in the hoses and connectors, constricting the flow like a hardened artery and leading to a traffic jam of bodily wastes. To slow down the mineral buildup, I give the system a weekly treatment with "head dressing"—vinegar to counteract the calcium, followed by a tip of vegetable oil to lubricate the seals, with a little warm water and detergent in between. I moved this chore permanently to my side of the boat-work ledger after I caught Steve pouring my precious cold-pressed extra-virgin olive oil into the toilet bowl.

No matter how diligent I am with the head dressing, the sea eventually gets the upper hand and Steve has to disassemble the head. "Look at this," he says one day, triumphantly brandishing a rock-hard lump of calcium salts in a surgically gloved hand. (We have a box of one hundred disposable latex medical gloves aboard for just such purposes.) He had chiseled the lump out of a valve, and is positively cheerful in the middle of this ugly job. "I'm off the hook tonight," he says. Any time he has to tackle a head-related problem, he's excused from dish duty.

Back home, Steve would have called a plumber and I would have loaded the dishwasher. But back home, I can't put on my snorkel gear, climb down the swim ladder, and watch spotted eagle rays rooting for dinner in the sand beneath me.

Ever since a cockroach escaped from a visiting cruiser's Scrabble box and tried to move aboard *Receta*, I don't take any chances—

even though Steve nailed it instantly with a direct hit of Baygon, our made-for-the-Caribbean bug spray that delivers on its promise of "fast knock-down." (I've never had the courage to look at the ingredients list. "Use only if necessary," the can says.) When we acquire books in exchanges with other cruisers, I surreptitiously slip them into Ziplocs, blast in some Baygon, and seal the bags for a few days. When we're on the hard, I make an embarrassed Steve spray our ladder and the stands that support *Receta*, so bugs don't stroll over from a nearby boat and climb onboard. And on the rare occasion that *Receta* is tied to a dock, I spray our mooring lines, in case any bugs get it in their minds to scurry aboard and sample the cruising life. One day a fishing boat pulled in next to us. I had heard bad things, *very* bad things, about fishing boats and their burgeoning *cucaracha* populations. So undeterred by the crowd on the dock, realizing that I looked like an out-of-control obsessive-compulsive, I got out my supersized can and sprayed the dock. Steve says we should buy shares in Baygon. I don't care: What matters is that except for the brief incursion by the Scrabble-box hitchhiker, *Receta* remains a roach-free zone.

My sternest anti-bug measures are reserved for groceries. Cardboard boxes—roaches eat the glue and lay eggs in them—never, *ever* come aboard *Receta*. Before we even leave the supermarket, we jettison as many as possible; the contents of the others get transferred to other containers before they go belowdecks. And every single piece of produce we buy gets rinsed with a bleach and water solution in the cockpit. Dry goods like rice and sugar get double-bagged in Ziplocs. (Steve says we should buy stock in that company, too.) No wonder grocery shopping takes all day.

Steve finally convinces me it's time to sell *Snack*. But it's illegal for cruisers to sell stuff in Trinidad, just as it's illegal for them to work, so Steve commits a semantic fiddle: He *trades* Snack instead—for a pile of U.S. greenbacks, which he immediately injects into the local economy by purchasing a new, larger dinghy and new, larger outboard.

I don't need much convincing, actually: I had long ago become tired of the cruising affliction known as dinghy butt—the salty wet bum that results from traveling in an underpowered dinghy on an overactive body of water. The only thing I need convincing about is the expense.

For the first time in my adult life, I don't have a paycheck. All I see is money going out. I know the bank statements that catch up with us sporadically show the accounts are healthy: The house is happily rented, the cruising guides we publish are continuing to sell. But *still*. Cruisers—even the wealthy retired-for-life types—wear frugality like a badge of honor. In Toronto, we had heard about "gold star days": cruisers proudly putting a gold star in their logs any day they hadn't spent a cent.

I'm in charge of keeping track of our finances onboard. So I carefully note every peso and dollar we spend—from the $2 EC (77 cents) we paid for a round trip for two to St. George's from Lower Woburn, to the $766.90 TT ($124) for a major provisioning in Port of Spain. (There are an appalling number of entries marked "beer.") At the end of each month, I tally it all up in an Excel spreadsheet on the laptop, and report how we've done compared to our plucked-almost-from-thin-air budget back in Toronto.

Early on, the monthly bottom lines are scary—mostly because of the equipment category, as Steve continues to find stuff that *Receta* absolutely *has* to have. But by the time we reach Grenada, the bottom lines have swung the other way, and for a few months we're actually well under budget.

The 75-mile crossing from Trinidad back to Grenada is ugly.

We leave about two in the afternoon, with the new *Snack* on deck, knowing we'll be watching the sun rise as we approach the anchorage at Hog Island. But a succession of squalls—nowhere in the forecast—starts soon after we are through the Boca, the mouth leading out of Trinidad's protected inshore waters. The 2 A.M. note in the log is a succinct one-worder: "Awful." We have to reef the sails because the wind is so strong—but between squalls, it slacks off, and we corkscrew limply up and down the waves, lacking enough drive to slice through them. This jerky up, down, and sideways motion is too much even for iron-stomach Steve. We take turns steering and leaning over the side to puke, attached to the boat by our safety harnesses so there's no danger of losing one of us overboard along with our lunch.

I had been looking forward to making the passage on this particular night, when the Leonid meteor shower is passing overhead. But watching the sky for any length of time exacerbates the seasickness: When I look up, the only obvious light is the one at the top of our mast, describing huge arcs across the heavens. Baaaacccckkk and forrrthhhh. Baaaacccckkk and forrrthhhh. *Blech*. I don't look up very often.

And this is how I arrive back in Grenada, where the sun is rising on a glorious tropical day: dehydrated and exhausted by a night of vomiting, and seriously depressed. After my bow-to-stern, every-inch-of-woodwork cleaning in Trinidad, the boat has been trashed. Not only is there wet clothing strewn everywhere, but waves found their way—yet again—through the leaky forepeak hatch.

"*Receta, Receta*. This is *La Esmeralda*. Welcome back to Grenada." We're still a mile offshore when the radio booms to life. *Receta*'s shape has been spotted on the horizon, and the call from *La Es* is followed by other welcomes. We've come home.

The road to Dingis's house is as steep as ever. But now, in late November, after another month-and-a-half of the wet season, the landscape is an even denser green. The flamboyant trees, blazing red a few months ago, now sport 2-foot-long pea-green pods; a few months from now, they'll be "shak-shaks," hard and brown, their seeds loose inside, perfect for shaking to a soca beat. The air seems freshly washed, with the unreal clarity of a retouched post-card. The wet season doesn't mean gray days of constant drizzle; the sun still blazes most of the time, with rain dancing down for only an hour or so in the afternoon. Then the sun returns—with such ferocity that the potholes steam like volcanic craters. Perhaps because we've been away and haven't seen it in a while, or perhaps because we're just so glad to *be* here, the road seems lovelier than ever.

Gennel had turned fifteen while we were in Trinidad, and we're eager to deliver her birthday gift. We had thought hard and lingered long over its selection. What would a fifteen-year-old girl like? What would a fifteen-year-old *Grenadian* girl like? Eventually, we settled on a wide woven copper bracelet, made by a Trini crafts-man; we both agreed it would look lovely against her skin. Of course, we have a souvenir for Dingis, too, a brightly painted ceramic jar decorated with Trinidad's national bird, the scarlet ibis.

"Let's not bother calling first," Steve had said. "Gennel will be home from school by now." So we had bypassed the pay phone outside Nimrod's and headed directly up the road.

But the house is silent as we turn into the drive. No familiar voice sings out hello, and no noisy gaggle of little girls plays under the fishnet-strung carport. The only person we can see is "Gennel's father," as Dingis introduced him to us once, and only once, who nods hello and continues sharpening his cutlass. The quiet is broken only by the menacing scrape of the cutlass on the sharpening stone. This, plus several goats tethered just outside the carport, makes me think we've arrived as the animals are about to be dispatched to the stewpot. I start to walk away. "I don't want to see this."

Steve takes my arm. "He's just cutting their tethers." Then, to Gennel's father: "Is Dingis here?"

He shakes his head no. Gennel, still wearing the pleated gray skirt and short-sleeved white blouse that are her school uniform, appears from the house, having heard our voices. "Mommy down in deh bay," she says, and then explains why the house is so subdued. Dwight had an accident while diving for lobster—the bends, it sounds like—and Dingis had to have him flown to Barbados, the closest decompression chamber. He's doing okay, but the strain on the household—loss of the breadwinner, the exorbitant cost of out-of-country medical care, daily long-distance phone calls—is clearly enormous.

"Gennel's father helping out," Dingis says, when we've again climbed the hill, this time calling first, "but still I had no money to get Gennel a birt'day cake." She has shown us a letter from the hospital in Barbados: The bill for Dwight's care is going to cost thousands, dollars that Dingis clearly doesn't have. The good news is that he will recover, though it will be a slow process; however, his days of diving for a living may be permanently over. Dingis's face shows the strain of the last week.

For the first time, she invites us inside the house to talk. Spotting the lineup of flip-flops at the top of the steps, we pull off our sandals before stepping inside. A TV on a small table dominates one end of the living room; a wall phone, the other; a few chairs are arranged around the perimeter, and a couple of inexpensively framed prayers and religious pictures hang on the walls. Several rooms are directly off the living room—bedrooms, I assume—their doors pulled most of the way shut. Gennel is wearing her bracelet; she had thanked us when we arrived, just as soon as she could politely break in on her mother's account of Dwight, but a little later, when she leaves the room to get a photo album to show us, Dingis says, "Gennel even sleep with her bracelet on."

Her musical voice is mournful. "But I couldn't do anything on her birt'day." Steve and I exchange quick glances. "Come to *Receta* for dinner on Sunday with Gennel and the girls and Allan," Steve says. "We'll make it a belated birthday party."

On the way back down the hill, we stop at Nimrod's to say hello and buy a loaf of bread. Before we even realize what he's doing, Hugh has two cold Caribs open and in front of us on the counter. Saying no thanks would be rude and out of the question. The problem is, we spent longer with Dingis and Gennel than planned, and it's almost sunset. When the sun drops below the horizon 12 degrees above the equator, it's day one minute, night the next; there's very little twilight. And with no flashlight, opening *Snack*'s combination lock on the unlit dinghy dock will be a little tricky.

We drink up quickly. I leave Steve to pay, run to the dock, and spin the lock in the last remaining minutes of daylight. But Steve doesn't appear. I wait. And wait some more.

The hazard of being considered a regular at the local rum shop: Before letting him out the door, Hugh had shanghaied him into a shot of rum. "Welcome back to sweet Grenada," Steve announces, grinning broadly, when he finally arrives.

The cockpit and cabin are decorated with balloons from a store in St. George's. I'd made a last-minute visit to Mr. Butters's the previous afternoon, my first since we returned from Trinidad. The fields looked more neglected than they had two months earlier, but he was still there. So was the bulldozer—still composting nicely.

"How are things, Mr. Butters?"

"Dey still makin' me leave. Maybe tomorrow. Most of my stuff finished." He had the tomatoes I needed, though.

The menu has been carefully planned. No way I'm going to attempt island fare with Dingis at the table—and, in any case, I figure it will be more fun if the food is typically North American—so pots of good-old North American–style spaghetti and meatballs and sauce are simmering on the stove. Remembering the finicky tastes of my niece and nephew, about the same age as the girls and Allan, I've toned down my cooking: The sauce has only a little garlic and no hot stuff in it; one loaf of the homemade bread that's warming in the oven is slathered with garlic butter, but I do a second loaf with plain butter, too. And, figuring it will be the least popular part of the meal with my younger guests, I've made only a modest amount of salad.

It's instantly clear I've made a gross cross-cultural mis-calculation. As Steve and I hand plates around the cabin table, each one with a hefty meatball perched on top of a mound of spaghetti, I explain which loaf of bread has garlic butter and which has plain. *Everyone*—the little girls included—digs into the garlic bread. They only move on to the plain buttered loaf when the last crumb of garlic bread is gone. "This is grated cheese." I point to a bowl of my freshly grated top-of-the-line Parmesan. *Everyone* spoons it on. Except for Allan, who carefully piles it next to his pasta, like a scoop of mashed potatoes, and proceeds to eat it with gusto, like a side dish.

"Do you have any hot pepper?" Gennel asks. I deliver a bottle of hot sauce to the table and *everyone*—again, the little girls included—sprinkles it liberally on the sauce.

Oh, dear. So much for toning down my cooking. I'm sure Dingis is by now convinced I don't know a thing about proper spicing. But she kindly tells me how delicious everything is, how it's the first meal she's really eaten since Dwight's accident.

And the kids: By the time Steve and I clear the table, they have each consumed two large meatballs. Beef is not a big part of the local diet—and certainly not in the form of meatballs. But these kids don't turn up their noses at unfamiliar foods. They've cleaned their plates, salad and all. There are no parents here urging them to eat or they won't get dessert. They eat with enthusiasm, taking real pleasure in my cooking.

And once Gennel has blown out her candles, of course everyone finishes a big square of chocolate cake thick with chocolate icing.

After lunch, "Uncle Steve" takes the kids and Gennel on a fast ride in the new *Snack* to Mt. Hartman Bay, the next bay to the west, then back to the Hog Island beach for a swim, this time with a wave and a welcome from Phillip. Dingis and I stay on board to talk—about Dwight, of course, but also, as always, about food. Despite the turmoil in her household, she had once again arrived bearing a gift: green coconuts from a tree on her property. "Do you know coconut water?" I assure her we both really like coconut water—leaving out that I particularly like it mixed with gin. I also omit that we've yet to open a green coconut onboard ourselves.

We've watched the coconut vendor in the St. George's market on every trip to town, however. He wears bib overalls woven entirely out of coconut palm fronds, with the bib top usually pushed down around his waist. A high-crowned hat, also woven from fronds, shades his face. Holding a green coconut in one hand, he gives the top a couple of quick whacks with his cutlass, its 20 inches of curved blade flashing in the sun. He slices off just enough of the shell to create a small opening in the end, small enough that none of the coconut water spills out before the customer tips it up to drink.

Coconut water—not to be confused with coconut milk—is found in young or green coconuts that haven't yet developed their hard, hairy inner brown husk and firm white meat. Green coconuts are also called "water nuts" and, in some places, "jelly nuts," because of the soft, quivering flesh inside, which can be eaten with a spoon. A good-sized young nut will have as much as three cups of almost-clear thirst-quenching water. "Very good for you," Dingis tells me. "Very nutritious." She neglects to mention its other local claim to fame: Coconut water is reputed to be an excellent hangover cure.

As the nut ripens, the flesh thickens and hardens, and the hairy brown husk develops. The smooth green or yellowish outer shell of the young nuts turns tan or brown; but this outer shell is usually removed before the coconuts are exported, so what you see in North American markets is just the hairy brown inner husk. These mature "flesh nuts" have a lot less water inside, the space now filled by dense white coconut meat—which the island women grate and soak in boiling water to make coconut milk and coconut cream. On islands such as Grenada, where there are many more coconut palms than cows, they take the place of dairy milk and cream in everyday cooking.

As I tuck the green nuts under our canvas spray dodger where they won't roll around, Dingis warns me to open them soon. "Deh water go sour if you leave it in deh coconut."

Steve's bought himself a cutlass—less than $6 at Arnold John's hardware store in town—so he can open coconuts and clean lambi the way the locals do. But, now, eyeballing the wicked blade and its proximity to the fingers holding one very smooth, very hard green coconut, we agree that using it seems like a very bad idea indeed. I substitute the Chinese cleaver from the galley, the 8-inch blade of which seems downright modest.

The guy in the market made it look easy. After losing a good portion of the sticky liquid from the first nut on *Receta*'s cockpit cushions, we decide opening a green coconut is a two-person operation. For the next one, we both lean overboard, Steve with the nut and cleaver, and me, holding our biggest bowl underneath. He thwacks and I catch the water that splurts out. Then I break out the ice cubes and Clarke's Court rum ("cabin table, aft compartment: good for mixing"), to put a proper Grenadian spin on the gin drink we loved in the Bahamas.

I mix the clear coconut water with the Clarke's Court, then stir in a couple of teaspoons of sweetened condensed milk. The translucent mixture immediately turns a lovely opaque milky white. Poured over ice into tall glasses, with one of our own nutmegs grated on top, it is a seductive, dangerous concoction: barely sweet, slightly coconutty, and very refreshing. Steve votes it a permanent place on my sundown repertoire.

Steve's parents are coming from Canada to visit next week, meeting us in Bequia. It's time to leave Grenada for good. Dingis insists we come visit once more. "You need more coconuts," she says, "and the golden apples are ready."

When we arrive, she has already filled one large canvas sack with golden apples. Slicing one for us to try raw, she tells me I can also stew them with sugar. Following Gennel's lead, we dip the wedges in a saucer of salt: A type of citrus fruit, the golden apple is tart and sweet at the same time, and full of sharp fibrous slivers that have to be cut or pulled away—a world removed from the apples we know. Meanwhile, one of the older local boys is shinnying up the trees to get coconuts, Dingis tells us, and a sack of them soon arrives.

But she also has several surprises, and she is almost girlish in her excitement as she presents them one at a time. "Merry Christmas," she sings, holding out a carefully wrapped package decorated with a plastic long-stemmed rose. "Open it on Christmas. But dis for tonight." She holds out the plastic container I had sent home with her from *Receta*, after Gennel's birthday party, with the leftover meatballs, spaghetti, and sauce. Now it's full of homemade chicken curry. The foil-wrapped package she hands me next contains still-warm roti breads. "If you could only stay, I could show you how to make them," she says wistfully.

Steve has a last errand in Mt. Hartman Bay and promises to

return and meet us in an hour at the jetty—which gives Dingis a little more time to load me up with more essentials.

"You need seasoning peppers." It's a statement, not a question, and she plucks some off the bush in front of the house. "Do you like grapefruit?" She doesn't wait for a response before picking a few off that tree. She also gathers passion fruit and celery stalks as we go, to add to the pile under the carport.

Finally, laden with sacks and bags, we start down to the jetty: me, Dingis, Gennel, the ever-present Stinky, the four little girls, and Alisha's mother, who has also come to the house to say good-bye. Even as we walk, Dingis is cramming me with a few last-minute bits of info. "Those are pigeon peas." She points to a bush covered in delicate yellow blossoms. "Dey will be ready at Christmas. If you could only stay." It is so very tempting.

About halfway down the hill, we pass two cruisers, strangers to me, heading up. They don't raise their eyes from their feet. They don't say "good afternoon," as local custom demands. In fact, they don't say a thing, don't acknowledge our presence in any way, just push the rambunctious Stinky aside and continue climbing. The Grenadians might as well be invisible—a fact that is not lost on them. I am appalled by the cruisers' behavior—they are *guests* on this island—and say so, loudly, to Dingis and the others. They just shrug. Unfortunately, I get the feeling they've seen it before.

Steve is waiting at the jetty, and Gennel immediately climbs into the dinghy. She's coming with us, she says. Dingis continues to admonish us, as she has all afternoon. "Take care of yourselves. I don't want anything to happen to you."

We hug good-bye, and I slip into the dinghy as Gennel reluctantly returns to shore. They all stand at the very end of the jetty, waving good-bye, as the dinghy pulls away. They continue waving, waving, waving, arms outstretched overhead, silhouetted against the green hillside of Lower Woburn, for as long as I can see them. I wave madly back as we cross Clarke's Court Bay, my vision blurred by tears.

Rum and Coconut Water à la *Receta*

If you don't have access to green coconuts, coconut water is sold in cans and little juice box–type cartons in West Indian grocery stores and some supermarkets. It's often sweetened, so you may want to add a touch less condensed milk.

MAKES 1 DRINK

2 ounces white rum

4 ounces (approx.) coconut water

1 tablespoon (approx.) sweetened condensed milk (or to taste)

Whole nutmeg

Shake or stir the rum, coconut water, and milk with ice. Taste, and add more milk if you want the drink a bit sweeter. Liberally grate nutmeg on top.

Sharing the Dream

Well, we didn't kill off my parents. In fact, they wouldn't make bad cruisers—although they might not tell you that. They'll probably bemoan little things, like risking life and limb clambering in and out of the dinghy, and practically needing a university course to use the head . . .

E-mail from Steve to his aunt and uncle in Canada,

December 1998

*M*YRNA AND MURRAY, STEVE'S parents, have sailed on *Receta* only once, on a carefully orchestrated afternoon on Lake Ontario, when the forecast promised flat calm and a gentle whisper of wind, and the sailing was followed by a convivial dinner onboard while safely tied to the dock. It was the kind of day that seduces non-sailors into buying boats, and I could see even nervous Myrna's view of sailing soften. Her only other outing on a sailboat had been years before, on *Overkill*, the 31-footer that preceded *Receta*. *Overkill* was a tender boat that leaned over easily under the pressure of the wind, regularly canting the cockpit to a funhouse angle. With an orange Coast Guard–issue keyhole-style life preserver tied tightly around her torso, Myrna clenched her teeth and clutched the handrails the entire time, certain her prankster son (the same son who would never leave a trail of plastic ants crawling all over her freshly baked pies as they cooled on her kitchen counter) was going to tip the boat and send her flying into the water. "When we sold *Overkill*," Steve told friends, "you could still see my mother's fingernail marks in the teak trim."

But now Myrna and Murray are not only coming to stay on *Receta* for a full week, they have chosen to visit us in Bequia, one of the small languorous islands that make up the nation of St. Vincent and the Grenadines. "Bequia sweet, Bequia sweet," sings the Carib grackle in its unmistakable two-note call, and those who wash up here quickly agree. However, Bequia is a fair stroll off the beaten tourist path and an unlikely destination for a pair of ultra-conservative travelers aged sixty-six and seventy-one.

For centuries, Bequia's residents made their living by whaling, and even now a few island men still have the skills and the nerve to kill whales with hand-thrown harpoons. During the whaling season—February to April—they keep watch for spouting hump-backs heading north after mating and calving; when one is spotted, they take to sea in an open 27-foot wooden whaling boat propelled by wind and oars. Bequians are still permitted, under the terms of an agreement with the International Whaling Commission, to catch two humpback whales a year for local con-sumption. Last year was a good one, we're told, with a full catch. Everyone on the island knows when a whale has been killed, because the monstrous carcass is towed to Petit Nevis, a tiny island a harpoon's throw off Bequia's southern edge, and the whalers build huge fires to render the oil from the flesh. The smoke and stench hang in the air for days. Bequia is decidedly not Nassau.

Five miles long by 3 miles wide, it is an island of empty beaches and small guesthouses framed by red and purple bougainvillea, perhaps with a pretty white arch over the front gate made from the jawbone of a whale. Traditional boatbuilders work with hand tools under palm trees, and Rastafarians sell tomatoes and papayas in the small market. Sure, there's an "Internet café" where we plug in our laptop to pick up e-mail: It's in a shack, up a path that's either dust or mud depending on the weather. Inside, the table that holds the aging computers also hosts a regular parade of sugar ants up and over the keyboards, and faces glassless, wood-louvered windows. One day, a squall raced overhead while we were there alone, the proprietor having wandered off to other business; it was left to us to dash about and close the louvers, leaving us in the dark but with the equipment only dampened rather than doused.

This has been a record wet year for Bequia—three times the normal rainfall. The cisterns on the roof of every house are full to overflowing. Even if the rain stops, the arrival of the blustery annual Christmas winds is imminent, fierce gusts that slide off the hills, sending boats hobbyhorsing in the heavy chop and sometimes even dragging anchor, usually in the black of night. The odds of seven straight days of blissful weather for our guests are very long odds indeed.

Common cruising wisdom says: Don't do things any differently because you have guests. Do what you usually do, eat what you usually eat, and get them involved in your usual daily routines. They're coming to visit because they want to experience *your* way of life.

Right.

The plane from Canada is late, and Myrna and Murray miss the first connecting flight. The next—a puddle-jumper from Barbados—arrives in the evening, which means their introduction to cruising life is a bouncing dinghy ride across the harbor chop in full darkness and a steady drizzle. "You're gonna love this new dinghy," Steve says as he holds it steady in the dark and helps his mom climb in. But Myrna and Murray never rode in the old *Snack*, so the relative improvements are lost on them. From their point of view, it is simply a small, rocking rubber boat—without a seat. Like most cruisers, we don't bother with such niceties; a seat simply gets in the way when you're carrying jerry jugs of fuel and water and bags of groceries. Perched nervously on the inflatable's pontoons, without any teak to clutch, Myrna (who doesn't like to swim unless her feet can touch bottom) and Murray (who doesn't like to swim *at all*) seem decidedly uneasy.

By the time they've climbed from the dinghy onto *Receta*'s swim ladder, an athletic endeavor at any age, and been coached from there into the cockpit—"*please* don't grab that, it's our radio antenna; no *NO*, not that either; it's a wind generator support"— they sink onto the cushions with obvious relief. They have clearly had enough adventure for one day. Perhaps for the entire week. Perhaps for a lifetime.

Welcoming hugs over, I leap into the breach. "How about a glass of rum punch?"

"No, I don't think so," says Myrna. I'm not surprised: Although back home she would occasionally join us in a glass of wine with dinner, I can't recall her ever having a cocktail. "Try just a sip of mine, Mom," Steve offers.

"Mmmm, that *is* good."

"Here, I'll pour you a small glass." By the time we sit down to a late dinner of chicken pelau, the small glass has been drained. And Myrna is looking decidedly more relaxed.

Prior to their arrival, we've had only one set of stay-aboard guests, but they hardly count: They were experienced sailors who knew the routines of life on a cruising boat as well as we did and fit right in. We know the stories from other cruisers, though: the terrifying but true tales of how the Good Friends from Back Home transmogrified into the Guests from Hell: dangerous creatures who—horror of horrors—left the water running while they brushed their teeth, drank the supply of expensive Diet Coke without offering to replace it, tracked sand through the boat, burned precious amps by neglecting to turn off lights, and—the worst offense—clogged the head necessitating ugly remedial work by the skipper.

We have four more sets of guests lined up to visit in the months to come. We want to make sure we get this guest thing right.

Don't do things any differently than you usually do. "You have a choice, Myrna," I explain. "You can take a shower in the head, where you'll have complete privacy. But you'll have to wipe everything dry and you won't have hot water." With the trade winds now keeping our wind generator spinning steadily, we don't need to run the engine to charge the batteries—which means no engine-heated water. "Or you can do as we do and shower outside in the cockpit, with nice hot water from our solar shower."

"Don't worry, Mom. You can keep your bathing suit on." Steve is trying to make amends after completely intimidating both parents last night with his detailed instructions on how to operate the toilet: "Pump at least ten times when you pee, at least double that when you do anything else. And don't forget to pop the pedal up after you're finished, or water will continue to come in and you could sink the boat." *How many times? Sink the boat? Was it pedal up or pedal down? I COULD SINK THE BOAT??* For the first two days, they ask for refresher directions every time they flush.

Myrna opts for the cockpit shower, with her bathing suit. Steve and I duck below to give her privacy, and to put together a pitcher of sundowners before we dinghy into town for dinner. "We still have fresh coconuts from Dingis, right? Make rum and coconut water tonight," he says. This time Myrna accepts a drink without urging, and when I top up everyone's glass a little later, she doesn't decline.

"I think she's settling in," Steve whispers.

Dinner is at Daphne's. "Daphne Cooks It," the worn sign says, pointing the way to a white frame house off the main street of Port Elizabeth, Bequia's one town. Daphne's is a restaurant only in the loosest sense of the word, more like eating Sunday dinner at the house of a favorite aunt. There's no menu, and the food—classic West Indian fare—is served family-style at a scant handful of tables covered with worn flowered cloths. Steve and I already know that Daphne certainly can cook it: We've eaten extremely well here before. We also know that, from the food to the loo, it will be a real adventure for Myrna and Murray. (Daphne cooks, but she doesn't necessarily clean.)

"It will be my pleasure to serve you tonight," Alwyn said when we stopped by in the afternoon to let Daphne know we'd like dinner. Alwyn is as lean as Daphne is rotund, with a warm broad smile that shows off his gold front tooth. The only disconcerting thing about Alwyn is that each time we see him, his belt hangs undone under his T-shirt, as if he has been suddenly interrupted from other pressing matters to serve his customers.

Daphne could cook fresh tuna tonight, Alwyn told us, or fresh lobster. "And there's chicken," he added, with only the slightest change in inflection to suggest this would be a really dumb choice. Since I've already promised to make lobster onboard, we all pick tuna. "But can you tell Daphne we'd like Steve's parents to try some traditional Caribbean side dishes with it?"

"It will be my pleasure," he said.

That night, Daphne serves thick callaloo soup, followed by the tuna, stewed in a Creole-style sauce of tomatoes, onions, and peppers. There's rice, to soak up the spicy sauce, and heaping platters of breadfruit salad, conch fritters, steamed red cabbage wedges, cucumber and tomato salad, and provision, the ubiquitous boiled starchy vegetables. As we're wiping the big plates embarrassingly clean, Daphne comes out of her kitchen to chat, as she usually does. "My stove's been givin' me trouble," she complains. Steve assures her that her cooking is better than ever, Myrna and Murray request another dinner later in the week, and I try to winkle out instructions for how to make the tuna. She's helpfully vague—at least until she can execute a diversionary tactic: the delivery of homemade vanilla ice cream, which immediately sets everyone *ooh*ing and *aah*ing in a different direction.

When we return a few nights later, Daphne has stewed the tuna—again, everyone's choice—in a buttery brown sauce that's fragrant with lemon. And taking seriously her responsibility to introduce Myrna and Murray to West Indian cuisine, this time she's accompanied the fish with squares of the polenta-like coo-coo and cole slaw. The fritters are different too, made with some other, more delicate, seafood than conch.

"Tree-tree," she explains when she again emerges from the kitchen. "Tiny, tiny fish you can only get for a short time around Christmas."

"Tree-tree" refers to all kinds of river fish that hatch in the ocean at this time of year and then, less than a half-inch long and not yet fully formed, migrate inland to live in rivers and streams. When the "tree-tree" run, people flock to the mouths of rivers to catch them, using very fine nets or sheets, since they're so small. We're lucky, Daphne tells us; tri-tri—I later see the name written down—are considered a delicacy, and they run for such a short time that most visitors never get to try them.

As she ambles back to the kitchen, Murray asks Alwyn if he can take a picture of them both. "It will be my pleasure," Alwyn says with his charming gold smile. "But I will have to ask Daphne." She agrees, removing the apron that covers her flowered dress but keeping on her color-coordinated ball cap, before posing in a corner of the dining room with Alwyn, his belt still undone.

But Steve wants a picture of her in her real domain: her kitchen, in front of her wonderful old monster of a stove. "It still givin' me trouble," she says, hefting a freshly roasted breadfruit from its oven. "Ah'm gonna trash it yet."

* * *

Bequia is the leaping-off point for the Tobago Cays, a 2½-mile-long horseshoe of coral reef 25 miles to the south, protecting small poster-perfect islands. The cays are pristine and un-inhabited—just a few coconut palms and glittering white sand beaches, the embodiment of the Caribbean. We want to take Myrna and Murray there for a day or two, but common cruising wisdom also advises it's bad form to make your guests seasick. The Christmas winds need to lay down if we're going to make the trip.

While we wait, we explore the island by day and teach them to play the island version of dominoes at night. Myrna builds a shell collection; Murray handlines from our deck, happily landing small squirrelfish and snappers, though nothing of edible size. They start to go barefoot onboard and in the dinghy, only putting on shoes when they get to the dock in town.

"Can the people on that boat see into our cockpit?" Myrna squints at our closest neighbor. "Not unless they're looking through binoculars," Steve replies.

And so Myrna decides showering naked in the cockpit is okay. As she's toweling dry, she sticks her head down into the galley. "Will you be making up some of that coconut water stuff tonight?" she inquires.

"I think she's *really* settling in," Steve whispers.

The water enclosed by the crescent of coral reef behind Petit Rameau and Petit Bateau, the two small islands that form the entrance corridor to the Tobago Cays, is so shockingly turquoise that it seems unreal: the blue of a newly painted swimming pool or a bottle of Bombay gin. Even before *Receta*'s anchor has dug into the sand, a small wooden boat roars up. "Do you want lobster?" asks the young driver. "I Desperado. I get you what you want."

The Tobago Cays is a national marine park, where fishing and lobstering aren't permitted, so cruisers who want seafood here have to buy it. A local boatman adopts each new arrival, providing not only lobster—alive or cooked, your choice—caught outside the protected area but also other essentials such as fruit, vegetables, and ice.

We only need lobsters from Desperado, though, since we'd stopped at the produce market yesterday to stock up before sailing out of Bequia. Every morning, the dreadlocked Rastafarians—members of a religious sect who regard blacks as the chosen people, smoke ganja as part of their religion, and believe Haile Selassie (once called Ras Tafari) is God—arrive with their produce on the ferry from St. Vincent. The Rastas are all over potential customers like flies. Aggressive and pushy, each one insists that you look at his table, then demands that you buy. "What do you need from me? What do you need from me?" "You bought from him—what will you buy from me?" Fending off one after another invariably leaves me irritated and out of sorts.

Then I learn the secret: Shop in the afternoon. By midafternoon, the Rastas don't care whose tomatoes or avocados you buy. By then, they've smoked enough "holy weed" to be substantially . . . mellowed. Their banter is lighthearted, no longer insistent; they flirt rather than threaten. When I ask one of them why his christophenes are white rather than the usual pale green, he takes my arm and holds it next to his: "Just like you and me," he says. "No difference under deh skin."

Whatever the time of day, Steve enjoys the parry and thrust of doing business with the Rasta men; he dishes the banter right back and buys a little from each. But he has a ready strategy when anyone tries to hound him into buying too much. "No, no," he says. "I can't. You have to ask my wife." They nod understandingly—and focus their attention on me.

Desperado returns, the bottom of his boat awash with live lobsters. "Dey very big." He hefts a pair by their antennae to calculate their weight: five pounds, he says, for $75 EC, or about $30. Sounds good, although I have no idea what the price *should* be, because we've yet to *buy* a lobster. Until now, they've always been delivered on the tip of Steve's spear or as a gift. But price isn't the real concern: I'm worried about squeezing these two into my big pasta pot.

Several hours before sundown, Myrna inquires, "Which of those rum drinks will you be mixing up tonight?"

"She was born to be a cruiser," Steve whispers.

With the wind still almost nonexistent, we decide to spend a second night in the cays, at nearby Mayreau, a slightly larger, slightly inhabited (three hundred people) island with a stunning beach for walking. More importantly from my point of view, it has a charming restaurant, on top of a steep hill on the windward side. Walking there is out of the question—I know the trail from Saltwhistle Bay, our leeward anchorage, is too rugged for Myrna and Murray—but a water taxi around the island can be arranged.

Our guests have settled into our way of life so beautifully that we forget how new they are to all this. "Water taxi" is a euphemism for a small open wooden boat like Desperado's, with a couple of planks for seating and a tiny decked area at the bow, where a bit of gear can be stuffed.

The ride back will be in the dark, of course, a minor detail that Steve and I had overlooked. There's no moon, no stars, and the water taxi has no lights. As we walk back down to the dock with our flashlights after dinner, Myrna and Murray are holding hands, a sure sign that Myrna is already nervous.

The bartender—who doubles as the water-taxi driver—sets his course by following the steep, rocky shoreline. Myrna and Murray aren't saying a word, just huddling together on one of the benches, clutching hands. That's when the squall passes overhead. Within seconds, the ocean, which had been pancake flat, is kicked up into short steep waves and rain pummels its surface. The boat bounces and the guiding shoreline disappears. "I don't have a clue which way we should be heading," I say quietly to Steve, hoping like hell the bartender/driver hadn't been sampling as well as pouring. "He's heading the right way," Steve answers loudly, but I can see Myrna and Murray are petrified.

A couple of minutes later, the bartender's helper, a scrawny kid of about eleven, dives under the small decked area at the front of the boat and starts tossing out life jackets. Now Myrna and Murray are *certain* the boat is sinking. Myrna clasps her hands and starts to pray.

But the kid is merely clearing himself a place to burrow, out of the driving rain. "Relax, everything's just fine," Steve says cheerfully. "Just a little rain." In fact, the rain is *pounding* on the ocean and the boat is slithering up and down the waves like a drunken snake.

The twenty-minute trip is taking *forever*. The bartender doesn't say a word. "Shouldn't we be there by now?" I whisper. "Almost there, everybody happy?" Steve answers loudly. I can't believe it. I think he's having fun.

After an eternity, the lights of the boats at anchor in Saltwhistle Bay come into view, and for the first time the bartender speaks: "Which one?" I don't have a clue, but Steve points through the raindrops with certainty, and the bartender heads that way. As we get closer, my flashlight picks up the reflective *T* at the top of our mast and Myrna unclutches her hands. Her turquoise shorts and yellow hooded windbreaker plastered to her body, her sodden hair flattened on her face, she looks like a tropical parrot caught in a hurricane. Murray, recognizing a good story to take home, is already grinning from ear to ear.

On board, in dry clothes, I unearth bottles of aged sipping rum and a rum liqueur from Trinidad. Myrna doesn't hesitate.

* * *

More common cruising wisdom: Never let your guests know that anything is out of the ordinary. Whatever happens, pretend it's just part of the cruising life.

The next morning dawns sweet, the sky again flawless, the surface of the water sugary in the sun. But the wind is up, way up, and the forecast is for more. In two days, our guests will fly home; we have to return to Bequia. Today.

"What a great day for a sail," Steve exclaims for the umpteenth time. Even with both sails reefed, we're making 7 knots, and *Receta* is heeled well over. We take turns delicately hand-steering the boat up and down the waves, trying to keep the ride as smooth as possible—a difficult job with 6-foot building seas and 20-knot gusts—and trying to keep Myrna and Murray distracted with the constant babbling of a tour guide on speed. "Ooh, look at the flying fish! Did we tell you they're delicious? Keep an eye out for dolphins! And whales! Ooh, look, more pelicans."

Murray exits the cockpit and disappears below for an exceptionally long time. Uh, oh, party's over, and the cookies will soon be overboard. But he reemerges, looking fine.

Back anchored in our old spot in the relative calm of Bequia's Admiralty Bay, he and Myrna talk happily about how great and how fast the passage was. They never knew they were supposed to be seasick. Meanwhile, Steve and I are *exhausted*.

Forget Murray and Myrna. *We've* had enough adventure for a while.

For their last morning onboard, I make a proper breakfast instead of the usual papaya, mangoes, and toast: eggs and hash browns—made from boiled eddoes, a knobby brown root with a creamy white interior that tastes a bit like potatoes; my latest experiment. Halfway through, Steve slides wordlessly off the settee and disappears into the cockpit. "Annie, can you come up a sec?" I follow him topsides. "So, uh, you think we're dragging?" he whispers rhetorically. Yikes. No question about it. *Receta* is drifting back, and the distant boat Myrna had worried about while showering is now perilously close. In fact, unless we spring into action immediately, we're gonna bounce she, as our friends in Grenada would say—slam right into our anchorage neighbor.

I start the engine and Steve springs to the foredeck. "We'll be back down in a minute," I call inside, as if we start the engine every time we sit down to eggs and eddoes. In fact, it is the *first* time we've dragged anchor, and had Steve waited another minute between sensing that the boat was moving differently and checking, we would *really* have given the parents something to remember their trip by.

Ten minutes later, we've reset the anchor and killed the engine. "Aren't these eddoes just terrific?" Steve says as he slides back onto the settee.

With Myrna and Murray back home safely and Christmas approaching, the Christmas winds kick in for good. The boats anchored in Admiralty Bay skate back and forth, outlined at night in dancing red and green lights, which form Christmas tree shapes between mast and rigging. Steve has scoured Bequia and totes home a package of Christmas lights which he strings around *Receta*'s cockpit. He's already rewired the end so it will plug into our 12-volt socket before he notices that in a misguided desire to save two bucks, he has bought lights intended only for indoor use. The wire is as thin as angel hair, and it breaks whenever I absentmindedly walk into a strand of lights—which is frequently. By Christmas, loose strands dangle on all sides of the cockpit, and festive gray duct-tape repairs adorn the intact sections. But all the lights still work, though we don't trust the weather or the wiring enough to leave them on when we're off the boat. Our Grenada-bought Christmas tree—a 12-inch-high foldout of green, gold, silver, and red metallic paper—sways from the oil lamp above our cabin table, sparkling as it catches the light, awaiting a delivery from "Soca Santa," as he's called in one popular island carol. (A couple of mixed religious backgrounds, Steve and I are equal-opportunity celebrators; a week earlier, we had lit Hanukkah candles onboard.)

In town, traditional carols like "Silent Night"—but set to reggae and soca beats—blare from the stores. Their windows are adorned with incongruous paper cutouts of white-skinned, white-bearded Santas wearing heavy red suits and black boots that would surely give a fat man heatstroke at this latitude. The artificial trees for sale are traditional evergreens—but the poinsettia bushes in full flame on the hillsides seem an entirely different species from the anemic potted plants back home: each one taller than a person, and completely blanketed with dozens and dozens of deep red leaves.

Admiralty Bay becomes more crowded every day. We tour the anchorage in *Snack*, checking out the new arrivals; sailboats from the British Isles and Europe—including a large number of Norwegian-, Swedish-, and Finnish-flagged vessels—far out-number the North Americans. I count only three other Canadian boats besides *Receta*.

Maybe that's why Santa finds us without difficulty. He even leaves a note near the little mound of gifts that has appeared on the table under our glittering Grenadian tree. "You oughta try anchoring a heavy sled a couple of times in these waves," it reads in suspiciously familiar handwriting. "Took a Carib from the fridge—thanks—and one for Blitzen, too. Ho, ho, ho—Santa."

You can indeed have secrets on a 42-foot boat. Steve is speech-less (a rarity) to discover the big golf umbrella with the Carib beer logo that he had coveted in Trinidad. I had managed to buy it, sneak it aboard, and keep it hidden through three countries. And I in turn can't believe he found his way a second time to the obscure backstreet bookstore in Port of Spain to get me the Caribbean cookbook I had regretted not buying. We've each received a piece of folk art that we noticed the other admiring—mine, a gaily painted wooden duck from Trinidad; Steve's, a simply carved wooden humpback whale from Bequia—and a few other goodies. We open the gifts in our bathing suits, very slowly, savoring every little thing, stopping in the middle to sip champagne in the cockpit—and leaving Dingis's long, narrow package till last. "It's a pair of candles," Steve guesses. I'm sure it's a Grenadian swizzle stick.

We're both wrong. Steve carefully unrolls the object inside: a small wall hanging that's a map of Grenada showing the island's tourist attractions in DayGlo colors. On black velvet. But it is absolutely right, an absolutely perfect gift. We hang it immediately. "I miss my sweet Grenada," Terry on *La Esmeralda* had said last night, when we reached him in Trinidad via SSB to wish him and Nancy a merry Christmas. We know exactly what he means. Sweet, sweet Grenada indeed.

When you're in Bequia for Christmas, you must have Christmas dinner with us," Sue and Dennis had told us last July, when we stopped here briefly on our way south. Not *if* we're in Bequia for Christmas, but *when*. "Everybody comes to Bequia for Christmas and New Year's," Dennis had said. "There will be four hundred boats in the harbor, from around the world."

Sue and Dennis are Canadians who retired early to live on Bequia. Like me, Sue is an escapee from publishing. We had met by accident on the road that runs alongside Admiralty Bay: She spotted my Ontario T-shirt; I noticed her tote bag with the logo of a Canadian bookstore. A minute's worth of conversation revealed mutual Canadian friends in the publishing business and led to an invitation to their house that afternoon for drinks.

They live high above the harbor, in a spectacular place they designed and built themselves called The View. The front is a series of arches, with floor-to-ceiling louvered doors that fold back, entirely opening the living and eating areas to a jaw-dropping view of the water below. The back wall of the living room has floor-to-ceiling bookshelves. More books—cookbooks, this time—cover an entire wall in the kitchen, whose centerpiece is a six-burner restaurant-quality stove. A gleaming full-size espresso maker sits on the counter. I've been living on a 42-foot boat and cooking in a 4-foot-square galley too long: I had to stop myself from visibly drooling.

Friends in publishing send her the books, and she in turn operates an informal lending library for friends on the island, Sue explained, as we sipped Dennis's excellent rum punch. She's also got an adult literacy program going, and already has a couple of graduates; she's not just teaching people to read, but also teaching a few islanders how to teach reading. Dennis, meanwhile, helps other ex-pats build their houses. And clearly these are people who love to entertain, with a house meant for entertaining.

Still, the old Ann would never have dreamed of imposing on virtual strangers for Christmas dinner. But when Sue reiterated the invitation on our return to Bequia, the new Ann accepted with alacrity.

Fourteen of us gather at The View on Christmas, an eclectic assortment of ex-pats who live here and visitors who've been coming to Bequia during the holidays for years. Dennis has been smoking a turkey over mango wood since early morning, and the smell rising from the barbecue is insanely delicious. By the time he's moved it to a big platter on the kitchen counter to carve, everyone is gathered around him, to sneak bits of crisp skin and moist meat. The rest of us have brought the accompaniments, a combination of traditional North American Christmas-dinner dishes and island cuisine. There are mashed potatoes, gravy, and cranberry sauce—and baked christophene with cheese, and rum punch—and French wines.

As the sun sets and the harbor darkens, Christmas lights blaze from the boats. Filled with holiday optimism that there would be no sudden squalls, we had switched *Receta*'s indoor-only lights on when we left. Now, I can pick out her colored pinpricks far across the harbor. Our beloved home.

"Thank you for the loveliest Christmas," Steve says as he kisses me goodnight. It *was* the loveliest Christmas—and I had been worried about it being lonely and disappointing, far from family and friends. But in our phone conversations back home, everyone, to a person, had described how hectic the season was: how rushed they were, how tired, so much to do, the shopping, wrapping, baking, decorating, cooking, partying. And I realized that only by sailing a couple of thousand miles away had we succeeded in gracefully escaping the usual competitive celebrating. Instead of doing frantic last-minute holiday preparations, we went to the beach on Christmas Eve afternoon, where we blissfully swam (and finally painted our registration number on the new *Snack*). I baked just one type of Christmas cookie, not dozens, and—limited by what I could find in the local markets and *Receta*'s storage lockers—made unelaborate goodies to take to a Christmas Eve gathering on a neighboring boat, and to Sue and Dennis on Christmas day. People still gobbled them up and asked for the recipes. This was the simplest Christmas ever, and we loved the feeling.

We've declined invitations to go out on New Year's Eve—Old Year's Night, it's called here—opting to see the new year in alone together on *Receta*. This year has given us a closeness—a pleasure in each other's company—that I know many couples yearn for. We trust each other too, in a different, deeper way. After all, day in and day out now, we're regularly trusting each other with our very lives. Steve has confidence in me—he's told me he trusts my boat handling and sail handling in all sorts of weather and waves, whether he's asleep or strapped to the mast, tucking another reef in the sail—which in turn gives me confidence in myself.

We talk together more, about more things. The past. The future. Our hopes, fears (still mostly mine), dreams. And the weather, always still the weather. We discuss, in detail, what we're seeing, and what we're reading. (Our worst choice for onboard reading material so far: Sebastian Junger's *The Perfect Storm*.) I laugh now at one of my concerns before we set off on the trip: Without the stimulus of our related jobs, I worried that Steve and I would have little to talk about each night at dinner. Ludicrous. Removed from the breathless pace of our old life, we have created space for a breadth of ideas and interests. Music. Food. Fish. Stars. Trees. Birds. Insects. Shells. Coral. Flowers. I am more aware of the moods and rhythms of the natural world around me than I ever have been, or probably ever will be.

This trip is allowing the sides of ourselves we like best to flourish.

Perhaps most amazingly, I have slowed down. Time has become more fluid, less rigid. Our days unfold; they don't just *bing-bang*, do-this, do-that happen. I lime. "I'm content to do *nothing* for stretches," I write in one of my last journal entries of the year (shortly after the one where I clock the Christmas winds at 40-plus knots and describe a wakeful night of boats dragging all around us). "I can just lay on the settee with my legs stretched out in front of me, watching the sky through the hatch. I can stare at the water for hours, utterly content." Me. Unbelievable. How will I cope in the real world?

To which Steve responds, "This *is* the real world."

Here, to our great satisfaction, we are no longer defined by our jobs. In our former life, we would meet people and one of the first questions would be: "What do you do?" To people in our new world, we have no last names and no professions. We are merely "Ann and Steve on *Receta*"—and that says it all.

We are saying good-bye tonight to a difficult year for first-time cruisers. Its fourteen named storms, from Alex to Nicole, ten of them hurricanes, have given the year a dubious distinction: It has made 1995–98 the most active hurricane period *ever*.

In our old neighborhood, the tradition at the stroke of twelve on New Year's was to go out on the front porch and bang spoons on pots and pans. If we banged pots and pans in Admiralty Bay at midnight, no one would hear us. Here the boats sound their horns, long loud lavish blasts, and shoot flares into the sky, maritime fireworks. A man-shaped silhouette sends up a flare from a nearby sailboat, but it plummets straight back down onto his foredeck, where it glows like a campfire on the fiberglass until he can scamper forward and douse it. We fill a bucket with sea-water—just in case—and cuddle in the cockpit as we watch the flares illuminate the tail end of the year.

Cream of Callaloo Soup

We've never met a bowl of callaloo soup we didn't like, but we were particularly partial to the one made by Jane, the owner and cook at Rosemount Plantation House, part of a working estate at the northern end of Grenada. Unlike more traditional versions, such as the one we had at Daphne's, Jane's is a creamed soup, and completely vegetarian. She came out of the kitchen after lunch and was happy to share her recipe—in reality, a skeleton of a recipe that I developed with a little trial and error. I borrowed the decadent crabmeat-and-cream garnish from another version that we also loved.

A swizzle stick—like the one Ed gave us for mixing 'ti punch—is traditionally used to "purée" the callaloo. An electric hand mixer will give you the same texture. You can also use a blender or food processor, although this will create a smoother soup.

And if you can't find callaloo, Jane suggested spinach as a fine substitute.

SERVES 4

2 tablespoons vegetable oil

1 large onion, chopped

1 clove garlic, chopped

1 stalk celery, with leaves, chopped

1 small cubanelle or green bell pepper, chopped

1 tablespoon chopped fresh thyme or 1 teaspoon dried thyme

Salt and freshly ground black pepper

1 bunch callaloo, ribs removed and leaves chopped, or about 1
    pound spinach, large stems removed

2 cups evaporated milk

1 cup (approx.) vegetable stock or water

4 whole cloves

Dash hot sauce

Squeeze lemon juice

1 cup cooked crabmeat

¼ cup heavy cream or crème fraîche

1. In a heavy saucepan, heat oil. Add onion, garlic, celery, and pepper and cook over medium heat until softened but not brown.

2. Sprinkle with thyme and season with salt and pepper. Add chopped callaloo or spinach and stir to combine. Add evaporated milk, stock, or water, and cloves, and cook over low heat for about 45 minutes.

3. Remove cloves. Purée soup until fairly smooth. (There should still be distinct pieces of callaloo or spinach.)

4. If soup is too thick, thin with additional milk, stock, or water. Taste and adjust seasoning, adding a dash of hot sauce and a squeeze of lemon as desired.

5. Pour soup into warm bowls. Sprinkle ¼ cup crabmeat on each, and swirl in a spoonful of cream.

Spicy Island Gingerbread

Gingerbread always reminds me of Christmas, but this version is quite different from the stuff used for holiday houses and people. It's a dark, almost chocolatey-looking cake, very moist, and not too sweet. The four types of ginger—fresh, dried, crystallized, and ginger beer—give it a really spicy, almost hot, kick.

MAKES ABOUT 20 SQUARES

¾ cup dark molasses

¾ cup packed dark brown sugar

½ cup butter

½ cup ginger beer

2 tablespoons grated fresh ginger root

2 tablespoons chopped crystallized (candied) ginger

2 cups flour

1 teaspoon baking powder

1 teaspoon baking soda

½ teaspoon freshly grated nutmeg

1 teaspoon ground ginger

½ teaspoon salt

2 eggs, beaten

2 tablespoons dark rum

1. Preheat oven to 350°F. Grease a 9-by-9-inch pan and cover bottom with baking parchment.
2. Combine first six ingredients in a large saucepan. Stir over low heat until butter melts, then set aside to cool.
3. In a bowl, combine dry ingredients and spices.
4. Stir eggs and rum into cooled molasses mixture, then stir in flour mixture. Mix well.
5. Pour batter into prepared pan and bake in preheated oven for about 30–40 minutes, until a toothpick inserted in the center comes out clean.

Part Three

To Leeward at Last

The Leeward Islands span some 200 miles and include 10 major islands operating as different nations. The variety is unparalleled. Many areas make for easy, comfortable cruising: others are more tricky. There are islands where you need both patience and luck to find a comfortable anchorage.

Chris Doyle, *Cruising Guide to the Leeward Islands*,
1998–99 edition

WHEN CHRISTOPHER COLUMBUS PRESENTED the findings of his second voyage to Queen Isabella, he used a crumpled sheet of paper to describe the terrain of Dominica. From offshore at sunset, this island looks like soft piles of emerald crushed velvet, haphazardly dropped by a wanton seamstress. The high, rounded mountains poke through pink-tinged clouds, each peak separated from its looming neighbors by deeply cut valleys.

If only it weren't for the swell, the constant, almost unseen undulations of the otherwise oily-calm sea, the area south of Roseau, Dominica, would be a perfect—and popular—anchorage. This, I've decided, is how God keeps the most glorious parts of the Caribbean uncrowded and pristine: Weed out all but the most committed by first making the beauty spots tricky to enter and then uncomfortable once you arrive. *Receta* is rolling and clanking from side to side in the swell, irritating when I'm onboard, but worse—nauseating, even—when I'm in the water, trying to scrub the sea scum off the waterline during my usual sunset swim.

A local kid is paddling toward me in the gilded late-day light. He's lying stomach-down on a battered white surfboard, arms windmilling steadily. The board, a scarred remnant of some ancient cast-off windsurfer, coasts to a stop a few feet from *Receta* and the boy sits up. Barely a teenager, wearing just a pair of soggy shorts, he asks shyly, "Do you need bread? I bring you fresh bread in the morning."

I tread water with my toothbrush in one hand and a sponge in the other. *Of course* we need bread; we *always* need bread. And having just arrived here after a boisterous sail from the north end of Martinique, *Receta* roaring like a freight train across the 26 miles of open water, I'm in no mood to bake. But I'm highly skeptical: What condition will this kid's bread be in after being transported a quarter-mile offshore on a chewed-up surfboard in a rolly ocean? I decide to pass the buck: "Steve, should we have some bread delivered in the morning?"

"Of course," he calls down from the cockpit. Given a choice, Steve *always* opts to support local commerce. "What's your name?" he asks the kid.

"Brian. I be here by seven, half-past seven, tomorrow morning." And with that he lies down and windmills away.

I'm dubious, but I keep my doubts to myself, not wanting to give Steve another excuse to remind me of Tyrrel Bay, off the island of Carriacou. There, a battered wooden skiff had pulled alongside as we were anchoring at dusk, on our way to Grenada. "Do you need anything?" the older man inside had asked. "Bananas, mangrove oysters, French wine, beer . . ." He'd rowed out the better part of half a mile from shore to see if he could do any business with us. I had already issued orders that we would never eat mangrove oysters on *Receta*, having seen what flowed past them in Luperón. And although we had heard the prices on wine and beer were good here, since it's usually "duty free"—meaning smuggled—we were already well stocked. Steve, however, was insistent that we buy *something* to make the man's row worthwhile. "Okay, we can always use some bananas."

"And how about a dozen limes, too?" Steve added. There were none in the skiff, but the man quickly assured us he would return to shore to get them. Steve paid him for the whole order upfront.

As he rowed off, I bet Steve that we'd never see the man again. But the new Steve believes in the essential goodness of people. He was sure the guy would be back.

Darkness fell. I was making dinner in the galley, and Steve was plotting the next day's course on the chart. I'd already suggested, twice, that enough time had elapsed for him to pay up. Then we heard the knock on the hull; the rowboat was alongside, and limes were tumbling onto our side deck—way more than a dozen—joining the mound of bananas already resting there. But this was what our money bought, and so this was what the man delivered. I felt terrible, and Steve of course didn't let me forget it. For my penance, before bed that night I had to sit in the cockpit and obsessively wash a gazillion limes and two-gazillion bananas with my bug-busting bleach-and-water solution. (Note to self: When you're washing in the dark, never let the sap from the oozing stem ends of freshly picked bananas get on anything such as cushions, hands, or clothes. The rest of my penance was figuring out how to remove the gummy residue, which turned black and stuck around for weeks.)

The soft knock on the hull comes shortly after 7. Brian, again clad only in a pair of wet shorts, hands me a perfectly dry bag, with five miniature soft-crusted baguettes inside, still warm from the oven and giving off the most wonderful smoky aroma. Their arrival seems magical: How had he managed to keep them warm, completely dry, and in perfect shape on a *surfboard*?

Almost the whole bag disappears at breakfast, the fragrant bread slathered with Trinidadian pineapple jam. The short loaves are like French *ficelles*—skinny baguettes—but their narrow ends grow plump in the middle. They have clearly been shaped by hand and baked in a wood-burning oven. I imagine Brian's mother forming them in the early-morning darkness, so they'll be ready for him to load on his surfboard at dawn. For bread in the islands, they carried a premium price—about $3 for the bag of five—but I would happily buy them again and again.

Therein lies the problem. At sunset, I keep an eager eye for Brian's surfboard as I swim. But he doesn't paddle by. We look for him and his board on shore the next morning. "Do you know Brian, the bread boy?" I ask at the hotel where we tie the dinghy. The answer is a definite, even quizzical, no. "Maybe his mom's baking stuff to sell at the market," Steve suggests; it's Friday, and Saturday is the big market day in Roseau, Dominica's capital.

No luck. The Roseau market is a profusion of flowers. People cradle enormous bunches of leggy birds of paradise and hold aloft long stems of ruby-red wild ginger like fanciful umbrellas as they make their way through the crowd. Obscene crimson anthuriums, with waxy erect spikes, poke out of yellow plastic buckets, next to fuschia bottle-brush flowers, which look like the kind of cleaning implement a fairy godmother would use. Much of Dominica is rain forest—the mountains trap moisture from the trade winds, giving the island at least 300 inches of rainfall a year in parts of the interior—and more than 1,000 species of flowering plants grow furiously here. There are more tropical flowers on a single market day in Roseau than I have ever seen.

But there are no long, thin, dark-crusted loaves.

On subsequent days, we poke our noses into the little shops that line the road into the capital, hoping to find Brian—or at least his mom's rolls. We buy several bags of lookalike loaves. None has the same smoky taste.

Christopher Columbus named this island for the Lord's Day, *Domingo* in Spanish, because he discovered it on a Sunday. His brother Diego, meanwhile, gave the same name for the same reason to part of the island of Hispaniola, to the northwest. To avoid confusion, one is officially called the Commonwealth of Dominica and the other, the Dominican Republic. It doesn't. Mail is sometimes misdelivered 600 miles in the wrong direction. Both islands, too, have a nasty way of enticing people to spend longer than they planned.

Dominica is the southernmost of the Leeward Islands group, which includes Guadeloupe, Montserrat, Antigua, Nevis, St. Kitts, Statia, St. Barts, Anguilla, and St. Martin as it proceeds north. More so than the others, Dominica's precipitous slopes and incised valleys continue below the sea, creating an underwater landscape with towering pinnacles and steep drop-offs that hold as great a profusion of life as the rain forests on the mountain slopes: hundreds of species of sponges and corals, moray eels poking out from rock hidey-holes, seahorses floating under ledges, arrow crabs with legs no thicker than a needle, and the rarely seen, comic-looking frogfish. We spend one day diving, and then another, flying weightlessly between the mountains that extend beneath us into infinite blue. One dive site is called "Abyme" in Creole: the Abyss.

By the time *Receta* reaches Portsmouth, at the north end of the island, it's Saturday again, hooray, another market day. We dinghy into the beach without breakfast—we're out of bread, of course—so I'm hoping we'll be greeted by the smell of baking. Instead, we're greeted by the smell of frying fat. "I can't believe I'm eating this, and so early in the morning," I tell Steve, my mouth full of greasy, crispy, hot-peppery fried fish cake and fried (of course) bake.

"Yeah, wonderful, isn't it?"

This market meanders through the streets of town: People set out whatever they have for sale on groundcloths or tables at the roadside—a pile of grapefruit on one cloth, some wedges of West Indian pumpkin on the next. Although the market covers more territory than the one in Roseau, it's much smaller, much more of a local affair, like a friendly neighborhood street sale. The lady at one table, from whom I'm buying a cabbage, doesn't have any change. She points Steve toward another vendor, who not only breaks the small bill, but gives him a bouquet of parsley, on the house. Not to be outdone, the cabbage lady then insists I take along two sweet potatoes and a shaggy brown rooty thing free.

I don't have a clue what the shaggy rooty thing is, with its coarse brown hair growing between a series of circles inscribed around its girth. I've seen them before, but the truth is I still can't tell one gnarled rooty brown thing from another.

I'm fairly certain it's not a yam or a sweet potato, two other gnarled rooty brown things. Although the two names are used interchangeably in North America, they are two entirely different vegetables in the West Indies. A cruising friend discovered this to his dismay after he asked for yams in the market and used them to make a traditional family recipe for a cruisers' potluck Thanksgiving dinner. From firsthand experience, I can report that tropical yams are a very odd mix with marshmallows. (One could argue, as Steve did privately afterward, that marshmallows are a bad mix with anything except a campfire and a stick.) If you want the tuber that's sweet and orange, you buy sweet potatoes; if you want the tuber that's white, bland, starchy, and fairly dry, you buy yams.

"What's this?" I hold up the rooty thing. "Tannia," the market lady says. "Just boil it, like a christophene."

A little farther down the street, a woman squats behind a tarp covered with more hairy rooty things. They look like large tannias. Maybe they *are* tannias, and she's just a better gardener. Even though I don't want to buy any—the tannia I have is enough to experiment with this week—I have to ask. "Dasheen," she tells me, the tuberous root of the plant whose heart-shaped leaves are callaloo. And she launches into a dissertation on its preparation. "Wear gloves," she says. In her strong Creole-laced speech, it's not exactly clear why, but it seems to have something to do with fibers. It's also not clear what I'll be doing with the spoon she tells me to use. I hope I'll be able to figure it out once I cut inside—because what is clear is that I *will* be buying a couple. Once I've got it cleaned and cut into pieces, she says, just boil it and serve it as part of provision—"with a little liquor before," she adds, with a wink at Steve.

"And you be sure and come back and tell me how you like dasheen."

A couple of nights later, I decide to cook the hairy rooty things to make my own provision to accompany citrus-marinated chicken. Before I tackle the dasheen, I pull on a pair of our disposable latex gloves. But it seems perfectly inoffensive, and I can't figure out why I'm wearing protective clothing and wielding a spoon. My cookbooks are no help, though the one Steve bought me for Christmas offers the following: Vegetables that grow below ground should be cooked with the lid on; those that grow above, with the lid off. I cut the dasheen, the two sweet potatoes, the tannia, and a big green plantain into pieces, and—majority rules—boil them all, lid on, until they're soft.

The citrus chicken, done in the oven, is excellent, the sweet potatoes are good, the plantain is rubbery, and the dasheen, to put it charitably, is an acquired taste. The tannia is completely inedible. Clearly, more study with the market ladies is called for.

Sail a scant 30 miles and be catapulted into another culture. The effects of geographic proximity are overridden in the West Indies by the effects of history: the results of the power struggles between European nations. And nowhere is this clearer than in the contrast between Dominica and its neighbors to the north and south, Guadeloupe and Martinique.

The "discovery" of Dominica didn't particularly excite Columbus, and Spain never showed much interest in settling the island—no doubt deterred by Chris's crumpled paper and the understandably less-than-welcoming attitude of the fierce Caribs who already lived there. French settlers eventually arrived in the early eighteenth century and imported slaves from Africa to run their sugar plantations. During a series of spats in the eighteenth and early nineteenth centuries, the island passed back and forth between the French and British, until 1805, when French warships made their last attempt to enter Roseau's harbor—disguising themselves as British by flying the Union Jack—and were defeated once and for all. Dominica remained British until it was granted independence in 1978.

Martinique and Guadeloupe were sighted by Columbus on the same voyage that he sighted Dominica, but these held no interest to the Spanish either. As with Dominica, the French subsequently moved in—but here they remained in control, despite takeover attempts (very brief) by the British. Both are still part of France, officially classed as French overseas *départements*. And this is obvious: They look, sound, feel, and taste different than their mutual neighbor, Dominica.

Dominica's Creole roots lie right on the surface—you just have to listen: English is the official language, but it's spoken with a strong overlay of Creole patois. It feels like a small, friendly, rural, third-world island. Its neighbors feel modern, prosperous, developed, upmarket—and oh-so-very French. There's a Creole flavor, but it's got a sleek, sometimes sophisticated, pure French overlay. As one of our guidebooks succinctly puts it, "Often you will feel more like you're in some part of continental France than in the Caribbean." You can buy *rhum* from the local distilleries, and red wine imported from France, both at equally modest prices. You can get lamb colombo—curry made with the fragrant local *poudre de colombo* (curry powder)—and fragrant Mediterranean-style spit-roasted legs of lamb studded with cloves of garlic. You can get *accras*—the deep-fried saltfish fritters that are close cousins to Dingis's saltfish cakes—and flaky, buttery croissants; pencil-thin Creole sausages, and French peppercorn pâtés. The currency is the French franc (until the arrival of the Euro), the roads are wonderful, everyone speaks French (and only French), and the attitude is decidedly Gallic.

"*Bonjour*," I say brightly, as I thump down between a couple of families fishing off a marina dock at the bottom of Guadeloupe. The fisherpeople ignore me. We have just arrived, and this is the tie-up dock, but since no one had made any movement to take a line from us as *Receta* approached, I jumped ashore, being careful not to land on any of the squid (their bait) strewn on the dock. My accent is atrocious, granted—I don't speak more than a few words of French—but I have, quite clearly and cheerfully, said good day. Nothing. No response. The Dominicans and the Grenadians would have been appalled.

At the local *boulangerie* the next morning, I ask for "*deux baguettes, s'il vous plaît.*" My pronunciation hasn't improved overnight, but I've said the words clearly. The woman behind the counter shrugs. I repeat my order. She reluctantly puts one baguette in a bag and hands it to me. This routine repeats itself, with small variations, throughout our week-long stay. On the days I ask for "*une baguette*," I am given two. I can almost hear the Dominican market ladies *tsk-tsk*ing. (They had been sympathetic, by the way—although somewhat mystified—about my report of my inedible tannia. Nothing wrong with my cooking methods, they assured me, though one of them suggested I try frying the tannia after boiling it. She was *sure* I'd like it that way.)

Thirty miles apart, night and *jour*.

The sky is black velvet, with white stars appliquéd on top. I'm convinced I can reach up from *Receta*'s cockpit and pluck one off.

We're sailing from Guadeloupe to St. Kitts—sizzling through the water, leaving diamonds of bioluminescence glittering in our wake. The night is perfection: the wind exactly where it should be, strong and steady; the ocean kicked up just enough for *Receta* to show her thoroughbred lineage as she slices through the waves. A curry-colored three-quarter moon rises just before midnight, while I'm on watch, and sits directly above the mountain that defines the ghostly silhouette of Montserrat.

Ah, Montserrat, "feeling hot, hot, hot/down deh in your belly," as Trini calypsonian David Rudder sings in his popular lament for the island. The Soufrière Hills volcano, at its south end, had roared to life in 1995 after 16,000 years of dormancy, and since then has continued off and on to be active—an innocuous word for the sporadic eruptions that spew violent ash clouds up to 40,000 feet into the sky, pelt the island with red-hot boulders, and vomit streams of rock and ash down the mountain's flanks, across the landscape, and into the sea. The bottom half of the island—including its capital, Plymouth—is buried under tons of gray ash, knee-deep in places, and has been evacuated. This is painfully obvious from my vantage point in *Receta*'s cockpit about 5 miles off the middle of Montserrat's west coast: The only lights that wink from the island tonight are clustered tightly together in a tiny corner at the north tip. The rest of the island is blanketed in utter darkness—abandoned, off-limits. More than half Montserrat's population has left for good, dispersed across the Caribbean and even as far as England.

The volcano is unmistakable, even when it's sleeping peacefully, as it appears to be tonight, shrouded in gentle clouds. It's by far the tallest peak on the island, built up by the stuff periodically regurgitated from the earth's belly. Soufrière Hills is the only active volcano in the Caribbean—if you discount Kick 'em Jenny, which is underwater, about 525 feet below the surface. Jenny is right on the direct sailing route between Carriacou and Grenada. But Jenny hasn't kicked since the late eighties—and even then it was a restrained little dance step; the last eruption that made it above the surface was in 1974. We figured the odds were in our favor, and we had sailed almost over the top of it on our way to Grenada and back north again.

The odds are a little different with Soufrière Hills. It's *actively* active; it can get cranky *any* time. Volcano alerts are given daily by the Montserrat Volcano Observatory, ranging from green (volcano is quiet), through yellow, to orange (eruption possible within 24 hours), to red, which means an eruption may begin without further warning—or is already in progress. Boats are advised to stay 10 miles clear of the leeward side of the island during an orange or red alert, as the hot smoke and ash can carry for miles on the prevailing trades.

Which is why Steve spent the afternoon trying to call Montserrat. A phone book proved as elusive on Guadeloupe as someone who spoke English. Steve's French is serviceable, but rustic, and not up to the subtleties of climbing over stone walls. The French-speaking operators seemed to feel the number for using our AT&T long-distance calling card from Guadeloupe was a national secret to be protected at all costs, and that revealing any phone number on Montserrat—let alone one for the Volcano Observatory—amounted to an act of espionage. "It would have been easier if I'd tried to yell from one island to the other," he reported, now swearing fluently *en français*. Eventually, he pried the numbers out of someone—only to find that the phone rang endlessly at the other end. Unfortunately, we didn't know whether this meant everyone had fled because the volcano was raging or simply gone to the beach because it wasn't.

The bigger the berth we give Montserrat, the more miles we add to our trip, and the more time we spend at sea. We decide to hedge our bets, and plot a course that will keep us a good 5 miles off the southern end of the island, a little less as we move up the coast.

I know it's about 11:20 when the smell hits me, because I have just returned to the cockpit after noting the time and a course change in our log. We have just reached a waypoint exactly 5 miles offshore near the middle of the island, and I have altered our course to point us at St. Kitts. A powerful smell of rotten eggs. *Very* rotten eggs. *Oh, Christ, it's the head.* Occasionally, stuff back-washes out of the lines and into the toilet bowl, leaving an unpleasant aroma to waft through the boat. *Must be really serious backwash.* With the boat riding on autopilot, I unclip my safety harness and go below again, hoping to solve the problem with some vigorous flushing. But the horrid smell isn't coming from the head and, in fact, is barely noticeable in the cabin.

Back in the cockpit, my brain translates "rotten eggs" into "sulphur," a smell I've experienced at hot springs that bubble to the surface from deep inside the earth. The smell must be the volcano burping.

At 11:30, the appointed time for a watch change, I wake Steve. When he comes up on deck, I point out the now much-dissipated odor, then go below to sleep.

"Ann, *Ann—COME BACK UP HERE.*" Steve yells me awake after what the clock above my head says has been only five minutes, and I climb into the cockpit once again. Steve points behind the boat. An iron-gray column of smoke stretches from the top of the volcano to the bottom of the rising moon and then obscures it. As we watch, the column flattens out into an island-sized anvil, then drifts south, blotting out the horizon and the lights of Guadeloupe, completely obliterating the path we've just sailed. The air again tastes strongly of sulphur—and ash.

Two days later, we learn via reports relayed on the radio nets that a "pyroclastic event" had taken place, according to the volcanologists at the island's observatory. In unscientific terms, this means an eruption: hot gases, rock fragments, pumice, and ash shot from the dome at speeds up to 100 miles per hour. This "pyroclastic event" blasted an ash cloud 15,000 feet into the sky, covering the decks of boats downwind of it in hot ash and turning their sails to Swiss cheese.

Sometimes God protects the ignorant, even while giving them a good reminder of exactly how ignorant they are: Safe by maybe an hour, *Receta* was far enough toward the north end of the island to escape damage when, as David Rudder sings, "the mountain beast has come to feast and pain is on the way / lighting up the nighttime sky and flaming up the day."

So many of the islands we've stopped at have looked to us like paradise. Sure, we know there are social problems and poverty, that one hit from a hurricane can wipe out a fragile economy based almost entirely on tourism and agriculture. But it's all too easy for visitors like us—and even more so for casual tourists—to ignore the other side of paradise.

Every once in a while, though, it walks right up to you—shy and giggling and maybe ten years old and wearing a pretty pink dress—and smacks you in the face. And you can no longer pretend it doesn't exist.

"This is Valencia," says Sharon, as she and her partner, Gong, climb aboard *Receta*, which is tied to a marina dock in Basseterre, the capital of St. Kitts. You need a compelling reason to tie up here—ours is that we've just dropped off a departing set of guests—because the marina has the ambience of a construction site. Hot, dust-covered, and treeless, it (along with the rest of St. Kitts) is still rebuilding from the destruction of Hurricane

Georges. A solitary perfect cube of crushed metal sits like a piece of postmodern sculpture on the otherwise barren expanse of land in front of *Receta*. A few months ago it was a car, until it was reshaped by the mudslide that followed Georges's torrential rains. It wasn't the only such cube, but the mudslide, which filled buildings on the waterfront to the height of their first-floor ceilings, bulldozed others all the way into the sea. Just offshore, barges and tugs chug noisily, working to rebuild tourism: Georges also demolished the cruise-ship dock, scarcely a year old.

"Hello, Valencia. What a beautiful name you have. Would you like a glass of cold juice?" The skinny girl nods timidly, but doesn't speak; in fact, she seems embarrassed to talk, holding her hand up to her mouth and whispering to Gong behind it. I assume she's either painfully shy or has a speech defect. I also assume she is Sharon and Gong's daughter.

We had met Gong a week or so ago, when we were anchored, with Jo and Mike, our guests, in pretty Ballast Bay. St. Kitts is shaped like a chicken leg, and Ballast Bay is at the bottom of the leg where it flares out in a bony knob. In the center of the knob is a salt pond, with a trail around it and good bird-watching potential. Ballast Bay itself, a jumble of rocks, is good lobstering territory. (A few days ago, Steve had speared a monster there that was big enough—one lobster—to feed all four of us. Lavishly.) We had headed off for a late-afternoon hike, and though we didn't see much in the way of birdlife, we did spot several green vervet monkeys in the trees and a mongoose crossing the road. Both are introduced species that took to life on St. Kitts exceedingly well; the first green vervet monkeys arrived as the pets of an English plantation owner, while the mongoose was introduced to kill the rats that were eating the sugar cane. Unfortunately, it turned out the mongooses weren't particularly interested in rats: They eat during the day, and the rats come out at night. They *love* chickens, though, and nice fresh eggs. Which is why Kittitians now *hate* the mongoose, a taximan told us one day, as he swerved to run over the one that was crossing the road in front of his car. (He missed.) The monkeys, on the other hand, are tolerated—even encouraged, with handouts of fruit.

On the far side of the salt pond, an inconspicuous sign pointed down a track that led off the main road. "Gong on the Beach" is all it said, with an amateurish painting of a black-robed, dreadlocked man striking a large gong with a mallet.

After a few minutes' walk, the vegetation thinned and the track opened up on a deserted windswept beach that stretched ahead as far as we could see: Nothing but sand and seagrass and one sweet little, fresh-looking hexagonal bar plunked in the middle, the man behind it smiling an invitation to cold Carib. "Mike and I didn't bring any money," Jo said with dismay as we approached. "Me neither," said Steve, who should have known better. Lucky this group has me. Since stumbling penniless on MacDuff's a year ago, I *never* leave *Receta* with empty pockets. I pulled out $20 EC and bought us each a beer.

And that's how we get to meet the loquacious, charming Gong, purveyor of beer and burgers on Sand Banks Beach. He's just erected his tiny gazebo-like structure, after the hurricane took the old one completely away. In exchange, Georges left behind mile-long cornrows of seaweed, driftwood, and ocean debris. But no problem, mon: Gong just uses it to fuel the bonfire at his regular full-moon beach parties. On our next visit, we meet Sharon, who moved to St. Kitts from Vancouver, and now, on *Receta*, we meet shy young Valencia.

She's followed me into the cabin, where I am getting snacks and drinks. Hoping to make her feel a bit more at ease, I introduce her to Curious George, my stuffed monkey. George has been with me since childhood and has traveled on *Receta* every mile of the trip—my loyal confidant when the going gets rough.

In a corner of the cabin, Valencia begins to carry on a

full-fledged, full-volume, completely comprehensible conversation with George. "Do you think Valencia pretty, George?" she asks him, dancing him on his feet. "Do you like Valencia's dress?" I know George will tell her exactly what she wants to hear, so I leave the two of them and retreat to the cockpit, where I tell Sharon that Valencia is starting to feel at home. "Poor kid," she says.

"She lives in a children's home on the outskirts of Basseterre. When she was a few years old, her mother sold her to a woman on St. Vincent for a couple hundred dollars, and when that woman no longer wanted her, she ended up back on St. Kitts, at the children's home." Though she looks only nine or ten, this endearing kid is fourteen, and carrying enough emotional baggage for a roomful of adults. Four or five years ago, Sharon took her under wing, and though she still lives in the home, she spends weekends, and other times as well, with Gong and Sharon. "She's much, *much* better now than when we first met her."

Mothers who can't afford to keep their kids. Kids who can't afford to go to school. We'd heard stories of it on Grenada, too, and there, wanting to give something back to the island that captured our hearts, we made a tiny step toward getting involved.

Newlo—the New Life Organisation—overlooks the ocean halfway up Grenada's leeward coast and provides a "second chance at seventeen" for disadvantaged kids who never made it further than primary school. They learn a vocational skill and what Newlo calls "life skills"—high among them, self-esteem. Those without any other option can live right at the school. It's a warren of rickety stairways and cramped rooms that reminds me of the shoe inhabited by the old woman in the nursery rhyme. A bit of concrete wall rises tentatively in one spot, under construction by kids in the masonry program; in another area, the guts spill out of ancient fridges, in the midst of repair by the kids learning refrigeration. Up another twisting stairway, we're shown an office, straight out of the sixties, with young men and women concentrating hard at manual typewriters: the office skills program. "We're trying to get computers," Ann David-Antoine, the director, tells us, "but right now the duties are too high to bring them into the country."

Newlo gives us a warm feeling. In the Dove Café, students in "hospitality arts" get to practice on real customers at lunchtime one day a week. They take what they're doing seriously—*very* seriously—and we're served with gravity and impeccable manners, one hand behind the back and ladies first, no matter what. The menu is carefully handwritten and photocopied on colored paper: a choice of golden-apple juice or pineapple juice; pumpkin soup or chicken soup; stew fish or stew chicken. Students do all the cooking—from the warm yeast rolls that arrive first to the Jell-O and pound cake for dessert—under supervision of their instructors. The food is simple, just homestyle cooking, but with a few stretch-their-wings flourishes: The steamed carrot batons that accompany my stew fish are carefully arranged in a hollowed-out round of cucumber. There's an incentive to do well here: A lucky few will be placed in an internship on a cruise ship—an unimaginable opportunity for these kids.

"In three weeks I have done so many things I never did in primary school—talk about myself, stand up in front of the class and talk," one young trainee told the director.

"Miss, look at me. I okay now," said another.

"Miss" writes us a few weeks later with an update. She'd used the check we'd left behind to buy one promising student a set of his own carpentry tools, a second, his own tools for electronics repair. A third young man, she tells us, she'd found hanging around the school long after class was over. He simply had no money for bus fare to return home at night, so she made him a resident at Newlo "and he is making a valiant effort to use wisely the opportunity."

Months later, we hear from her again. All three young men have completed their programs, but she seems particularly pleased to tell us about the third: He is in the middle of on-the-job training for full-time employment with the Court of Grenada. Miss, look at him now.

Accras (Saltfish Fritters)

Accras (or *acrats*) *de morue* are saltfish fritters—the French island version of Dingis's saltfish cakes. (*Morue* is French for salted cod.) Serve them as an appetizer or a snack.

SERVES 4

½ pound salt cod or other saltfish, preferably boneless
1 lime
1 small onion, grated
1 clove garlic, grated
¼–½ hot pepper, seeded and finely minced
1 seasoning pepper or ½ green bell pepper, finely chopped
1 stalk celery, finely chopped
2 green onions, finely chopped
1 tablespoon chopped fresh thyme or 1 teaspoon dried thyme
Freshly ground black pepper
1 cup flour
1 teaspoon baking powder
½ cup water (approx.)
Vegetable oil for deep frying

1. The night before you want to serve the fritters, put the fish in cold water to soak. Change water 4 or 5 times, squeezing half the lime into the water during each of the last two soakings.
2. Rinse fish, drain, and remove skin and bones if necessary. In a

large bowl, finely shred the fish. (See Tips, below.) Add the onion, garlic, peppers, celery, green onions, thyme, and black pepper, and mix well.

3. Combine flour and baking powder and add to fish mixture. Stir thoroughly. Slowly add enough water to make a thick paste.

4. Heat oil to 350°F in a deep fryer or pot. Drop fish mixture by tablespoons into hot oil and fry until golden on both sides.

5. Drain on paper towels and serve hot with hot pepper sauce.

Tips:

- Some saltfish may not shred easily. If that's the case, chop it finely in a food processor or by hand with a knife. Alternatively, put it in boiling water, turn off the heat, and allow it to cool in the liquid. It should then flake easily. Whichever method you use, be sure to "chip it up fine," as Dingis says.

- Before proceeding with step 2, try a little piece of the soaked fish. If it is still too salty for your taste, soak it again in fresh water.

Curried Chicken in Coconut Milk
with Island Vegetables

This dish is popular on Guadeloupe and Martinique, where cooks prepare it with their own freshly made curry powder, *poudre de colombo*. Any good-quality curry powder can be substituted.

As they do with fish and lambi, island cooks "wash" their chicken with lime—squeeze a lime over it and rub it with the pith—to freshen it before cooking.

Serve the curry with rice and Steve's Favorite Plantains (see page 186).

SERVES 6

2 limes
4 pounds bone-in chicken pieces
3–4 tablespoons vegetable oil
1 large onion, finely chopped
2 cloves garlic, finely chopped
½–1 fresh hot pepper, seeded and finely chopped (or to taste)
2 tablespoons curry powder
1 tablespoon chopped fresh thyme or 1 teaspoon dried thyme
2 tomatoes, chopped
1 christophene, peeled and cubed
1 large Japanese eggplant, cubed
½ pound West Indian pumpkin, or butternut or Hubbard squash, peeled and cubed
1 cup coconut milk
Salt and freshly ground black pepper
1 tablespoon rum

1. Halve one of the limes. Squeeze the juice over the chicken pieces, rubbing it in with the cut lime.

2. Heat 3 tablespoons of the oil in a large heavy pot. Pat the chicken dry with paper towels. Over medium-high heat, brown the chicken pieces in batches until golden on all sides, adding more oil as necessary. Remove chicken and set aside.

3. In the same pot, gently sauté the onion, garlic, and hot pepper until soft and golden, about 5 minutes. Add curry powder and thyme, and continue to cook for about a minute, stirring constantly.

4. Add the vegetables and stir until they are coated with the curry mixture. Add coconut milk, return chicken pieces to pot, season with salt and pepper, and stir. Bring to a boil, reduce heat, cover, and simmer for about 30 minutes, until the vegetables are tender and the chicken is cooked, stirring occasionally.

5. Stir in the juice from half the remaining lime and the rum. Taste and adjust flavor with additional lime juice, salt, and pepper.

Tip:

• Add and subtract vegetables depending on what's available. Other possibilities include unripe papaya, zucchini, sweet potatoes, white Caribbean yams, or white potatoes.

Beautiful Babe Spit

Red and black—Wahoo attack.
Yellow and green—Dolphin fishing machine.
    Bahamian Chris Lloyd's rhyme about which color
lure to use when trolling offshore for fish; from
On And Off The Beaten Path: The Central & Southern
                                        Bahamas Guide by Stephen J. Pavlidis, 1997

"COME ON, SPIT. A *BIG* GOB. None of this dainty stuff."
Steve is dangling a large lime-green fishing lure in
front of my nose as *Receta* serenely sails along on
autopilot. Knowing there's no sense protesting, I work up a
mouthful and, *pitooey*, deliver enough saliva onto the lure to do
a baseball pitcher proud. Satisfied, Steve runs the fishing line out
behind the boat, then offers up another lure. I hark it up and spit
again.

I blame Ed, the Minister of Rum—at least indirectly—for this
unusual fishing practice, just as I blame him for the boat's still-
growing collection of spirits.

"Come over for a 'ti punch at sundown," Ed said one day at
Hog Island. "I want you to meet Cleo. He's in publishing, too.
You'll like him."

Across Ed's cockpit that evening sat a courtly man with the
look of a longtime sailor. Lithe, attentive, with laughing eyes—a
real ladies' man, my mother would have said—white-haired and

well-read. And extremely hard of hearing. With Lisa Soon Come as his only crew, he sails each year between the Virgin Islands and Trinidad, he told us, spending much of hurricane season in Grenada and much of the rest of the time in Culebra, a scrubby U.S.-owned island off the coast of Puerto Rico. Cleo is in his early seventies, Lisa Soon Come is scarcely two. She's a placid tabby, whose name captures the jus'-now essence of both cats and West Indian life and conversation.

Capturing stuff in words is what Cleo is about. A writer, poet, and retired professor of modern languages, he's also the publisher, editor, and everything else of *The Melibea Review*, an occasional literary magazine that takes its name from the place it's produced, Cleo's boat, *Melibea*. Each *Review* is a photocopied-and-stapled (as well as online) collection of writing that relates to the Caribbean, some by cruisers, some by islanders he's found and encouraged, some his own.

Even though we hadn't yet read anything he'd written when we met him on Ed's boat, we quickly realized Cleo could sure *tell* a story. I had no doubt his tales were true—but the truth plotted and prodded to serve a writer's ends. Could a Grenadian land crab really jump a man and chop his balls off? Could it really be hypnotized by a flashlight to prevent such a fate? Did Cleo *really* drop his flashlight with a monstrous crab just inches from . . . ? Not a word of a lie, his manner implies, and who would doubt this erudite gentleman? Cleo was a raconteur of the first rank.

The conversation on Ed's boat meandered from island life to writing, to reading, to rum. The subject of saliva on fishing lures, oddly, never came up. Nor did it in the days that followed, as we got to know Cleo better.

Frankly, fishing (unlike lobstering) just wasn't that important at Hog Island. Steve occasionally dangled a line over the side late in the day for the fun of it, sometimes picking up a two-person snapper or grouper that he cleaned and I fried for dinner. And he sometimes went off with his fly rod in *Snack* toward the mangroves that edged the anchorage. That dinner never resulted from these excursions was beside the point: Steve loved the solitude and took pleasure in simply casting the line, watching huge tarpon roil the water and ignore his flies, and letting his mind wander wherever the breeze took it. He always returned happy, and empty-handed. With fresh, cheap fish at the market in St. George's a short bus ride away, any notion we had of devoting serious attention to catching our own had long since drifted out to sea on the tide.

Even when we started moving back up the island chain—and traveling offshore, where big fish live—we were pretty lackadaisical about putting our lines in the water. The problem was we still weren't exactly fish deprived. "Just listen for the conch horn blowing," we were told by islanders from Bequia to Dominica. "That means there's fish arriving at the market." In fact, we didn't even have to listen for the horn at Dominica's north end: When we saw the local ladies clustering in the shallow water around the brightly painted open boats, we knew the fish were in. With their long skirts hiked up, the women bent over the catch, pointing and prodding, before wading back onto dry sand, dinner in hand.

Carol and Jack on *Splashdance* have been putting even less effort into catching fish than we have. We'd been introduced to them at the Mighty Sparrow concert in Grenada and really got to know them in Trinidad. With interests as wide-ranging as ours, always-exuberant Carol and quieter but equally enthusiastic Jack became our sometimes-partners there for exploring and liming. Now after several months of going our separate ways, we've caught up with each other again in heavily developed, touristified St. Martin, the island with the split personality near the top of the Leeward chain. The northern part of St. Martin is French, a *département* of France, like Martinique and Guadeloupe; the southern part, Sint Maarten, is Dutch. No customs or immigration checkpoints divide the two halves, but a wall of difference lies between them. The Dutch capital, Philipsburg, where the cruise ships stop, is crowded with casinos; expensive high-end jewelry and designer stores sit cheek by jowl with crummy souvenir shops and places selling duty-free booze and smokes. The French side is, well, French: chic, fashionable, and sophisticated, with elegant little boutiques, wine stores, brasseries, and cafés.

Like Carol and Jack, we anchor on the Dutch side of St. Martin's protected lagoon, and eat and shop on the French side. Take it as an indication of the style of the French side that the supermarket in the heart of Marigot, the capital, is called the Gourmet Boutique. Food is flown in daily from France. The Gourmet Boutique has at least a dozen types of goat cheese; an array of *saucissons* and pâtés, stuffed with bits of wild mushrooms or truffles; delicate greens like frisée, white radishes, and young asparagus; even fish from the Mediterranean. Worse than the Gourmet Boutique is Le Goût du Vin, the wine store across the street. Steve is simply incapable of walking by its sandwich board—which advertises a daily special for $2.75 to $3.50 a bottle, imported duty-free from France—without nipping inside to try a sip and make a purchase.

When I return from a brief New Jersey visit with Mom and Dad, Steve picks me up in the dinghy from a dock near the airport. *Snack's* bottom appears to be covered with collapsed cardboard boxes, but it's dark, I'm tired, and I don't bother to ask. The next morning I discover two things have occurred in my four-day absence: First, Steve learned Le Goût du Vin delivers to the waterfront; and second, he has spent four days "renovating," turning a couple of corners of the boat into storage cupboards for the case of champagne and the five—*five!*—cases of wine he has acquired in my absence. "I cut open the old holding tank and put a door on it," he says proudly. It had been connected to the second toilet, which we had removed when we bought *Receta*. I look at him with horror. "Don't worry—it didn't look like it had been used much, and I scrubbed it out with bleach. It holds a full case."

Our credit cards, which had a light workout in Grenada and the islands that followed, are feeling bruised. If we don't get out of St. Martin soon, we will be broke—and fat. We drink *café au lait* and munch *pain au chocolat* under big umbrellas at waterfront cafés; sip red wine and eat escargots in profiterolles in elegant Antillean houses; devour mussels in white wine and *frites* at a streetside brasserie with the regulars (we *are* regulars); and, in our bathing suits, down cold beer, smoky grilled fish and chicken, and deep-fried *accras* at the beachfront barbecue shacks called lo-los. "The game plan is to bus to Marigot and go hiking from there," I write in my journal one day. "The reality is we bus to Marigot and have lunch."

Little wonder no one's been thinking a whole lot about fishing lines. Now, though, we're getting ready to leave St. Martin. Carol and I are sitting in our respective dinghies, waiting for Jack and Steve to return from doing the checkout formalities with Customs and Immigration.

"We need a tournament," says Carol. "*That* will give us the incentive to start fishing."

I've been in the Caribbean for more than a year now, I've learned how to lime, and I've fully integrated "jus' now" into my vocabulary and lifestyle. But I haven't entirely lost my once finely honed competitive edge.

By the time Jack and Steve return, we've worked out the details. "Here's the scoring," Carol tells them, "five points for an edible fish landed, four points for an inedible fish landed, and three points for one that gets away before you land it. Winner gets a case of Presidente." Both boats are planning to again spend a few days in the land of Presidente on the way north.

Unfortunately, Carol and I have little experience with fishing tournaments—none, actually—so the Rules Committee neglects to mention size of fish: It's five points whether you land a four-foot tuna or a four-inch snapper.

"All on the honor system," I add. The whole point, after all, is to *eat* the proof as soon as possible. The tournament will last however long it takes both boats to reach Beaufort, North Carolina, Carol and Jack's home port, which is at least three months away. Since *Splashdance* is headed from St. Martin to the U.S. Virgin Islands and *Receta* is headed to the British Virgins, we'll keep track of tournament action via SSB.

We've barely got the anchor on deck that afternoon when Steve runs out the fishing lines. (He has a fairly strong competitive streak himself.) On one side of the boat, a length of plastic pipe hose-clamped to the rail holds a long-past-its-prime rod and reel bought at a Florida flea market. On the other side, a "Cuban reel" lies on one of the cushions. This oversized plastic yo-yo with fishing line wound on it is about as cheap and cheerful as fishing tackle can get. There's no rod; to bring in the line, you just wind it by hand back on the yo-yo.

Scarcely half an hour after we're out of the harbor, the radio crackles. "*Receta, Receta; Splashdance.*" Damn. They've caught a small tuna. A little later, they call again: another small tuna. They're already up ten points. Carol attempts to console us. "Don't worry—we'll freeze some and save it to eat with you." Steve isn't consoled. Dinner is now beside the point; the ego of a lifelong fisherman is at stake.

By the time the two boats share an anchorage (and the tuna) a week later at Watermelon Cay, off St. John in the U.S. Virgins, the score is thirteen to zip: *Splashdance* also hooked one that mercifully (from our point of view as well as the fish's) got away. Meanwhile, we hadn't had a strike.

"It's become an onboard joke," Steve e-mails a friend. "I let out the fishing lines and Ann checks the freezer for a dinner selection."

By the time we reach the Spanish Virgin Islands, and Culebra, where Cleo is by now anchored, Steve has tried every lure in his Tupperware box. He's switched squid skirts so frequently you'd think it was a fashion show. These brightly colored, soft, plastic, fringed thingies fit over hooks like grass skirts on hula dancers and are meant to mimic swimming squid. Chartreuse, hot pink, fluorescent green, sparkly yellow, silvery blue—none of them makes a difference. In fact, *nothing* makes a difference. He varies the length of the lines behind the boat. He varies our speed (though just a little: much as I like to win, I draw the line at slowing down when we're on a passage). No fish.

"What am I doing wrong?" he laments at dinner on *Receta* one night. Cleo is at the table, and so too is another set of guests from home, Sari and Pete. Steve's question hangs unanswered in the warm night air, but Cleo, a gleam in his eye, launches into a story about a young Grenadian girl he once took fishing. "It was her first time," he says, "so I explained the secret of successful fishing to her. If a pretty lady spits on the lure before it goes into the water, I told her, she will almost certainly catch a fish."

The girl would have been completely charmed by Cleo, I know, the same way that Sari and I, and every other female who's been introduced to him in my presence, have been completely charmed by him. She wouldn't have been able to resist his intimation of her beauty. The young lady spit, of course. And to her amazement, a fish was caught.

Steve's eyes light up in the shadows, and I know there will be no peace onboard *Receta* tomorrow until the lures have been anointed.

* * *

We thread our way into open ocean through the coral reefs that surround Culebra for the 20-mile run to Punta Arenas, Vieques, another one of the Spanish Virgin Islands that are part of Puerto Rico.

"Spit," says Steve.

"This is ridiculous."

"Does the spit of two pretty ladies work better than one?" Sari asks.

"Okay, both of you spit."

Zinnnnggggggggg. A scant fifteen minutes later, we're so surprised to hear the line sizzling off the reel that it takes a few seconds for anyone to respond. Steve grabs the rod.

Ten minutes, twenty minutes, thirty minutes. The fish clearly has the upper hand. Steve gives us a play-by-play as the fight continues. "*Big* tug," he reports at one point, his arms straining against the pressure. Then, suddenly, the fish is easier to reel in.

I dig out the tools we've had ready for weeks, just in case: gaff, bucket, garbage bags, and rum. The rum isn't for celebrating; cheap alcohol poured into the gills is a cruiser's trick for subduing a large fish before bringing it into the cockpit. "Carol emptied the better part of a bottle into our first tuna," Jack had told us while we ate five points' worth of fish at Watermelon Cay. "But in the excitement she used the first bottle she grabbed. Unfortunately, it was my Tanqueray." His *ferociously expensive, imported, hard to find Tanqueray*, he might have added.

Pete stands ready with the gaff as Steve brings the fish alongside. The head emerges. A big blackfin tuna . . . well, *part* of a big blackfin tuna. No need for the rum: That big tug a few minutes ago was another fish biting off three-quarters of the tuna for a snack. The cut is surgically, scarily clean, which makes the thief most likely a blue marlin, we learn later. The part he's left us is 19 inches around and 20 inches long.

It becomes the dinner that Steve rates the best onboard meal ever. Rubbed with a little olive oil and grilled rare, it is certainly gorgeous, but the circumstances—the first big fish we've caught ourselves—push it totally over the top. "The Beautiful Babe Spit did it," Steve crows between mouthfuls. And the now-proven-beyond-a-doubt fish attractant has a name.

Next day, Sari and I liberally gob the lures on both lines with scarcely a protest. Why quibble with being called a Beautiful Babe? The result is a 3½-foot great barracuda, not a wise fish to eat. (Large barracuda can carry ciguatera toxin, which causes a dangerous form of food poisoning.) We release it, but no matter: We have plenty of grilled tuna left. That night, I serve it cold, with lemon-dill mayo. One wonders how the stuff in cans can have so little flavor.

The next morning, more gobs. That evening, we have a choice: bonito or Spanish mackerel, both great eating, both large enough to serve four. As we eat baked mackerel fillets topped with olive oil, bread crumbs, and Parmesan, I suggest a moratorium on fishing the next day: The steaks and chicken Sari and Pete had brought vacuum-packed from Canada need to be eaten. No one will hear of it, and it's business as usual the next day: Sari spits, I spit.

Luckily, we only hook one.

"Oh my God, you mean it really *works*?" This, from Cleo, weeks later. We had sent him a postcard with a full accounting, which reached him while his son Will was visiting. And now he has sent us a full account of their conversation:

"Why'd you ever," Will said, laughing, "mention that old superstition, anyway?"

"Not a superstition. It's a fetish."

"Whatever. Why'd you tell them?"

"I don't know. A boat in the water, two beautiful babes. They wanted to catch fish. Noblesse oblige . . ."

"You know, Dad, you really have got to shape up. You're the one always saying speak nothing but the truth. Steve"—Will's brother—"and I got one hell of a dose of that when we were growing up. Now here you are telling women to spit on fishing lures. You need to be more careful with people."

"Yeah, sure. But just look at that postcard. I never really believed it, but a little female spit *does* bring in fish. Has to do with pheromones or something."

"Pheromones my ass."

"What?"

"Pheromones are species specific. You should know that."

"I couldn't argue the point any further," Cleo concludes. "Will has a degree in chemistry."

Chemistry be damned. The stuff *works*. Just ask the Queen of Expectoration or the Queen of Salivation. That's what Cleo now calls Sari and me.

Grilled Tuna, Three Ways

The only trick to this dish is to grill the tuna quickly over high heat, so it's seared outside and rare within.

    4 6–8-ounce tuna steaks
    2 tablespoons fresh lime juice
    2 tablespoons olive oil
    1 tablespoon dark rum
    Salt and freshly ground black pepper

1. Combine marinade ingredients and rub into both sides of tuna. Cover and let tuna sit about 10 minutes at room temperature.
2. Meanwhile, preheat barbecue.
3. Grill tuna over high heat about 2 minutes per side for rare, brushing occasionally with remaining marinade. Serve hot or cold one of the following ways.

- Grilled Tuna with Wasabi: Mix 2 tablespoons wasabi powder (Japanese green horseradish powder) with enough water to form a paste and allow to stand 5 minutes for flavor to develop.
- Grilled Tuna with Mango Salsa (see page 129-130).
- Chilled Tuna with Lemon-Dill or Lime-Cilantro Mayonnaise: Combine ½ cup mayonnaise with 1 tablespoon freshly squeezed lemon juice and 1 tablespoon finely chopped fresh dill; or 1 tablespoon freshly squeezed lime juice and 1 tablespoon finely chopped cilantro. Refrigerate briefly to allow flavors to blend.

The Passage from Hell

Lure-making on a boat in the middle of nowhere demands deep concentration. It's best accomplished by lounging in the sun for a couple of hours and sipping a beer or two.

E-mail from Steve to Todd and Belinda, May 1999

*B*Y THE TIME WE NEXT MEET UP with *Splashdance*, as planned, in Boquerón at the southwest corner of Puerto Rico, Beautiful Babe Spit has rocketed *Receta* into first place in the tournament. Since Sari and Pete have flown home, it has also been proved that the spit of one Beautiful Babe works as well as the spit of two.

Boquerón is the usual leaping-off spot from Puerto Rico back across the Mona Passage to the Dominican Republic, and *Receta* and *Splashdance* plan to cross together. The four of us work out the timing and the course over dinner on *Receta*: cero baked with lime and onion. Steve had landed the 17-inch mackerel-like fish (one of our smaller catches) on the day's sail from Ensenada, with help from my salivary glands, of course. If the forecast holds, we'll spend one more day in Boquerón, then leave at one the following afternoon. At a projected speed of 5 to 6 knots, we should arrive in Luperón two days later—in the morning, when the sun is high enough to give us the good visibility we'll need for the eye-of-the-needle passage between the reefs. It's been a full year since we were in Luperón, but its harbor entrance still holds first place in my memory for being the trickiest of the entire trip—the *only* spot we had needed a guide boat to lead us in. I'm not looking forward to the repeat performance.

In fact, the entire 244-mile, two-night, one-and-a-half-day trip between the two islands still stands as my most-hated passage. I haven't forgotten the thunderstorms that "charge like bulls," or the "steep seas" and "spurious currents." I haven't forgotten the churning water or my twenty-four hours of sporadic vomiting. Going this way, though, is supposed to be comparatively easy— because the wind's at our back and the waves are largely in our favor. Piece of cake, other cruisers tell us. Even our fear-mongering guidebook calls it a cinch. None of them, however, makes the trip on the good ship *Receta*.

Only fifteen minutes later than planned, the hooks are up, the sails are raised, and we're on our way out of Boquerón Bay. The start of the trip is a cruiser's dream: steady breezes and good speed throughout the afternoon, and some fishing action just before sunset. As the line whistles off the reel, Steve grabs the rod, but is unable to make any headway toward bringing in whatever's on the other end. It's heavy, and it's fighting hard. Suddenly, the 80-pound test line snaps and the rod goes slack. Gone. Steve's pissed off, even more so when Jack radios from *Splashdance* behind us to say he'd seen the black shape of the fish surface "and it looked like you had hooked a whale."

By the time I start my watch at 10 P.M., Puerto Rico's regular evening lightning is already crackling in the distance. But it's far away and we're smoothly steaming along at almost 6 knots. Because the wind had lightened at dusk, we've turned on the engine for an assist, to keep our speed up and the boat on schedule.

A few minutes after midnight I hear a gentle *clunk*, followed by a momentary change in the hypnotic drone of the engine. I'd instantly drifted off to sleep on the settee after coming off watch, but any little variation in the regular pattern of boat sounds, under sail or power, is enough to snap either of us into instant wakefulness. "Did you hear that?" I call up to Steve, but he's already lowering the throttle and checking the gauges. He's heard it, too. "Everything's fine," he says reassuringly, and increases the speed again. Within seconds, the engine's overheat alarm screams its omen-of-very-bad-things warning.

Engine off, all hands on deck. I struggle back into my evening offshore attire—pants, jacket, life vest, safety harness, armband strobe light, mini pocket flashlight, shoes—and back into the cockpit, taking the wheel while Steve goes below to troubleshoot. But the problem isn't obvious, and it's hard to keep my mind from leaping ahead and my anxiety from turning into full-blown fear.

We're sailors at heart. Even me. More so than many cruisers we've met (who invariably seem to motorsail everywhere even when the wind doesn't require it), we *hate* to turn on the engine. Yet here we are, not in the least bit of danger, sailing without an engine—and not the least bit happy about it. The engine is like insurance: It's sure nice to know it's there when you need it. Which we will, soon. Without it, the reef-strewn entrance at Luperón will be more than just a little challenging. And assuming we make it in safely, how will we get Mr. Engine, Sir fixed? Luperón gets the nod as the spot least likely to offer spare parts, let alone a mechanic acquainted with the likes of our aged Westerbeke 50. One step at a time, I tell myself. First let's get *to* Luperón.

But getting to Luperón isn't going to be quick. We're making less than 4 knots under sail alone, and the wind is lessening and shifty. Without enough air in the sails to drive us, the Mona Passage chop and slop has started rolling the boat, making my stomach, which is already knotted up nicely thanks to the engine problem, even less happy. We radio *Splashdance* to alert Jack and

Carol to our problem. Jack immediately says they'll slow down to keep within VHF radio range. I'm relieved to know we won't be out here alone, but feel horribly guilty, knowing how frustrating it will be for them to prolong their own time on passage. "That's what buddy boats are for," Jack says, shrugging off my concern.

Still, my off-watches are not marked by anything like sound sleep. And take it as an indication of my anxiety level that nowhere—not in my journal, not in the ship's log, not in my memory—is there any indication that we ate during this passage.

As soon as it's light the next morning, we agree to switch to our big headsail—678 square feet of Dacron—to help us get a little more speed in the light air. This giant has lived in the cockpit locker since we left Toronto, never used and "taking up valuable space," as Steve has reminded me every time he's had to shove it out of the way. (It can barely be lifted by just one of us.) Now that we actually need it, I feel vindicated about insisting we bring it along, but I refrain from making comment.

Steve got even less sleep than I did last night, and wrestling the small sail down and the big sail up is hard work—especially while clipped onto a rolling foredeck with a safety harness, and with *Snack* tied upside down right in the middle of the working area. The maneuver takes more than forty minutes, and by the time he returns to the cockpit dragging the smaller sail in its bag, he's drenched in sweat. But we pick up a little speed, the boat's motion in the waves improves, and he disappears below to crash on the settee before tackling the engine again.

Meanwhile, I call *Splashdance* and give them a cheery-voiced morning update. "Do you mind if we go on ahead?" Jack asks. "Of course not, no, not a bit, really, no, of course not"—and in the daylight, riding along at a reasonable clip with the big sail pulling nicely, I almost mean it. Since they will soon be out of VHF radio range, we set up a schedule to talk on the long-range SSB.

We may be sailing faster, but we can't sail directly at Luperón (like most boats without a spinnaker, *Receta* doesn't sail well dead downwind), which means a series of long jibes: a succession of 5-mile zigs and zags adding many extra miles to the straight-line course. Then, to heap further trauma on my already traumatized self, on one of these jibes a shackle lets go at the back corner of the mainsail where it attaches to the boom. The sudden bang is bad enough, but it's followed by a loud *rrrrrrrrriiiip*, as a long tear appears along the foot of the sail. Great: Now we have to reef the sail past the tear or it will blow out entirely. Almost one-third less sail area. Just what we need.

After more time contorted over the now cool engine, Steve's still found nothing wrong. Oil, coolant, belts, pump, impeller— they all seem fine. The only thing he can't check is the business end of the shaft and the prop, and we're suspicious this is where the problem may lie, given the *clunk*. But checking it would mean diving under the boat—impossible since the wind and seas have been steadily increasing since dawn. When you don't want wind, you get it.

Those thunderstorms that "charge like bulls"? The first one rolls over us around eight that night, when Steve's on watch. Pounding rain, lightning all around, and us once again the tallest object in any direction (the *only* object in any direction, for that matter). At ten, his terse notation in the log is another "AWFUL." I don't even realize how bad "AWFUL" really is, because Steve has suggested I stay dry below and he'll stand a longer watch. I just know I can see him in the flashes as clearly as if the cockpit were lit by huge film-set lights. They come one after the other, classic forks of lightning, stabbing the water on all sides—so many and so frequent there's no longer darkness between flashes, so close and so bright he has to hide his eyes behind his hand and peer out between slits in his fingers. Only later do I learn that he could *hear* the sizzle as the forks crashed into the water around us, and that he was truly frightened, fearing we would be hit. Steve, whom I have never known in twenty years to be afraid.

Usually, squalls cross our path quickly: a few wild minutes and then peace. But these squalls are traveling in our direction and, like hitchhikers, we are picked up by their wind and carried along. The lightning stays with us.

Below, I'm carrying on a lively interior monologue. "Okay, name ten ways this could be worse," I say, trying to trick myself into believing it's really not so bad. But I bog down after number 1, "We could be sinking."

By midnight, the fireworks are finally over and I'm back on watch. As often happens post-squall, there is zero wind. Zip. *Nada*. Absolutely nothing. We have virtually no forward motion—we just sit there, slatting around, rolling with the big waves that refuse to depart with the wind. The boom, with the flogging mainsail, is first on one side of the boat, then crashes over to the other; back and forth, with all the attendant banging, popping, and squeaking. For me, sitting stock-still in the middle of the ocean, knowing we have no engine to turn on to move us along, is worse than the squall. I am beside myself. I fiddle endlessly with the sails, but I can't make the boat move. I twiddle endlessly with my hair—the one nervous habit from back home that I haven't been able to break entirely in my new relaxed state; it still returns in times of stress. I want to scream. I could *walk* to Luperón faster than this. I resist as long as possible, but finally wake Steve, get him to reassure me that there is nothing I—or he—can do, and then let him go back to sleep.

"I'm going over the side to take a look," he announces when it's still very calm the next morning. Because of the current, our speed is a full knot even with the sails furled, so he ties himself to the boat with a long line, and we run another floating line with a life-ring on the end out behind the boat. It wouldn't do to lose him mid-ocean.

He's only underneath for a few seconds. As he surfaces, he spits out his snorkel and the news: "A fishing net's wrapped on our prop." Bingo! I hand him his dive knife and run yet another line over the side, this one amidships so he can hold on when he comes up for air between cuts.

Although we're rolling in a slight swell, the surface is calm, and the color is the exquisite cobalt of bottomless ocean. (The depth is over 3,000 feet here.) As Steve works under the surface, his black diveskin is cleanly etched into the rich blue, and the water is so clear, I can see beyond him into infinity. Beautiful— euphoric, even, now that we've found the cause of our problem.

Fifteen dives later, he surfaces waving a 3-foot square of thick, green, ratty cordage, probably from one of the dilapidated Haitian fishing boats that ply this coast. Each of its heavy strands required a full breath to cut. Steve heaves the net as far into the sea behind us as he can. We should have brought it onboard, of course, but at that moment he just wanted to cast our problem as far away as possible.

The engine starts, we put it in gear, and we keep our eyes *glued* to the temperature gauge. Five, ten, fifteen, twenty minutes. All seems well. We even leave the gauge to run to the foredeck when a dozen dolphins converge out of nowhere in the sparkling water, as if they've come to celebrate with us. Riding *Receta*'s bow wave, they shoot from one side of the boat to the other, somehow calculating their leap across our bow so they never touch the boat. What a party.

We take freshwater showers in the cockpit to continue the celebration as we race along (comparatively speaking) at 6 knots. We're even going in the right direction: straight toward Luperón. At our next radio check-in time, we let *Splashdance* know the good news.

As the day progresses, though, it becomes clear we're not going to make Luperón by sunset. The harbor entrance isn't lit, and neither are the markers inside, and we know there is no tolerance for error. We debate going into another, closer port, but Sosua is an unacceptable choice given the wind direction, and Puerto Plata is simply not recommended, a poor port of entry for a cruising boat. We debate standing off, spending a third night at sea, and entering harbor in the morning. But the sight of fresh lightning in the distance, as dusk begins to ride over the backbone of the Dominican Republic, makes that a pretty unpopular alternative too. Especially since Steve (although he hasn't yet admitted it) has been badly spooked by last night's storm. Especially since we're already very tired (both of us) and very seasick (me).

There's a cruising rule: Never enter an unlit and unfamiliar harbor at night. Especially if that harbor has claimed more than one boat on its treacherous reefs even in *daylight*. I radio *Splashdance*, who had long since arrived: Would they be willing to lead us into the harbor in the dark via dinghy? They radio back yes, saying they'll try to get some help, too, from an old Luperón hand. It's hard to get a sense from Jack's voice—Jack, who's so calm and reserved in any case—whether he thinks this is madness or the best of a bad lot of choices. What I do know is that it's a huge imposition on our friendship.

By the time we're off the harbor entrance, it's totally dark, except for the evening's lightning show, strengthening in the distance and clearly heading our way. Even without the help of a moon (barely half full and shrouded in cloud), I can picture the entrance from a year ago: reefs tight to both sides. We must pass very close to the red buoy (missing the last time, now back in place), but not too close: It's attached directly to the right-hand reef. Then head more-or-less for the first green stake, hard turn to starboard, and you're through the worst of it. I'm on the foredeck with the battery-operated handheld searchlight. Steve's at the helm with the handheld VHF radio. Jack, Carol, and Lisa (the old Luperón hand—her sailboat, *Serenity*, has been resident in the harbor for more than a year now) are in *Splashdance*'s dinghy at the unlit red buoy, flashing their light. Sweaty-palm nervous, I would be twiddling my hair if I had a free hand, but I'm clutching the searchlight in one and the forestay in the other. The wind has inconveniently picked up again, of course, so we're bouncing through the waves. This will be no romantic moonlit entrance.

Here we go. As we pass the red buoy, I can see and hear the breakers all too clearly—and we seem *entirely* too close to the left-hand reef, a bit of info I anxiously call back to Steve. Luckily, I can't hear the radio conversation between the skipper and our guides. Only afterward do I learn that our depth sounder had suddenly dropped to less than 10 feet from more than 20, an indication we'd strayed dangerously from the channel, and the dinghy crew didn't know which way to tell Steve to head. He inched the boat first to starboard, then to port, until he saw the depth begin to increase.

It seems a lifetime, but it's probably only thirty seconds until my light hits the first green stake. (My mind foolishly flicks to the Energizer bunny: My light is now guiding our guides, whose flashlight has already weakened.) We head for it, make the turn, and have another heart-pounding few moments until we spot the next stake. But the water has become flat calm; it even smells different—lush, fertile. We're through the reefs.

You can feel the tension drain from the boat. From here on, if we miss the stakes and go aground, it will only be in mangrove mud and we won't punch a hole in *Receta*'s bottom. A good thing, since the dinghy crew—their light dimmed to an emaciated glow by this point—can't find the rest of the stakes. Steve steers from memory, and after what seems another lifetime, we are pointed at *Splashdance*, which is lit up like a Christmas tree—masthead lights, spreader lights, cabin lights—and told we can safely drop the hook on their starboard side.

We're giddy with relief, my arms and legs weak, with the

adrenaline no longer pumping. Laughter and too-loud jokes echo in the anchorage, replacing the tension. "You know they say a sign of alcoholism is when you say, 'I *need* a drink?'" I announce. "Well, *I NEED A DRINK*." With Caribs popped open all around, we rehash the trip with Jack and Carol. "We were really, really worried about you last night," Carol says, uncharacteristically somber. "We could see a wall of lightning way behind us, and knew you'd be going through that." And it's here that Steve confesses how really, really worried he was, too.

I let myself sleep in—screw getting up to listen to the weather reports, I'm not going *anywhere* for a few days—and when I pull myself out of the berth at eight, it is already dripping hot, a typical Luperón morning. Flat calm, blazing sun, little breeze, no worries. Bliss. (Jack has already offered up his sewing machine for the torn mainsail, the only thing that now needs fixing.) The tide is receding and the water around us is littered with white feathers. I assume someone is plucking chickens by the town dock, and only days later do I realize they are from the elegant long-necked egrets that roost in the mangroves at night and fly off to feed in the morning.

In the early afternoon, a frantic call is broadcast on the VHF radio by a sailboat trying to enter the harbor: It's gone up on the reef, and its panicked owners are calling for help in getting off. Knowing that there but for the grace of God go we, Steve roars off in *Snack* and is the first to arrive on the scene.

The British-flagged *Milda Rose* has already been pounded by the waves so far over on its side on the reef that *Snack*'s bow is soon covered with the boat's bottom paint. For some reason, probably tiredness, new arrivals Stan and Sue had passed on the wrong side of the red buoy, and the Luperón entrance is completely unforgiving of such errors. In fact, the reef is so close to the surface just beyond the buoy that some of the rescuers stand on it, the water barely over their knees, making it all too obvious how easily we could have come to grief last night.

A dozen dinghies, a big charter trimaran, a heavy local fishing boat, and several hours of pushing and pulling are required to free *Milda Rose* and get her back into deeper water. The dinghies then push her into the anchorage (her engine had ceased functioning while on the reef), with one of the other cruisers at her helm. Stan's nerves are too shattered at this point for him to negotiate the rest of the turns through the stakes and, besides, his eyes are needed below—to make sure *Milda Rose* hasn't been holed and isn't taking on water.

The next day, the word goes out on the radio: *Milda Rose* is fine, and Stan and Sue are hosting happy hour at the Puerto Blanco Marina bar, in grateful thanks to those who saved their boat.

This evening, though, we're off to a noisy cruisers' dinner announced by another sailor that morning on the VHF net. It's at the "chicken shack," a nameless, signless restaurant on Luperón's main street. The outside is painted robin's egg blue, the inside cool and dark, with bare wooden tables and mismatched chairs. No menus—the food just arrives: crispy fried chicken, more than I can manage (Steve, of course, offers to help); rice and beans, served as they had been in Puerto Rico, the beans a spicy soupy mixture to be ladled on top of plain white rice; and creamy cole slaw. Dessert is caramelized papaya, the sweet fruit cooked in an even sweeter syrup. The meal, including a rum-and-Coke for everyone, costs 35 pesos each—$2.21 at the current exchange rate. Only the beer is extra, and the buck-a-bottle *grande* Presidentes taste as *grande* as ever. I am positively gleeful to be here.

A week later, *Receta*'s lockers freshly stuffed with cases of MasMas bars, Presidente, and Santo Domingo coffee, the fridge crammed with cheese and yogurt, the hammocks sagging under full loads of fruit and vegetables, we're ready to tear ourselves away again from the Dominican Republic. Remembering the *comandante's* finely engineered bridge, I try to weasel out of the excursion to his hilltop headquarters to check out, but Steve won't hear of it: What if he needs a translator? Jack and Carol decide to come along at the same time, figuring they might as well enjoy a free translation service, too. "*Milda Rose* told us there's a new bridge," Carol says.

The wobbly branches and trick planks have indeed been replaced—by two heavy steel beams. Unfortunately, that's it: No crosspieces, just two steel beams separated from each other by more than three feet of empty air, over the still-fragrant sewage stream. I step up on one beam, Steve on the other; we grasp hands and wobble across like a circus act in training.

The junior official who handles our *despachos* tells us, in English, we need to pay him a fee. The *comandante* himself—a different one than a year ago—had visited us on *Receta* to check us into the country, and when he relieved us each of $10, he had explained clearly that no additional payment would be required. And so I say gently and quizzically in Spanish to the junior official, "There must be some misunderstanding." And then I get to the magic words: "*El comandante* told us . . ." The junior official instantly leaps in and agrees that yes, of course there is no fee. Just a little attempt to extract a *mordida*, a tiny bite, an un-official supplement to the government's paltry wages, from visitors who don't know better. Steve figures if they want to charge us to leave the Caribbean, maybe we should just stay.

But, no, the next day we're on passage back to the Bahamas, both fishing lines streaming out behind the boat. The tournament is still on, so I had worked up a couple of big, satisfying goobers for the lures. "Good work," said Steve.

Zinnnnnnnnnng. SNAP! The line starts screaming out of the

rod and reel, and almost simultaneously a clothespin pops off the lifeline. The clothespin is the low-tech alert system that lets us know a fish is on the line attached to the Cuban reel. The clothespin holds a loop of nylon cord; one end of the cord is attached to the heavy monofilament run out behind the boat, the rest is wound on the yo-yo. If a fish hits the lure, it puts pressure all the way up the line and, *SNAP*, sends the clothespin flying. We have two fish hooked behind *Receta* at once.

A few seconds later, a *massive* dorado leaps out of the water and tailwalks about 100 feet behind the boat, hooked on the lure attached to the rod and reel. Called mahimahi in the Pacific, the dorado is a stunning fish, iridescent blues and greens, the colors of the sea, shot through with purple and gold. It's also quicksilver fast—it has to be, to catch one of its favorite foods, the flying fish, which it can grab out of the air—and when it runs with a lure in its mouth, it really *runs*. More importantly, it makes delicious eating, though it's sometimes shunned in North America when it's called by its other common name: dolphin. This fish is no relation to the air-breathing aquatic mammal, but those who think they'll be eating one of Flipper's relatives steer clear. I *adore* dorado.

Graciously, I offer to wind in the yo-yo, letting Steve fight what is obviously "the big one" and avoiding the possibility of losing dinner because of a tangle with the other line. It doesn't seem like there's very much tension on the line coming out of the yo-yo in any case, so I suspect if a fish is still there, it's quite a small one.

But, geez, winding in the line is hard work. "Hurry, or it's gonna tangle for sure!" I can hear Steve's impatience with my seeming lack of gusto for the job—but I *have* to keep resting and switching hands. My arms ache and my fingers are cramping. I've never reeled in the yo-yo before, so I simply assume it's difficult because the cheap and cheerful yo-yo lacks the gearing and handle of a conventional reel.

And then the "small" fish on the end of my line decides to

tailwalk too, with Steve watching. (I'm too busy concentrating on the yo-yo to look up.) "Holy shit." He dumps his rod—with "the big one" still on the end—back in its holder and runs to the other side of the boat to help me. Now I have a reason to keep a death grip on the yo-yo: We have two big dorados hooked at once.

I'm determined to finish what I've started, and refuse Steve's offer to take over the yo-yo. I manage—albeit very slowly—to wind my dorado all the way to the side of the hull, where Steve gaffs it. I can't believe my eyes, and arms. This fish is *way* bigger than anything we've dealt with before: much too big to dump in our bucket, no garbage bag handy that's big enough to hold it. (Bagging or bucketing helps keep the cockpit reasonably clean of the assorted fluids of a gaffed and dying fish.) So a little side-deck butchery is called for before we bring in the other fish. "But get the tape measure first."

My "small" fish measures 41½ inches from the tip of its blunt head to the end of its forked tail. I don't know whether I'm more pleased about my strength or my spit.

Even after dorado number 1 has been dispatched into numerous Ziploc bags, it's still another twenty-five minutes before Steve brings dorado number 2 alongside. By now it must be close to dead. No such luck: Just as Steve's reaching over with the gaff, it does an effortless flip, snaps the heavy leader, and swims away. But we get to eyeball it long enough to agree that it was indeed "the big guy," well over 4 feet long. "But mine," I hasten to remind him, "is worth more points."

What do you do with 41½ inches of dorado? You throw a dinner party, with sautéed dorado in Creole tomato sauce as the main course. Luckily, we're just two days away from George Town, our old nemesis on Great Exuma Island. *Splashdance* and other friends are already there waiting.

The problem with all this piscatorial activity is that it's decimated

Steve's small collection of lures. The few he has left are as bedraggled as revelers after Carnival, the fringe on their skirts torn and tattered, their once-brilliant pinks, yellows, and greens faded, their feathers half-chewed off.

Basking in the pleasure of self-sufficiency, Steve decides to manufacture his own replacements. We've heard of cruisers who trolled the fingers of yellow rubber gloves behind their boat with success, but Steve shuns inelegant solutions. He goes to the hardware store and returns with a bright green $1.49 featherduster. Back in Ontario, he tied his own flies to cast for bass and trout, and his fly-tying equipment and supplies are onboard, though depleted by the small flies he's been making for his own reef-fishing attempts and as gifts for friends. For big game, he needs a somewhat different approach, something that will mimic a fleeing baitfish when it's dragged behind the boat.

From our plumbing supplies, he retrieves two short pieces of nylon-reinforced clear plastic water hose—"the nylon reinforcement kinda resembles fish scales"—epoxies a sinker inside, and strings them onto a wire leader to create a jointed body with a hook on the end. He ties on green feathers from the freshly plucked featherduster, adds a few strands of shiny tinsel and the last yellow feathers from his fly-tying box, and glues on a pair of fake eyes.

"It looks," I tell him, "like an overdecorated Christmas tree." He takes it as high compliment.

Next, he plans to carve a mold out of bath-size bars of Ivory soap and fill it with silicone sealant to make replacements for the mangled squid skirts. "But I need something to color the sealant with," he says. I think for a minute: What do we have onboard that's fish-friendly fluorescent green or yellow?

I remember a kids' craze from a couple of years back where Jell-O was used as a hair dye. "How about Jell-O?"

"Worth a try. I'll take the lime."

* * *

The Jell-O is evidence of something I've been noticing lately: I've become a much better lateral thinker. Not only has my brain not got out of shape without the daily stimulation of my job, but I've also learned to use it differently. Completely nonmechanical in my old life, I can now help Steve troubleshoot a balky water pump or diesel engine. Independently, I had deduced that our engine-overheating problem in the Mona Passage most likely had to be something obstructing the prop.

Steve calls me *Receta*'s weather goddess. Those days when the offshore forecasts were like a foreign language, reducing me to tears as I struggled to transcribe them, are long gone. Now I not only confidently take them down in weather shorthand—I filled a 200-page notebook in ten weeks during hurricane season—I also work with Steve to analyze them and plan passages. "It takes a huge load off my shoulders," he tells people. "Her understanding and judgment are sound." Who would have guessed? This is not the sort of thing I used to be good at.

Other changes have been sneaking up on me too. The old Ann fussed and fretted about her appearance, never left the house without makeup. Most days now I barely glance in *Receta*'s one mirror, which is in the head. Very occasionally, on shore, I will catch my full-length reflection somewhere and I am taken aback, barely recognizing the tanned, slender, fit woman who stares out at me. I look better than I ever did at home.

I can't believe I'm spitting on a Jello-O-infused hunk of silicone and the remains of a featherduster.

Mid-morning, just when we're changing watch, Steve looks back and sees the bull head of a dorado making a beeline for the ex-featherduster. It takes a full hour for him to tire it enough to bring it alongside and get it on the gaff. Finally, we heft it aboard, snap the requisite photos, and lay it out on the side deck for measuring: 49½ inches. Good Lord. Let the filleting begin.

"*Splashdance, Splashdance; Receta.* Can you come for dinner tonight?" Steve tells Carol why we slowed down, allowing *Splashdance* to do a horizon job on us.

"Meanwhile, we lost two new lures on two strikes," Carol says glumly. "Two dorado, couldn't land either one."

Damn. That means they got *six points.* The ten pounds of fillets now jammed in our freezer got us only five. Who designed this tournament anyway?

Sautéed Dorado with Creole Tomato Sauce

"First, catch a 3-foot dorado," my step-by-step notes for this recipe begin. That part over, the preparation is simple—all that fabulously fresh fish requires. With white-fleshed, delicate fish such as dorado, I prefer to garnish it with the sauce, rather than cook it in the sauce, as Daphne did with her tuna in Bequia.

SERVES 6

For the sauce

4 tablespoons olive oil

2 cloves garlic, chopped

2 medium onions, sliced thinly

3 sweet bell peppers (a combination of red, green, and/or yellow), thinly sliced and slices cut in half

½ teaspoon hot pepper, seeded and finely chopped

Salt and freshly ground black pepper

2 green onions, thinly sliced on the diagonal

1 tablespoon chopped fresh thyme or 1 teaspoon dried thyme

2 tablespoons cilantro, chopped

3–4 tomatoes, chopped

½ cup white wine (approx.)

For the fish
    2 limes
    2½–3 pounds dorado or other fish fillets
    1 cup flour
    Salt and freshly ground black pepper
    2 tablespoons butter
    2 tablespoons olive oil
    2 cloves garlic, thickly sliced

1. To make the sauce: In a large, heavy pan with a lid, heat the olive oil. Add the garlic and onions and cook gently over medium heat, stirring frequently, until the onions are meltingly soft and translucent (but not brown), about 10 minutes.

2. Add the sweet and hot peppers, and cook about 10 minutes more, stirring occasionally. Season with salt and pepper and add green onions, thyme, cilantro, and tomatoes. Cover and cook until the sauce has thickened a bit, about 10 minutes.

3. Add the white wine and simmer a bit longer for the flavors to blend. Taste and adjust seasoning, adding a bit more wine, stock, or water if the sauce seems too thick. Keep warm over low heat.

4. Meanwhile, squeeze the limes over the fish, and rub with the pith. Season the flour with salt and pepper and dredge the fillets in the mixture.

5. In a large skillet, heat the butter and oil. Add the sliced garlic cloves and allow them to sauté for about 5 minutes over low heat.

6. Remove the garlic and raise the heat to medium. Sauté the dorado fillets, about 4 minutes per side (if thick), turning only once. Fish is done when it just flakes. Serve with rice and the warm tomato sauce.

The Northbound Blues

Two bucks per guess. Specifically, we want to know the exact time
and date that Ann and Steve will cross a line between the Ward's
Island ferry dock and the end of the *Rapids Queen* [the grounded
barge that marks the entrance to Queen City Yacht Club, *Receta*'s
home berth in Toronto]. The person with the closest guess will win
the incredibly huge pot. . . . The last information we have on their
whereabouts was an email sent in early June from Nassau. . . .

E-mail sent by one of our Toronto friends to
fifteen others, June 1999

The locals are still talking about your piña colada cheesecake. Please
send recipe.

From an e-mail from *Splashdance*, July 1999

"HOPE YOU LIKE OLD BAY." Not waiting for a
response, Mike, a beefy guy in his early fifties,
fires a blizzard of the seasoning into the cauldron
of beer and water that's bubbling over a propane burner in his
backyard. Mike and Caroline live on the outskirts of Charleston,
not right on the water but close enough: On the drive here this
afternoon, I'd spotted a crocodile ambling along the grass a couple
of blocks away. Old friends of Jack and Carol, they have invited
them and, showing real southern hospitality, us, two strangers, to
their house on a hot June Sunday for a "low-country boil."

I've already sneaked a peek at the stained recipe resting on the counter in their kitchen. Anyone who doesn't like Old Bay Seasoning is seriously out of luck today, since making a low-country boil involves five generous applications.

A low-country boil—also known as Frogmore Stew—is the Carolinas equivalent to a New England clambake. Some people claim the dish originated in Frogmore, a town on South Carolina's Helena Island. But it's also called a Beaufort Boil, after Beaufort, South Carolina. And a Shore Dinner in Beaufort, North Carolina—where Mike and Carolyn lived until a few years ago.

Instead of the clambake's pit in the sand, the low-country boil involves a massive pot. The ones sold expressly for this purpose have an equally massive steamer basket that fits inside. ("Around Thanksgiving, everybody uses them to deep-fry turkeys, too," another low-country boiler subsequently tells me. I'm sure she's kidding, until she describes the two-and-a-half gallons of cooking oil required, and the tender juicy result, with to-die-for crispy skin.) You're not going to fit one of these pots too easily on your stove, however, so the other part of the package is a stand-alone propane-fired burner. Besides that, the only thing you need is a crowd with a healthy appetite.

With the beer and water bubbling, Mike layers in his ingredients, letting each layer cook for the prescribed time before adding the next. First come chunks of kielbasa—although Andouille sausage is the traditional choice, he says—followed by a flurry of Old Bay. Then small new potatoes, and another sprinkling of Old Bay; then chicken pieces, and yet more Old Bay; then ears of fresh corn, broken in half and sprinkled with . . . Others swear by other brands of seafood boil, but Mike is adamant. You can adjust the other ingredients to suit your taste, but "you gotta have Old Bay."

Finally, when everything else is almost cooked, Mike tumbles in eight pounds of raw shrimp in their shells. Sometimes crabs and clams are added too, but it's not a low-country boil without shrimp. As *Receta* and *Splashdance* entered Charleston harbor at dawn a few mornings ago, I had looked over my shoulder. Silhouetted on the horizon behind us, in a pink glow, were several large commercial shrimpers, their nets hanging at their sides, returning home after a night of work. The low country is shrimping country.

Receta and *Splashdance* had lingered in the Caribbean as long as possible. But the beginning of June meant the start of another hurricane season, and now it was time to hustle north. We had really stepped up our pace about two weeks ago.

We checked back into U.S. waters from the Bahamas at Cape Canaveral—celebrating our arrival over an all-American dinner out together: steak and fries and live rock-and-roll—and then quickly hopped back offshore again to head directly to Charleston. No way we would have done *that* a year and a half earlier: Me, happily choose a forty-eight-hour ocean passage when there's an option of the protected, stop-each-night (but longer and slower) Intracoastal Waterway route? It's yet another sign of my hard-won confidence. For ten hours, we ride the swift northbound Gulf Stream, hooting at our speed (up to an unprecedented 11 knots, like *Receta* has been fired from a slingshot), eyes glued to the radar at night as oceangoing tankers take the same fast ride we do, and then we run out our fishing lines come daylight. The tournament's not over yet.

Unfortunately, *Receta* has been showing her displeasure at being pointed inexorably north. Her fridge and freezer stopped working on the way to Grand Bahama Island, our last stop in the Bahamas, and we've been dependent on ice blocks ever since. (Luckily, we caught only one small—27-inch—dorado on the passage to Charleston.) And her battery-charging system now works only when it feels like it. When we arrived in Charleston, however, Steve's plans to fix the fridge and the electrical system immediately got back-burnered by more pressing problems: "Toilet's not working," he announced, shaking me awake when he returned to the berth after a midnight visit to the head. "You can't use it at all." Knowing exactly how unpopular this announcement would be, he graciously offered to get me a bucket from the cockpit locker.

My body has also been showing displeasure at moving north: My pollen allergies, which laid dormant in the Tropics, now have me sneezing and red-eyed whenever we're on land. Steve has taken to calling it "latitude disease."

While the shrimp steam, Mike covers a long outdoor table with a thick layer of newspaper and Carolyn melts a bucket of butter for dipping. Then, when they judge everything to be done, Mike puts on a pair of heavy oven mitts, lifts out the steamer basket, lets it drip for a moment, and then dumps the contents down the length of the table.

This is a reach-out-and-grab, eat-it-with-your-hands meal. The trick to preparing it is clearly in the timing, and Mike's got it right: The shrimp are just-cooked juicy and plump. The overtones of Old Bay infuse everything, of course—making this a meal that goes extremely well with beer. A mound of detritus grows in front of each of us: shrimp shells, corn cobs, chicken bones, and greasy spent paper towels. Everyone claims they're full to bursting—though hands keep snaking out for a few last bites.

Jack and Carol think they have first place in the bag, when they catch four small tuna on the two-night trip from Charleston to Beaufort. But *we* catch a 3-foot king mackerel, a 3-foot Spanish mackerel, and a small tuna, which we think cements *us* firmly in the winner's spot. It had better—because I declare a moratorium on fishing: The freezer is absolutely full. (Fortunately, Steve had fixed the refrigeration in Charleston—*and* the toilet, *and* the charging system, this last with the assistance of a troubleshooter from the company that manufactured one of the components. "Push to energize," said the man on the phone, and when Steve clearly didn't have a clue what this meant, he explained. "Just bang the hell out of it." Steve did, and the $2,000 piece of troublesome equipment began working perfectly again.)

The tournament awards banquet is held the night we arrive in Beaufort, at Lookout Bight, a sheltered harbor on the Atlantic a few miles outside the town. In the afternoon, we each present a tally of our catches to *Splashdance*'s Beaufort friends, who are joining us for dinner. "Independent auditors," says Steve. "From Pricewaterfish."

There are ten of us gathered on *Splashdance* that evening, ten people who *love* to eat well. One of the Beaufort couples brings a mountain of chilled local shrimp. Another couple had dug clams on the tidal flats, which they steam and we eat with a squeeze of lime and a drop of hot sauce. For the main course, Carol grills tuna, and I do Spanish mackerel in a Caribbean coconut milk sauce. There is rice and cole slaw, and, a southern specialty, green beans cooked with salt pork.

The auditors fudge the results. They refuse to allow full points for our first fish, the partial blackfin tuna from Culebra, and they give Carol and Jack credit for an additional fish—the one painted on the flag they're flying from their backstay—making the final tallies closer. But *Receta* is still the winner. "Uh, we have a confession," says Carol. "We drank the Presidente. Will you accept a case of Carib instead?" In a fit of our own southern graciousness, the crew of *Receta* delivers half the case back to *Splashdance* for taking second.

Beaufort is the end of the line for Carol and Jack, *Splashdance*'s home port. The morning that *Receta* gets underway to head north again, we hug each other tightly, with tears in our eyes. "I now know what the toughest part of cruising is," a friend of theirs says to me quietly. "It's saying good-bye."

In Coral Harbor, on the island of St. John in the U.S. Virgin Islands, one of the businesses had an array of clocks on the wall, showing the time in places around the world: Moscow, Stockholm, London, New York, and Coral Harbor itself. The Coral Harbor clock had no hands. As we get farther and farther up the Eastern Seaboard, I want to put time on hold like that clock. Steve buys a pair of real-world shoes and is morose for the rest of the day. That night, on the weekly SSB radio net we had used in the Caribbean to stay in touch with other cruising boats, we can faintly hear *Splashdance* in Beaufort calling *La Esmeralda*, still in the Caribbean. But we're too far north now to be heard ourselves on that frequency, which makes Steve more despondent still. He desperately wants to put on the brakes, to "throw the compass over the rail," as Jimmy Buffett sings.

Catching bluefish as fast as he can clean them temporarily cheers him up along the New Jersey coast, but we pull in the lines as we approach New York Harbor, and a deep funk descends on *Receta*, along with a pea-soup fog. A couple of days' travel north of the city on the Hudson, I see Canada geese, honking overhead and then skidding to a landing in the river, a sure sign that we're on our way home.

The blanket of heat that laid constantly over us seems distant and hard to imagine now, an impossible memory. Could it have really been so hot that Steve ate dinner belowdecks in nothing more than his underwear, that I slept in the cockpit to keep cool, not even needing a sheet? So hot that I had soaked the ladies next to me on the Woburn bus with my sweat?

We begin to meet a boat or two heading south, just starting off on their own grand adventure, not realizing how truly grand—

how life changing—it will be. I can't believe how *envious* I am of them. "Please come over for a beer and let us pick your brains," they ask. They seem inexperienced, naive even. That was us, two years ago.

Dear Splashdance,
Last night when we were programming waypoints into the GPS (to cross Oneida Lake, part of the New York State Canal System), we determined the following: As the crow flies, we are 160 miles from Toronto, and 2,005 miles from Hog Island. Steve is whimpering, and still threatening to throw the compass over the rail. . . .

Two of my cousins come to visit us one night while we're transiting the canal. They had done the same thing twenty-three months earlier, to wish us Godspeed. *Receta* is inhospitable, a forgotten chill in her cabin from the intermittent drizzle. I'd been forced to hunt up socks and a long-buried sweater, and I now exude a faint aroma of mildew. We quickly retreat from the dankness to a cozy restaurant. It's around sunset when we leave the boat, but there's no color on the water here. The world around us has seemed flat-gray for days.

"Tell us about your trip," they urge. But I hesitate, momentarily speechless, not knowing quite where to begin. I find myself groping for the "best" answer to every question they ask because there are a hundred, a thousand bests. "You better get used to it," Steve says afterward. "Or you'll be tongue-tied in Toronto."

We are determined to sneak back into our home port without fanfare, and our Toronto friends are apparently just as determined that we shall not. Spies have been recruited in ports on Lake Ontario to report *Receta* sightings, and when we meet people who have been thus enlisted, we are forced to buy their silence with Carib beer and St. Martin wine.

Now that we're so close, we make excuses to delay: We hide out in Rochester for a couple of days to clean and polish *Receta* from top to bottom. (We can't arrive home without her looking her best, we tell each other.) We stay an extra day in a port an hour's drive from Myrna and Murray's home, so they can come to *Receta* for lunch. They climb onboard like old pros, and slip off their shoes before they're even in the cockpit. "I hope you'll be doing this again before we're too old and decrepit to come visit," Myrna says. "I hope so too, Mom," Steve says with real feeling. And we stop a scant 9 miles from Toronto to spend a night because the lake is rough. Granted, *Receta*'s speed is a bit slow in the chop, and her motion is uncomfortable, but we've been in much worse conditions. The truth is, we just can't bear to see the trip end.

Almost exactly two years to the day since we left, we cross the line between the Ward's Island ferry dock and the *Rapids Queen* with the courtesy flags of a dozen countries flying from the rigging. Five o'clock, on a Thursday afternoon. The owner of Toronto's nautical bookstore wins thirty-six bucks in the *Receta* pool—but only because *we* later report the exact time of our arrival. At that hour on a weekday, people are still at work, and no one is around. Our homecoming is a complete anticlimax.

Shortly afterward, friends arrive at their boats and island houses, and a spontaneous party happens. But for us it's bitter-sweet. I know the last two years have to end, but I can't bear the thought. I don't want just to sink complacently back into our old existence. I've seen too clearly there's more to life than that.

When we climb back onboard late that night, almost hoarse from telling stories (Cleo would have been proud), my loyal stuffed pal Curious George is sulking. I reassure him—and myself—that we will indeed go to sea again.

Sleep comes with great difficulty. Instead of sheep, I count goats—the ones that graze on the hillsides of southern Grenada.

In a downtown Toronto business-district building about a week after our return, Steve steps onto an elevator. "Good afternoon," he says, looking the other passengers in the eye and smiling broadly. They shuffle nervously to clear a wide space for him and avert their eyes. In a downtown Toronto market, I stop to buy fish. Fresh tuna is $18.99 a pound, and I catch tears running down my face. It's not the price, but what the sight of that tuna represents: Two years overflowing with an embarrassment of riches.

We make a trip to the storage locker where we had left our possessions when we moved onboard. Furniture. Clothing. Appliances. Tchotchkes. When Steve throws open the big steel door, we stand and look at each other, mystified. All that *stuff.* We forgot we had it. We don't want to take it back.

As we unpack *Receta*, preparing to move back into our house, I find two whole canned chickens at the very back of one of the food lockers. They have traveled 5,500 nautical miles, at least. And I never thought once of opening them.

Low-Country Boil
(A.K.A. FROGMORE STEW)

A fab, fun way to serve a crowd. The only thing you need to accompany the stew is lots of melted butter—and lots of paper towels. This isn't genteel dining.

2 12-ounce bottles of beer
Kielbasa or sausage (¼ pound per person), cut into chunks
Large container of Old Bay Seasoning
Chicken thighs or legs (1 pound per person)
Small new potatoes (3–4 per person)
Corn on the cob (1 ear per person), cut in thirds
Shrimp (¼ pound per person; more if not including clams and crabs)
Clams (8 per person)
Crabs (1 per person)

1. Pour enough beer and water in a big steamer pot (see Tip, below) to reach the bottom of the steamer basket, and bring to a boil.
2. Put the kielbasa or sausage in the steamer basket and sprinkle liberally with Old Bay Seasoning. Cook 3–5 minutes.
3. Add chicken, potatoes, and more Old Bay. Cook 12–15 minutes.
4. Add corn and Old Bay. Cook 10 minutes.
5. Add shrimp and Old Bay. Cook 2 minutes.
6. Add clams and crabs and Old Bay. Serve when clams open and crabs are cooked, about 5 minutes more.
7. Dump the whole steamer basket out on a table covered with newspaper. Let the crowd dig in.

Tip:
• Proper Frogmore Stew–making equipment consists of a stand-alone propane-fired burner on which sits a massive pot equipped with a steamer basket. These are available at hardware stores throughout the South.

King Mackerel Escabeche

Escabeche, or escovitch, is pickled or "soused" fish. Most recipes call for a white-fleshed fish such as snapper, but king mackerel (kingfish) or Spanish mackerel also works well—especially when you've just caught one of each and each one measures 3 feet. The technique involves first frying and then marinating the fish, a marriage of two culinary traditions: African (frying the fish) and Native American (preserving or pickling the fish in vinegar or lime juice, as with ceviche).

Islanders serve escabeche both chilled and hot, as an appetizer and as a main course. Because it can be made in advance and kept in the fridge, it's a lovely dish for a warm-weather dinner party or buffet.

SERVES 4 AS A MAIN DISH, 8 AS AN APPETIZER

4 tablespoons olive oil (approx.)
1 large white or yellow onion, thinly sliced
1 red onion, thinly sliced
2 green bell peppers, thinly sliced
2 cloves garlic, thinly sliced
½–1 teaspoon hot pepper, seeded and finely chopped (or to taste)
2 pounds fish fillets or steaks
Salt and freshly ground black pepper
2 bay leaves
1-inch piece fresh ginger, peeled and chopped
6 whole black peppercorns
6 whole allspice berries
⅛ teaspoon mace
¾ cup white or malt vinegar
½ cup black olives
2 tablespoons capers
½ cup roasted red peppers, sliced

1. Heat 2 tablespoons of the oil in a large frying pan. Add the onions, green peppers, garlic, and hot pepper, and cook over medium heat, about 10 minutes, until the onions are soft and golden. Remove from pan and set aside.
2. Dust the fish with salt and pepper and fry in the same pan until lightly browned on both sides and just cooked through, adding more oil as necessary.
3. Place the fish in a large, nonreactive dish. Put the onions and peppers on top.
4. In a saucepan, combine the spices with 1 cup water and salt and pepper, and simmer gently for 15 minutes. Add the vinegar and simmer for 2 minutes more.
5. Strain the liquid and pour over the fish. Serve hot or let cool and chill before serving. Garnish the fish with the olives, capers, and red peppers right before serving.

Piña Colada Cheesecake

This tropical twist on my mother's old-fashioned cheesecake was a hit at cruiser gatherings.

SERVES 16

For the crust

    1 cup graham cracker crumbs
    ½ cup sweetened shredded coconut
    ⅓ cup melted butter

For the filling

    1½ pounds cream cheese, softened
    ⅔ cup sugar
    4 eggs
    3 tablespoons dark rum
    1 cup sour cream
    ¾ cup cream of coconut (see Tips, below)
    ⅔ cup well-drained crushed pineapple (about 1 19-oz can)

1. Preheat oven to 350°F.
2. To make the crust, combine graham cracker crumbs and coconut with melted butter. Press into the bottom of a 10-inch springform pan. Bake for 10 minutes until lightly browned. Set aside to cool while you make the filling.
3. To make the filling, beat cream cheese and sugar until smooth. Add eggs one at a time, beating until blended. Mix in rum, sour cream, cream of coconut, and well-drained pineapple.
4. Spread evenly on prepared crust and bake about 50–60 minutes on middle rack of preheated oven, until edges are set and center moves just slightly when you shake the pan.
5. Run a knife around the inside of pan to loosen cheesecake. Allow cake to cool completely on a wire rack. Cover and

refrigerate until well chilled or overnight. Remove from springform pan before serving.

Tips:

- Garnish the cheesecake with slices of tropical fruit, such as fresh pineapple or mango.
- Don't confuse cream of coconut with coconut milk or coconut cream. Used to make drinks (such as piña coladas) and desserts, cream of coconut is thick, syrupy, heavily sweetened coconut milk. Coco Lopez is one popular brand.

One Last Lesson

. . . Sticky mango juice, running down my naked chest
And sturdy people who can still smile a mile of love into their pain
Put their shoulders to the wheel
And their Gods will do the rest
And in the end they will pass the test
Soca music, take me back to my island.
> From "Song for a Lonely Soul" by David Michael Rudder

*F*OUR YEARS AFTER WE LEFT, we return to Grenada—by plane—for a brief late-November visit. We stay in a small cottage on a low hillside overlooking the sea, and Hog Island, and the anchorage we loved.

As we lie in bed, we can see the masts of the sailboats at anchor in the distance. From our vantage point on the hill, the lines of reef we once blithely threaded are scarily visible.

But it is the wind that frightens me most now. It whistles through the palm fronds night and day, and when the regular wet season downpour arrives each afternoon, it drives the rain through our screens with such force that there are spatters clear across the room. On the other side of the bay, we can see plumes of spray shoot skyward where the waves crash on the rocks on the windward side of Hog Island. The wind is such a strong, constant background sound that I awaken when it stops briefly, in the hours just before dawn. Surely it was never like this when we were here on *Receta*? It *couldn't* have been—I would have been anxious all the time if we had been living on a boat in this wind. It was, Steve assures me. I've simply forgotten. And I am astounded that this much wind once seemed commonplace. At night, the piping frogs still provide steady accompaniment.

When we pull a borrowed dinghy onto the little sand beach where the path led to Mr. Butters's farm, the rusted Cuban gunboats seem to have settled lower in the water. The path is so overgrown now that, like the first time, I lose my way climbing the hill and return to the beach, my legs scratched and mud squishing out of my sandals. At some point, Mr. Butters was finally forced to leave. There's no sign of his shacks, or any cultivated land. A bit of rare steak, however, still grazes on the hillside.

The goats still graze, too, outside Nimrod's rum shop in Lower Woburn. But Hugh Nimrod passed away a couple of days before our return. It wasn't the rum that killed him, but his heart.

We keep our eyes open for a 45-foot cutter named *Triton*—the Minister of Rum's new office—but Ed must have already started his seasonal migration from Grenada up-island. *Tafia*, his previous boat, had been holed off the coast of Antigua about two years earlier, carried onto the fringing reef by the currents while Ed was making a solo night passage from St. Barts. Before she went down, Ed had time to escape in his dinghy—with his satellite phone and a bottle of twenty-one-year-old rum. Although the boat was lost, he went back in daylight and salvaged sixty-four more bottles.

In St. George's, the Music City Record Centre is gone, and so is Pyramid, Steve's favorite lunchtime haunt. Doc has moved to the northern end of the island; Basil has returned to Trinidad, the new tenants tell us. A big, bright fish market has been built across the street from the old one, which is now padlocked shut, and a couple of traffic lights have sprouted. But the produce market is unchanged—still a fragrant confusion of fruit and spices. Golden apples are in the greatest profusion at this time of year, but we hunt among the market ladies and find one glorious late-season mango to carry back to the cottage for breakfast.

A public bus takes us up the coast to Newlo. But unaccustomed to the roller-coaster roads, the sardine-can packing of passengers, and the all-encompassing heat, we are both woozy by the time we arrive for lunch. Secondhand computers have replaced the manual typewriters in Office Skills, but otherwise the place looks much the same—a jumble of crooked stairways and cubbyhole classrooms—belying its growth: Two satellite centers operate elsewhere on the island and an adult literacy program has been started.

We're taken to the shed up the road, where students learn to build fiberglass sailing dinghies. A year ago, we had heard about a program started by former cruisers, now Grenadian residents, to teach the kids of Lower Woburn to sail, using dinghies constructed at Newlo. We loved the circle this closed and had immediately commissioned one: to be built by the kids at Newlo, to be given to the kids at Lower Woburn—and to be called, Steve's choice, the *Annie V.* It was christened with Carib, we were told, and we see it later in the week, resting on the shore of Clarke's Court Bay.

On our second morning on the island, we climb the road to Dingis's house, and the colors—intense greens against flawless sky-blue above and turquoise below—are shocking to us, freed now only briefly from the monochromatic grays of a northern November. Each of us carries a bag with some gifts, including— as on one of our first trips—a batch of brownies. We had brought the ingredients from Canada, and I baked them this morning in our cottage. But we don't know who or what we'll find at the house behind the coconut palms and the breadfruit tree. Our most recent letters weren't answered.

As we round the final curve before the blue-green house—me, dripping with sweat as ever—we see an oh-so-familiar woman tending the goats halfway up the hillside behind the house. "Good day," Steve calls loudly from the foot of the drive. "I be down in a minute," a voice sings back. I'm sure Dingis thinks a couple of strangers have arrived to buy lobster or lambi. But as she gets closer, she raises her hands to her cheeks. "It Ahhnnn and Steve, it Ahhnnn and Steve. Gennel, come quick, it Ahhnnn and Steve."

Fifteen years old when we left, Gennel has become a raving beauty, just graduated from high school a few months ago and ready to enter a nursing course. "With God as my witness, I know in my heart you be back this year," Dingis says. "You told us you return by Gennel graduation. I look for *Receta* each time I down in deh bay."

Dingis has not forgotten that she never had a chance to show me how to make roti, and she's simply *not* going to let this sudden opportunity escape: We *must* come back to the house in a day or two, she says, so I can properly learn to cook chicken curry and roti. That bit of planning out of the way, she and Gennel catch us up on what we've missed: Dwight is back, still limping and in some pain, but again fishing and lobstering; the four little girls are growing up, and Alisha soon arrives to prove it; the village is unchanged, except that the postmistress has become increasingly unreliable (explaining our unanswered letters, which Dingis and Gennel never received).

If you'd walked up the steep drive on Saturday, brushed by the two sleeping dogs—the excitable Stinky is gone ("someone tief him," Dingis says)—and the clucking chickens, and peered into the dimness under the house, you would have seen me crushing cooked split peas with an empty rum bottle, kneading dough, pinching off little balls, hiding smashed split peas inside them, rolling out the balls into thin pancakes with the rum bottle and, finally, cooking them one by one on a hot greased griddle, my clumsy hands mimicking Dingis's practiced motions.

And if you'd peered through the dense foliage behind the house, freshly washed by the afternoon rain, you would have seen Steve knocking young coconuts out of a tree to get us all coconut water to drink and, later, on the road with Gennel, helping Dwight bring a wheelbarrow of lobster, lambi, and fish up from "deh bay." Later still, you would have seen him perched on a stool in the corner, knife in hand, up to his elbows in lambi slime and for once happy about it, helping Dingis and Dwight clean conch.

"Ahhnnn hand sweet," Gennel pronounces when she tries the chicken curry and roti. "Ahhnnn hand very sweet," adds Dingis.

Dingis's Chicken Curry with Dhal Puri Roti

Not for the time-pressed. With two sets of hands, it took a good three hours to prepare this dish. Of course, at the same time, Dingis was telling me how to make pumpkin curry, mango chutney, and rice and peas with coconut milk, and stopping to chat with neighbors who wandered up to the house to buy a bag of lambi or a fresh fish.

MAKES 12–16 ROTI

Roti

For the dough

    8 cups all-purpose flour

    1 heaping tablespoon baking powder

    1 teaspoon salt

    1 cup lard, shortening, or margarine

    2–3 cups water (approx.)

For the dhal puri

    1 cup dried yellow split peas, rinsed and picked over

    2 cloves garlic, minced

    ½ teaspoon freshly ground black pepper

    1 teaspoon good-quality curry powder

    2 teaspoons vegetable oil

    Salt (to taste)

    1 cup vegetable oil (approx.), for frying

1. To make the dough, in a large bowl, combine flour, baking powder, and salt. Cut in lard, shortening, or margarine with your fingers or two knives. Make a well in the center and add water a little at a time to make a soft dough. Knead lightly until smooth and elastic. Cover and "put it to rest for an hour," as Dingis says.

2. While dough is resting, prepare dhal puri: Place split peas in a large saucepan with 6 cups of water and bring to a boil. Partially cover and cook over medium heat until peas are tender, about 20–25 minutes. Drain thoroughly, and return peas to pot with the garlic, pepper, curry powder, and the 2 teaspoons of oil. Cook, stirring occasionally, over low heat for about 5 minutes. Add salt to taste. Allow to cool.

3. Grind peas in food processor (or mash by rolling with a rum bottle or rolling pin) until mixture resembles coarse meal.

4. Spread a tea towel on the table or counter and sprinkle with flour. Knead the dough briefly again. Pinch off pieces and form into balls. (Each one should be a little smaller than a tennis ball; you should have about 12 to 16.) Flatten one of the balls until it is about the size of a saucer. Holding it in the palm of your hand, put a heaping tablespoon of the split-pea mixture in the center. Carefully pinch the dough closed to again form a ball, and smooth it by turning it in your hand. Repeat with the remaining balls, placing them on the tea towel and covering with another cloth.

5. Heat a griddle or large frying pan on the stove. Working on a floured surface, flatten one of the balls with your hand and then roll it into a circle (using a rolling pin or rum bottle) until it is about 8–9 inches in diameter.

6. Oil the hot griddle. (Dingis dips the bottom of a metal cup into a saucer of oil and then runs the cup over the surface of the griddle.) Using a spatula, carefully transfer the roti to the griddle. Blot the top of the roti with oil (the metal-cup method works well). Cook for 1–2 minutes. When the dough begins to bubble, flip the roti with the spatula and cook the other side for another 1–2 minutes. (The roti should be lightly browned on both sides.)

7. Remove roti from griddle and keep warm in a towel that has been lightly sprinkled with water. Repeat with remaining balls, wiping the griddle clean with a towel between roti.

Chicken Curry

SERVES 6–8

3–4 tablespoons vegetable oil

3 pounds small bone-in chicken pieces (cut chicken breasts in
   half or thirds if including)

1 large onion, chopped

2–3 cloves garlic, finely chopped

2 tablespoons good-quality curry powder

1 teaspoon turmeric

½ lime, juiced

6 whole cloves

2 tablespoons ketchup

¾ cup water or chicken stock (approx.)

Salt and freshly ground black pepper

3 white potatoes, cubed

1. Heat 3 tablespoons of the oil in a large heavy pot. Over
   medium-high heat, brown the chicken pieces in batches, until
   golden on all sides, adding more oil as necessary. Remove
   chicken and set aside.

2. In the same pot, cook the onion and garlic until the onions are
   golden. Sprinkle with the curry powder and the turmeric and
   stir for a minute or two. Return chicken to the pot and stir
   until the chicken has been coated with the curry.

3. Add remaining ingredients except for potatoes, cover, and
   simmer gently until the chicken is falling-off-the-bone tender,
   about 1–1¼ hours, stirring occasionally. Add the potatoes for
   the last 30–40 minutes of cooking time, putting in a little
   more water or stock if the mixture seems dry.

4. Taste and adjust seasoning. Serve hot, with dhal puri roti on
   the side.

Tip:
• To shorten the cooking and preparation time (and make for easier, if less authentic, eating), use boneless chicken and serve the curry with rice instead of roti.

One-Pot Coconut Brownies

Leave out the coconut and coconut milk, and you have the basic brownies we took to Dingis and Gennel. The recipe, which was adapted from one in *Cottage Life's Summer Weekend Cookbook*, by Jane Rodmell, is ideal for making in a galley, since you're left with only one pot to wash. The original calls for melted marshmallows on top—a bit of finesse that I dispensed with onboard. But I "islandized" the recipe after seeing a suggestion on a box of coconut milk powder.

MAKES 16–20 BROWNIES
3 ounces unsweetened chocolate (3 squares)
½ cup butter
1¼ cups sugar
3 eggs
1 teaspoon vanilla
⅔ cup flour
⅓ cup coconut milk powder (see Tip, below)
½ teaspoon baking powder
½ teaspoon salt
½ cup chopped walnuts or pecans
½ cup fresh shaved or coarsely grated coconut

1. Preheat oven to 350°F. Grease a 9-by-9-inch pan.
2. In a medium saucepan melt chocolate and butter. Remove from the heat, and add sugar, eggs, and vanilla. Stir until smooth.

3. Stir in flour, coconut powder, baking powder, salt, and nuts. Mix well.
4. Spread mixture in prepared pan. Sprinkle coconut shavings on top.
5. Bake for about 25–30 minutes, or until brownies dimple slightly when you press them in the center. (If coconut shavings begin to get too brown, cover top loosely with aluminum foil.)

Cool and cut into squares.

Tip:
• Instant coconut milk powder is available in boxes in U.S. and Canadian stores that carry a selection of Caribbean foods. If you can't find it, substitute 1 teaspoon coconut extract and omit the vanilla.

Acknowledgments

Many, many thanks to Charlie Conrad, my editor at Broadway Books, for all his professional help, ideas, and attention every step of the way. And special thanks to Jackie Kaiser of Westwood Creative Artists for her boundless enthusiasm from the start. Maya Mavjee and Brad Martin at Doubleday Canada were among the first to champion this book; a particular thank you to them. I am also extremely grateful for the assistance of Alison Presley at Broadway Books, who did many things—including baking some of my recipes.

A big thank you as well to Mom and Dad, who instilled early on a love of travel, a love of food, and a love of the kitchen; to Myrna and Murray Manley, the ultimate good sports; to our cruising buddies Belinda and Todd Jackson, Carol and Jack Farmer, Nancy and Terry Newton, and all the other cruisers we laughed and learned with along the way; to Elizabeth Narayan and Gennel Narine, who opened their hearts and home to us; to singlehanders Cleo Boudreau and Ed Hagar, who shared arcane knowledge; to Herb Hilgenberg, who helped us avoid bad weather; to home economist Jill Snider, who tested many of my recipes; to Christina Hartling, keeper of my e-mail correspondence; to Sari Bercovitch, Peter Broecker, and John Warren, who kept business running back home so we could concentrate on cruising; to all the islanders who welcomed us; and, above all, to Steve, who convinced me I could do it.

References

Books and periodicals

Doyle, Chris, *The Cruising Guide to the Leeward Islands: 1998–1999 Edition* (Cruising Guide Publications, 1998).

——, *Sailors Guide to the Windward Islands* (Cruising Guide Publications, 1996).

Fuson, Robert H., transl., *The Log of Christopher Columbus* (International Marine, 1987).

Glinton-Meicholas, Patricia, *How to Be a True-True Bahamian* (Guanima Press, 1994).

——, *More Talkin' Bahamian* (Guanima Press, 1995).

Grenada Today: The National Newspaper of Grenada, Carriacou and Petite Martinique, August 7, 1998.

Hamilton, Edward, *Rums of the Eastern Caribbean* (Tafia Publishing, 1997), www.ministryofrum.com.

Hendrickson, Robert, *The Ocean Almanac* (Doubleday, 1984).

Moeller, Jan, and Moeller, Bill, *The Intracoastal Waterway: Norfolk to Miami, A Cockpit Cruising Handbook* (McGraw Hill, 1997).

Parsons, Kathy, *Spanish for Cruisers: Boat Repairs and Maintenance Phrase Book* (Aventuras Publishing Company, 2000).

Pavlidis, Stephen J., *On and Off the Beaten Path: The Central and Southern Bahamas Guide* (Seaworthy Publications, 1997).

Sheriff, Marguerite, "A Ride on the Board Bus," *The Melibea Review*, March 1998 (on-line at www.cruisingthecaribees.com/boardbus.htm).

Van Sant, Bruce, *The Gentleman's Guide to Passages South: The Thornless Path to Windward* (Cruising Guide Publications, 1996).

Warner, William W., *Beautiful Swimmers: Watermen, Crabs and the Chesapeake Bay* (Little, Brown and Company, 1976, 1994).

Music

Baha Men, *Junkanoo!* (Big Beat Records, 1992).

Buffett, Jimmy, *Somewhere over China* (MCA Records, 1981).

Quinn, Eileen, *No Significant Features* (1997) (www.eileenquinn.com).

Rudder, David, *Beloved* (Lypsoland, 1998).

——, *The Gilded Collection 1986–1989* (Lypsoland, 1993).

Organizations

New Life Organisation/Newlo (P.O. Box 609, St. George's, Grenada, W.I.; (newlo@caribsurf.com).

KIWIS MIGHT FLY
Around New Zealand on Two Wheels
by Polly Evans

When Polly Evans read a survey claiming that the last bastion
of masculinity, the real Kiwi bloke, was about to breathe his
last, she was seized by a sense of foreboding. Abandoning the
London winter she took off on a motorbike for the windswept
beaches and golden plains of New Zealand, hoping to root
out some examples of this endangered species for posterity.
But her challenges didn't stop at men.

Just weeks after passing her bike test, Polly rode from
Auckland's glitzy Viaduct Basin to the vineyards of Hawkes
Bay and on to the Southern Alps. She found wild kiwis in the
dead of night, kayaked among dolphins at dawn, and spent
an evening on a remote hillside with a sheep-shearing gang.
As she travelled, Polly reflected on the Maori Warriors who
carved their enemies' bones into cutlery, the pioneer family
who lived in a tree, and the flamboyant gold miners who lit
their pipes with five-pound notes, and wondered how their
descendents could have become pathologically obsessed
with helpfulness and *Coronation Street*.

The author of the highly acclaimed *It's not about the Tapas*
reaches some unexpected conclusions about the new
New Zealand man – and finds that evolution has taken
an unlikely twist.

0 553 81557 1

BANTAM BOOKS

FROM HERE, YOU CAN'T SEE PARIS
by Michael Sanders

A fascinating memoir about life in Les Arques (population 159), a hilltop village in a remote corner of France untouched by the modern era. It is the story of a dying community's struggle to survive, of an artist whose legacy begins its rebirth, and of chef Jacques Ratier and his wife, Noelle, whose magical restaurant – the village's sole business – has helped ensure its future.

The author set out to explore the inner workings of a French restaurant kitchen but ended up stumbling into a wider, much richer world. Whether uncovering the darker secrets of *foie gras* or absorbing the lore of the land around a farmhouse Kitchen table after a boar hunt, Michael Sanders learned that life in Les Arques was anything but sleepy. You will discover its vibrant history and traditions of food, cooking and rural living, sharing a family's adventures as they find their way in a place that is sometimes lonely, often wondrous, and always fascinating.

'A RICH TEXTURAL TAPESTRY OF EVERYDAY LIFE IN THE LOT . . . HONEST, FUNNY AND ENDEARING'
Ken Hom

0 553 81566 0

BANTAM BOOKS

MONSOON DIARY
Reveries and Recipes from South India
by Shoba Narayan

Monsoon Diary weaves a fascinating food narrative that combines authentic vegetarian recipes from South India with tales from Shoba Narayan's life, stories of her delightfully eccentric family, and reflections on Indian culture.

Shoba recounts her childhood in South India, a portrait of small-town life richly populated by characters like the flower woman who brings jasmine for the gods, the milkman who names his cows after his wives, and the iron-man who picks up red-hot coals with his bare hands. Food is so important to her family that when Shoba wins a scholarship to study in America, they only agree to let her go if she prepares a successful banquet. She returns home to an arranged marriage – to her surprise, the family have chosen well – and later there are visits from her many relatives, old and new, to her home in New York City.

In *Monsoon Diary*, Shoba Narayan's culinary talent is matched by stories as varied as Indian spices – at times pungent, mellow, piquant and sweet. Her characters, like Shoba herself, have a thing or two to say about cooking and about life.

'HUMOROUS, TENDER PROSE...NARAYAN'S
SPARKLING, INSIGHTFUL NARRATIVE MAKES FOR A
DELIGHTFUL CULTURAL AND CULINARY READ'
Publishers Weekly

0 553 81635 7

BANTAM BOOKS